PEPPER

PEPPER

Eyewitness to a Century

by

Claude Denson Pepper

with Hays Gorey

Harcourt Brace Jovanovich, Publishers

San Diego   New York   London

To my late
beloved wife
Mildred

Requests for permission to make copies of any
part of the work should be mailed to:
Permissions, Harcourt Brace Jovanovich, Publishers,
Orlando, Florida 32887.

Library of Congress Cataloging-in-Publication Data
Pepper, Claude, 1900–
Pepper, eyewitness to a century.
Includes index.
1. Pepper, Claude, 1900–   . 2. Legislators—
United States—Biography. 3. United States. Congress—
Biography. I. Gorey, Hays. II. Title.
E748.P455A3 1987 328.73'092'4 [B] 87-8662
ISBN 0-15-171695-1

Designed by G.B.D. Smith

Printed in the United States of America

First edition

A B C D E

Contents

Photographs follow pages 96 and 192.

Prologue

In broad terms, I assert that modern society,
acting through its government, owes the definite
obligation to prevent the starvation or dire
want of any of its fellow men and women who
try to maintain themselves, but cannot.

—FRANKLIN D. ROOSEVELT

On a bright September day in the twentieth century's first year, Lena Talbot and Joseph Wheeler Pepper knew visitors would be calling in at the little frame farmhouse near County Line Baptist Church in eastern Alabama's Chambers County. Relatives and friends would have attended second-Saturday services at the church and then would be anxious to see Lena's new baby, a little boy. It didn't take a whole lot to excite the neighbors in rural Alabama in 1900. There was no television, no radio—indeed, no electricity. News traveled by word of mouth, and it was mostly about births and deaths and marriages, or about the weather or the doings at County Line Baptist Church or Hominy Methodist Church. After a rendition of "All the Doo Da Day" on his harmonica, my father—J.W. or Wheeler Pepper, as he was called—told the visitors that he didn't care about the baby's first name—Lena could choose that—but he wanted the middle name to be "Denson" after the finest lawyer in all of eastern Alabama, Judge John D. Denson. Well, they teased Wheeler about that—"The little fellow's only a few days old and already you got him headed to law school"—but he paid them no mind. "Mebbe," he would say. "What's so wrong about that?"

Lena had her mind made up, too. She wanted to call her firstborn Paul. How did it all sound together—Paul Denson Pepper? Not bad. But then one of Lena's sisters spoke up: "Lena, when he goes to school the kids aren't going to call him Paul Denson Pepper. They're going to call him Paul Pepper, and then someone will say Peter Piper Paul Pepper." Everyone had a good laugh about that. So Lena gave it some more thought and decided no whimsical alliterations were likely if her son was named Claude. The formal christening would come later, but the name was decided on right then and there. The newest citizen of Alabama's red clay country would henceforth be known as Claude Denson Pepper.

If, as told in Lincoln lore, someone said "Bet he won't amount to much," no one heard, or at least no one remembered. In those days and in that part of the country, nobody had very great expectations for himself or for anyone else. Those were hard-scrabble times. People farmed and picked cotton, planted vegetables, carried water up from the wells, and had to rely completely on themselves—their broad backs and their gnarled hands—and on their neighbors. A few taught school, and there was always at least one minister to a county. They prayed every day and went to church on Sunday. Though Baptists weren't supposed to dance, they danced a little. Baptists weren't supposed to drink, either, but they did a little of that, too, on occasion. Papa played his harmonica and Mama played the foot-pedaled organ at the church; not until years after I was born did she manage to buy a piano for our home, on the installment plan (eight dollars a month). I never saw a paved road until I went away to study at the University of Alabama. The first automobile I ever saw was in 1905 in Waco, Texas—the noisy contraption so startled a team of horses that, whinnying with fright, they bolted and ran away, and I wanted to do the same thing.

Alabama was heading into the new century, but even more it was still a part of the Old South. The War between the States had ended only thirty-five years earlier, and the wounds—physical, economic, and psychic—had not begun to heal. Much more than the victorious North, the vanquished South had suffered mightily from the war and the so-called Reconstruction that came after it. Everybody's grandfather, including both of mine, had fought for the Confederacy and had tales to tell about depredations by the Union armies and about former slaves who had been made governors and legislators in the South by the vengeful conquerors from the North. Nearly everybody in the South was a Democrat, and the hated Republicans were in charge of the White House—under William McKinley as the century turned, and then Theodore Roosevelt. But national politics was not the major concern; eking out a living was. That, and trying to provide a little education for the children—with time out for some singing and dancing and maybe a little nip on Saturday nights—used up just about all the time there was.

For the most part, people stayed close to home and mingled with their own kind, which to us was other hardworking white farm families. Negroes (they weren't called blacks in those days) didn't come around much, except to earn a little money picking cotton or doing some other farmwork or housework. Generally on the farms, young Negroes worked alongside us white children. A few rose to the status of sharecroppers with the owners of the farms. It was taken for granted that Negroes were inferior to whites, and nobody spent a lot of time think-

ing about their rights as human beings. For the most part, they
were treated with kindness but expected to "stay in their place,"
which meant a very distant second place to the whites. They
generally were prosecuted even for petty crimes, and for murder or rape they frequently were lynched. A half century after
my name was chosen for me I was seeking reelection to the
United States Senate and was the subject of a whispering campaign that I was a "nigger-lover." The charge hurt me at the
polls in 1950 as, alas, it would today. Racism, like cancer, still
awaits a cure.

Despite my beginnings, I was destined to live a long, busy,
and for the most part productive life away from that farmhouse.
I went to college, hardly routine for Chambers County boys of
my generation and nearly unheard of in those days for girls. I
made Phi Beta Kappa and then obtained a law degree from
Harvard University in that bastion of abolition and anti-South-
ern intellectualism, Cambridge, Massachusetts. I would win and
lose battles in legislative chambers in Tallahassee, Florida, in
the United States Senate, and in the United States House of
Representatives. From my origins, from the struggles I shared
with my family and my neighbors, I formed a personal philosophy that later proved remarkably adaptable to a political philosophy—to which I have adhered unwaveringly even when
the price was defeat, humiliation, obloquy, and near bankruptcy.

Looking back now on nearly nine decades, I wonder if an
unseen hand, aware that Destiny would place me at the center
of many of the great events and terrible tragedies of the twentieth century, saw to it that the century and I arrived almost
simultaneously. I was just a little late, born September 8, 1900.
But I was in time to:

—become a high school teacher at the age of seventeen.
—serve long enough in the army to qualify for education
benefits that enabled me to study law at Harvard, which was

beyond my wildest imaginings had it depended on my own resources.

—win my first election to public office in 1928 and my most recent in 1986, a span of fifty-eight years.

—see Halley's comet in 1910 and again seventy-six years later.

—meet Orville Wright *and* greet the crew of the *Apollo* spaceship.

—lose my first bid for reelection to the Florida legislature because I would not support a resolution condemning Mrs. Herbert Hoover for inviting the wife of a black congressman to the White House.

—introduce, thirty-six years before it became law as Medicare, a bill to provide health care for the elderly.

—be courted by presidents, and try to depose one.

—be eyewitness to the emergence of the century's cruelest mass murderer, Adolf Hitler, and be received in the chambers of the runner-up dealer in wholesale death, Joseph Stalin.

—hear, with only three other persons, the first word that Franklin D. Roosevelt would seek an unprecedented third term.

—be informed that a president who came long after Roosevelt, Ronald Reagan, would not sign off on a Social Security rescue program until I approved it first (and therefore would not be able to "demagogue" the issue in the next election).

—appear on the cover of *Time* in 1938, and again forty-five years later in 1983.

—cast the only vote in favor of the Lend-Lease Act when I introduced it to the Senate Foreign Relations Committee and, when Lend-Lease finally became law, win the undying gratitude of Winston Churchill, and a hanging in effigy by members of the pre–World War II U.S. peace movement.

—be victimized during the McCarthy era for liberal views on United States–Soviet Union collaboration and on race and wage and hour laws, and be ousted from the U.S. Senate in the vicious "Red Pepper" campaign of 1950.

—serve in the U.S. House of Representatives, rise to chair the House Rules Committee, and for more than two decades help protect Franklin D. Roosevelt's greatest legacy, Social Security, for thirty-seven million current and untold millions of past and future beneficiaries.

—be in place in Washington to support and counsel President John F. Kennedy two decades after his father, Joseph Kennedy, turned against Roosevelt and against me.

—sit on a park bench with Bernard Baruch and fly on *Air Force One* with Jimmy Carter.

—know Helen Hayes and Bob Hope, and Brooke Shields.

—be retained by the most prestigious law firm in New York City, Cravath, Swaine, and Moore, to represent Bethlehem Steel Corporation, and win the case.

I entered public life because my early years in the destitute South convinced me that life for human beings should, and could, be much better than it was. What could make it so? Neighbors, churches, and private enterprise all had roles, but they all had limits, too, and those limits fell far short of providing security, health care, and some comforts of life for the many. It seemed to me that government policies and action were required to help in this nation's "pursuit of happiness" for its citizenry. What worthier purpose could government serve than to make life a bit happier and a lot less arduous for its people? I thought as I was growing up—and I think now—that a nation is stronger and better in every way if it concerns itself with the health, the education, the housing, and the economic security of its citizens. I am aware that such a philosophy is considered unfashionable today. In 1950, people told me that I could remain in the Senate as long as I wished, if only I would "change." Well, I had wanted to be in the Senate more than most: when I was fifteen years old, I wrote "Claude Pepper, United States Senator" on the office wall of a justice of the peace who let me use his library at night. But I could not change in the way people said I must, just to stay there. I could not reject my innermost feelings. My career, indeed my life, would have been rendered hollow.

Looking back, I wonder at what point in my Senate career I would have had to change in order to remain. Well, it doesn't really matter, because liberalism was and is my honest disposition. In the late 1940s, as Florida, the state that sent me to the Senate, became more and more conservative and as opposition to the New Deal, particularly by big business, became more and more virulent, I considered the only type of "change" I would be willing to make—resigning from the Senate, moving to New York, and trying to resume my political career in a more congenial ideological climate. But that was impractical. An outsider, particularly one with a Southern accent, would not likely break into the top rungs of New York Democratic politics. Florida business interests had opposed me ever since I unapologetically pressed for legislation calling for a minimum wage of twenty-five cents an hour, and at each election they tried harder to defeat or, better, destroy me. Men who controlled the large campaign donations told me to wise up or I was doomed. There was only one reason I would not change— I could not.

I was a New Dealer before there was a New Deal. I remained one when the ideology behind it came under bitter attack. I remain one today. I returned to public life after making lots of money practicing law because I preferred to be in the Congress, doing something that meant something. I learned long before I heard of Franklin D. Roosevelt that the private sector will not, and in many cases cannot, do all that needs to be done. It never has and it never will. Government will always have to help if there is to be fairness and a degree of equity in our society. How much health care would there be in this country for the poor and elderly if there were no Medicaid and Medicare? And what would be the plight of the elderly if there were no Social Security? Only 21 percent of Americans are protected by private pension programs; most employees work for small companies that cannot afford costly retirement benefits. Many large corporations are making remarkable progress in their retirement programs, and this is all for the good. I favor relying on private enterprise to the utmost. But where private enterprise leaves off, who besides the government can step in?

People frequently ask me, "Why are you still so liberal?" or "Why do you remain liberal when that word has become the kiss of death to white voters in the South?" Well, I have been around awhile, and liberalism and conservatism are like seasons—they come and they go. Why? I don't know. Why do fashions change? I suppose people grow weary of what they have at times and want to try something different, particularly if things are not going well. Some politicians, wiser or maybe just more survivalist than I, change with the fashions, some successfully, others not. I do not question their sincerity, but it just isn't in me to change politically unless I first have changed fundamentally in my character.

When I was twenty-eight years old (some readers may be startled to learn that Claude Pepper was once young) and a member of the Florida legislature, the first bill I introduced had to do with the elderly. It was legislation to waive the license fee for oldsters who wanted to go fishing. Where I grew up, old people were greatly loved and respected. I knew all four of my grandparents, so it seemed natural to me to be concerned about the elderly throughout my political career, not just after I had grown older myself. Some of my political opponents have tried to make it appear that my interest in senior citizens coincided with the increase in the elderly voting population in Florida, but when confronted with a record of support dating back to 1928, they have had to back off.

My record, open for all to examine, is equally long-playing in other areas. During my years in the Senate, for example, I strongly supported equal rights and equal pay for women, issues that many think are of recent origin though this was in the 1930s and 1940s. And the very first bill I introduced in the Senate was to extend federal assistance to handicapped children. I have been ridiculed often as a do-gooder for some of my concerns, but that doesn't bother me in the least. There are many worse terms of derision.

Back on July 2, 1938, I wrote in my diary: "My intense interest is in hospitals for all needing places, in schools, health, rural electrification, libraries, the art projects, etc., all indicating the real effort Government is now making to enrich the lives of its people. This is liberalism." I was excited by what was going on, delighted to be a part of a government that was doing what I, trudging along the dirt roads in the red clay country as a youth, had felt it should be doing. But I recognized that liberalism, according to my definition, was on a high that would not last forever. "How long will it survive now?" I wrote. "When will the people permit themselves to be deluded again?" Big business had had free rein for twelve long years and had brought the country to the edge of ruin. It could happen again.

In my years of public life, I have become convinced that two main philosophical or ideological strains exist side by side in America. One, the beneficiary of Ronald Reagan's remarkable personal popularity during the early 1980s, holds that anyone can become rich and successful and that anyone who does not "make it" is lazy, unwilling to work hard, envious of those who have moved ahead, and dependent on the government to take from others (through taxation or other means) and give to him (welfare, unemployment insurance, Social Security, etc.). This view is opposed by those who believe that a strong and prosperous society can and should lend a hand to those who are handicapped, poorly educated, sick, forgotten, or just plain down on their luck, people who can become productive and contributing members of society if just given a little boost. These competing viewpoints are at the heart of domestic political struggle in the United States and have been since the days of Thomas Jefferson and Alexander Hamilton.

Why should there be this struggle at all in a nation with such abundant resources? America's economic upper classes have always had a disproportionate share of the total wealth, a maldistribution that worsened during the Reagan years. How much is enough for these people? The New Deal didn't go "too far" as we often hear argued; World War II kept it from going far enough. Nor was the Great Society excessive; it did what needed to be done. But that's getting ahead of my story.

Providence has been generous to me, both in the number of years it has allotted to me and in the history it has allowed me to witness and be a part of. It blessed me with loving parents and with my beloved wife, Mildred, who shared every victory and every defeat with me until her tragic death in 1979 left me to carry on alone. It introduced me to the great and famous of my era, as well as to many of its worst scoundrels. It gave me the opportunity to help President Franklin D. Roosevelt in his lonely struggle to prevent the conquest of Europe by fascist dictators, and then gave me a chance to sponsor the National Institutes of Health, to help strengthen Social Security, and to resist and perhaps abate a little bit that cancer on the American body politic—entrenched privilege. It enabled me to demonstrate that a person can be useful and productive long after the "normal" retirement age, and to help eliminate mandatory retirement policies in both public and private employment.

Most of all, Providence has given me a life of personal satisfaction and fulfillment that comes only from knowing one has been able to make life a bit better for others—for many others. This is something that those who spend their lives trying to maintain and expand entrenched privilege will never, ever know.

1

A Subsidy for the Former Plowboy

Not in the clamor of the crowded street,
Not in the shouts or plaudits of the throng,
But in ourselves are triumph and defeat.

—HENRY WADSWORTH LONGFELLOW

We are all molded by region, era, antecedents, and chance. As a canyon is created by wind, rain, heat, cold, and flowing water, so is an individual the product of the family, the values, the prejudices, and the economic circumstances into which he is born. Thus, Thomas Jefferson held slaves and Franklin D. Roosevelt grew to manhood as an anti-Semite. In the postbellum rural South into which I was born, poverty and disdain—even hatred—for the Negro were the pervasive forces. But it was possible to overcome both.

The South! It had been home to generation after generation of my family. No close kin ever moved north to stay. My peo-

1

ple lived in Virginia, North Carolina, South Carolina, Georgia, and Alabama, and in my travels I have met and heard of Peppers who settled in Texas, Iowa, and Tennessee. The Peppers (the name originally may have been Culpepper) were in the colonies long before the Revolutionary War. In fact, a Pepper ancestor, my great-great-great-grandfather, died on King Mountain, North Carolina, in one of the fierce battles of that war. Exactly when the Peppers settled in the American colonies is not known. It is not even certain where they came from, although it most likely was England or Ireland. Dating back to at least 1774, the family was Baptist. Some family members belonged to other Protestant denominations, but there is no record of any Catholic. On a visit near Leeds, England, several years ago, I met some people who said the absence of Catholics in my ancestry made Irish origin unlikely. Noting my speech, they speculated that the family probably came from Yorkshire, for which there is some evidence. I have always wondered how echoes of Yorkshire could survive in competition with my pronounced Alabama accent.

There are records of a Samuel Pepper and a John Pepper, brothers, being signatories to a 1774 petition seeking to build a Baptist meetinghouse in Fauquier County, Virginia. This was long before Thomas Jefferson introduced in the General Assembly a bill establishing religious freedom (1779) and considerably before the assembly approved such legislation (1785). The names Samuel and John occur frequently in my family's history, as does the given name of the ancestor killed in the Revolutionary War, Elisha. There aren't many Claudes, although I did meet a Claude Pepper many years ago in Anderson, South Carolina. My family lived in Anderson for a time prior to 1800.

Court records I once examined in Anderson reveal that the Pepper family moved from Marshall, Virginia, through North Carolina and into South Carolina before 1800. By 1800, an

2

ancestor, Elijah Pepper, was living in Anderson County, South Carolina. He and his brother William and nephew John, my great-grandfather, moved from Anderson to southern Georgia. I have the original marriage certificate of my great-grandfather, John Pepper, and Sarah Oliver, who were wed in Pike County, Georgia, around 1840. Other family members, including my grandfather, moved to Chambers County in eastern Alabama. After the Battle of Tallapoosa, in which forces led by Andrew Jackson defeated the Creek Indians, many farmers, including my grandfather, moved into the rich river lands around Sanford's Bridge near Alexander City in eastern Alabama. When the Civil War began, my grandfather Elisha, at age seventeen returned to Georgia and, with his father John, joined the Third Georgia Volunteer Regiment. Their unit became part of the Army of Tennessee and fought at Chickamorga and Missionary Ridge. The two were discharged at war's end in North Carolina.

Many of my father's family are buried in eastern Alabama, including my great-grandfather. They have been silent now for decades, but stories passed down the generations suggest that they were anything but reclusive. The late Supreme Court Justice Hugo Black, who grew up in Clay County, Alabama, used to tell me that on many a Saturday afternoon he heard someone say, "Well, the Peppers are in town. There'll be some fighting in a little bit." A story—perhaps a legend—holds that when a bully attacked my great-grandfather, John Pepper, my ancestor responded by biting the fellow's ear off.

Grandfather Elisha Pepper was living on a small farm near Millerville, Alabama, when my father was born in 1873, one of ten children, five boys and five girls. At Grandfather's insistence, my father was named Joseph Wheeler, after the great Confederate general under whom Grandfather had served. My grandmother was Sarah Carriker, of Scotch ancestry, who came to Alabama from Georgia. My grandfather's home consisted of

3

a master bedroom, a parlor, a combined dining room–kitchen, front and back porches—and one bedroom for the five girls, another for the five boys.

I vividly remember Grandfather Pepper, a small man, about five feet seven inches, gray beard, deep, resonant voice. He liked to drink a toddy when he got up in the morning and in his younger days, I am told, drank fairly heavily until Grandmother ordered him to quit—or else. He and Grandfather Talbot used to tell me Civil War stories. I felt and still feel only one generation removed from that war.

The Talbots, my mother's family, were English through and through. They came to Maryland in the late 1700s and lived there for many years; there is a Talbot County in Maryland. But the Talbots, like the Peppers, moved progressively south— to Virginia, to North Carolina, to South Carolina, and finally to Georgia, where my mother was born in 1877.

My mother's mother was Sarah Armour, who came from a plantation family in southern Georgia. I remember learning as a little boy that Grandmother Talbot had inherited a thousand-acre plantation from her family in southern Georgia. She used to send one of her sons down there every year to collect the rents, but he was shot at so many times she sold the land.

The Talbot home was about a mile and a half away from our farm. It seemed like a very large home to me, two stories with a large front porch and an L-shaped porch at the rear. Grandfather Talbot, who had been a Confederate soldier, was a tall and well-educated man. My mother acquired her appreciation for the value of education from him.

My mother was a vivacious young woman, bright, and fond of music. She attended junior college, which was rare for women of that era and region. It was especially rare as she was one of eight children. It was not too common for men, either, but my father also went to junior college, he in Lineville, Alabama, and Mama in Georgia. Joseph Wheeler Pepper and Lena Corine Talbot met when J.W. went to Chambers County to visit his brother, who was teaching school in the very community in which the Talbots lived. They met, fell in love, and were married in 1896. Four years later, I came along, the third child after Mama lost a son and daughter in infancy.

Mama and Papa lived at first in a small farmhouse west of Dudleyville, Alabama, moving later to a 129-acre farm near the Talbot plantation on which my father built another small house, the first home I can remember. We moved in 1910 to Camp Hill.

But perhaps the most vivid of my early years was 1904, when I moved with my parents to Texas and got my first look at the world outside Alabama's red clay country. We had relatives in Texas, but the reason we moved was that the land was said to be fertile, broad, and flat, and Papa hoped to make a better living there. He was sufficiently cautious to retain our Alabama farm, however.

It was a venture for a four-year-old—the train, the ferry that carried it across the Mississippi, the big waterwheel that propelled the ferry. We settled in De Leon, Comanche County, which is in northeastern Texas. I remember Mama going to the doctor's office, and I was so lonely that, with my pet quail, I too went to the doctor's office. I acquired so much dust and dirt along the way that she was embarrassed to see me. Cowboys were commonplace, but a thrill to a small boy, even though they drank whiskey, and on one occasion, one of them fired a shot from his pistol. We moved after a few months to a tiny place called Ben Arnold in Milam County. It had a post office at least, and that may be where I first acquired the politician's trait of storytelling. The postmaster learned that I had a memory full of stories from my grandparents, and he would gather a few men around to listen. When I finished, the men would clap and give me pennies. After I had become a U.S. senator, the late Texas congressman, Bob Poage, called me to say a visitor in his office had said he used to pay me pennies to tell stories when I was a child. I met him and we reminisced.

The Texas experience did not lead to our hoped-for prosperity, so we returned to Alabama after about a year. The trip back, via Waco, was highlighted by an unforgettable incident: A team of horses was frightened by that strange new invention the automobile and ran away.

The farm home to which we returned was plain and small, like most in the area. Of course it had no electricity and no indoor plumbing. Not until the administration of Franklin D. Roosevelt would a significant number of American farm homes enjoy the luxury of electricity.

Family records do not disclose major involvement in public life by anyone on either side of the family. My father was a town marshal, a chief of police, and a deputy sheriff. He ran unsuccessfully for sheriff in Tallapoosa County, Alabama, his defeat being attributed to the fact that he openly declared he would enforce the Prohibition laws. But if the family tree is barren of statesmen, there is one case of a horse thief, although John Talbot's son was just a suspect. And I am indebted to my cousin John D. Pepper, Jr., for information that a Robert Pepper and 141 other residents of Burke County, North Carolina, were ordered to answer charges of high-treason felony and to show cause why they should not forfeit their real and personal property. This was in January 1783, and there is no record of the disposition of the case (many records in Southern states were destroyed during the Civil War). However, there is a document establishing that Robert Pepper died that same year, and in 1784 his widow, Catherine, was appointed to administer his estate. This suggests that he did not have to surrender his property and therefore could not have been found guilty.

The nearest post office to our farm was in Dudleyville and it was there that I went to school. We youngsters used to eat our lunches out of tin buckets while sitting atop a pile of lumber. For dessert, I used to bore a hole with my index finger in a biscuit and fill it with ribbon cane syrup out of a Macco Boy snuff box. Delicious! As much as they could have used my help on the farm, Mama and Papa insisted that I go to school and even bought a black mare named Maude for the two-mile trip to the two-teacher school. It was the same with my sister Sarah and my two brothers, Joe and Frank, when they came along: we were all going to go to school and there would be no argument.

I don't know at what age I began to help out around the farm, but all children in that region and time pitched in as soon as they were able, working on weekends and before or after (sometimes both) school. We picked cotton, backbreaking work; we plowed fields; we milked the family cow; we helped make syrup from sugarcane. I used to carry lunches to the men who made syrup at the cane mill. They would let me feed the cane into the mill, which was pulled by a mule hitched to a long lever. Of course, I would enjoy the taste of the good syrup my father had made. I helped pull fodder some, a very hot and dirty job, but the stalks were too tall for me to do much of that. We had a twelve-foot-high bell in our backyard, and I would ring the bell to summon people from the fields for lunch. Sometimes Mama sent me out to catch a chicken when visitors dropped by unexpectedly for a meal. There was a well on our back porch that served as a refrigerator—we would lower milk into the well to be cooled. Also in the backyard was a smokehouse where we kept large quantities of meat, salted for preservation. And, of course, we had horses and mules.

And always there was the County Line Baptist Church, a major social as well as religious focus of my early years. My grandfather Luke Talbot and his father John had been among the founders of the church. I was in a Sunday school class taught by a cousin, Will Jarrell. One day after an electrifying evangelical sermon, Cousin Will tried to get all of the boys to join the church. Only I demurred. "Claude, I don't understand you," Cousin Will said. "You're a good boy. Your parents are good churchgoers. Your classmates are all joining. Why not you?" Finally, I let him know the reason for my hesitation: "The last time I had a fight with Tom Cotton, he whipped me. I'm not going to join the church until I whip Tom Cotton." Whether or not I ever whipped him I don't recall, but I did join the church sometime later.

Holidays were special in our section of rural Alabama. On the Fourth of July several families would go together to a lake or stream, where the men would fish and we would always have a big meal with the day's catch as the main course. On Sundays, everyone would go to church, join in community singing after the service, and then have a big dinner together in the churchyard. Tables were laden with meats and vegetables, pies and cakes, and everyone joined in. At Christmas, our stockings hung over the mantel in Mama and Papa's bedroom, where they would be filled with an orange, an apple, raisins, some red stick candy, and various kinds of nuts. We couldn't have been happier if we had received bicycles, wagons, dolls, or sleds.

We did not realize until years later how poor we and most of our neighbors really were. We were never unhappy. Our family was close-knit, each member devoted to the others, and we remained so. In fact, in 1931 when I was practicing law in Tallahassee, Florida, I moved my family from Alabama to Tallahassee and we all lived together in homes Mildred and I rented. Ten years later when I was in the Senate, I built a four-apartment complex with the two ground-floor apartments joined, where Mildred and I lived on one side, Mama and Papa on the other, sharing living room, dining room, and kitchen. Although she rarely complained, and although we were in Washington or traveling much of the time, I am sure that Mildred,

like Eleanor Roosevelt,* would have preferred less together-
ness.

But when I was growing up, that very closeness and love
provided the sense of physical security that money brings to
children of the wealthy. We had few needs and wants, which
was fortunate since we had no means of fulfilling any but the
simplest ones. We knew nothing of the world outside the South
and little of the world outside Alabama. The odds were long
that I would grow up in the red clay country, take over the
farm someday or maybe start up a general store or other small
business in Dudleyville or Camp Hill. But Mama and Papa
were determined that this scenario would not be played out.
They wanted something more for their children.

For us, social life consisted of occasional parties in the
homes of farm families, many of whom were relatives. Someone (usually Mama) would play the organ or piano and everyone else would gather around to sing. One home was special—
the family owned a marvelous device, the Victrola, which miraculously poured forth music. Our home offered something
special in community entertainment, too: a violinist named
Connor traveled through the area and always spent the night
or evening with us. He was a gifted fiddler and loved to play
for square dances. When Connor visited, Mama would invite
friends and relatives to dance to his music, despite Baptist
teaching on dancing. Once Mama was mortified and angered
when one of her cousins, whose son was a suspected horse
thief, brought Mama and Papa up for disciplining at a second-
Saturday service at County Line Baptist Church—for "dancing
to music." The church acquitted them of wrongdoing and
afterward Mama turned to her accuser and snapped, "John
Talbot, you'd better sweep first around your own door." He
got the message.

*Eleanor and Franklin Roosevelt lived with FDR's mother, Sara Delano
Roosevelt, on the Hyde Park estate owned by the older Mrs. Roosevelt.

Music was a big part of my growing up. Mama was a real talent on the organ and, later, the piano. She tried to teach me, but I did not inherit her musical ability, although Sarah and Joe did. Mama was so musical that in later years she taught herself to play the violin and guitar.

There were other facets of this simple life. The farm women held "quiltings," where friends who had come from miles away would sit around frames suspended from the ceiling and make beautifully colored quilts. And there were logrollings, when farmers were clearing land and neighbors gathered to help. If a fire broke out in the community, volunteer wagons would drive through the countryside gathering furniture to be given to the unfortunate family. Later, everyone would help to rebuild the damaged structure.

Cotton was the only cash crop produced in the area. Often I would ride with my father on a wagon, carrying three bales of cotton, two or three mules pulling the wagon, to Lafayette, the county seat, and the market. Papa would take his samples from the warehouse to the town square, on three corners of which were buyers to offer him what they would. Nobody asked the farmers how much it cost to grow the crop, nor did anyone care about the 12 percent interest they had to pay on the money they borrowed. It would not be until Franklin D. Roosevelt's presidency that the farmer would be allowed to put his cotton "in the loan," get the market price, and later sell it for more if the market improved.

Another enjoyable activity centered around Tucker-Willingham's general store in Lafayette where my father traded and where he and I often enjoyed lunch together, meals more memorable than many I have had at the most famous restaurants and hotels of the world. We would dine sumptuously on canned oysters, potted ham, cheese, crackers, and mixed pickles, washed down by Coca-Colas.

In our area, all the farmers owned their farms, which ranged up to several hundred acres. At 129 acres, ours was one of the smallest. Whenever the farmers went to market at Lafayette or Camp Hill, they would bring back ice, and this signaled another community activity: homemade ice cream gatherings, with pound cake served up by the women. Another big event was known as "shooting the anvil," which occurred on Christmas Day: black powder placed between two anvils, one reversed on top of the other, would be exploded, the noise reverberating for miles around. It's a good thing we didn't have movies or television; we would have had no time for them.

Perhaps the most exciting event of my youth on the farm occurred when my father got me up about three o'clock one morning in 1910 and took me to our backyard to see Halley's comet. It was a bright light, with a long fiery tail, streaking across the sky like a Roman candle. Another great adventure of those farm years was visiting my father's parents near Millerville in Clay County. En route, we (Mama, Papa, and myself, and after 1909 my brother Joe) had to cross the Tallapoosa River at Germany's Ferry. The river was two or three hundred yards wide there, with a swift-flowing current. The horse (or horses if we borrowed Uncle Sanders Talbot's surrey) would nervously step down on a flat, which was hauled up against the bank. A man would then pull the ferry to the other side by means of a wire strung across the river. As we entered the current, the ferry would swing downstream. Although there was a chain that slid along the wire, attaching the ferry, Mama and I were as frightened as the horses, and we remained so until the horses excitedly scrambled up the bank on the far side.

One additional highlight of my boyhood was the Howard Owens store in Dudleyville. After school, I would ride to the store atop Maude, buy a nickel's worth of red peppermint stick candy mixed with crackers, and charge the purchase to Papa, who never objected though at times he must have been hard-pressed to come up with the nickels.

Papa did object, however, to some of my conduct. The youthful Claude Pepper was not a rural version of Little Lord Fauntleroy. Once I was toying with my father's .38 pistol and fired a hole through the wall of our home. Another time, curious about his .44 pistol, I fired a shot into the fireplace. Papa took the switch to me both times. Once some older boys in Camp Hill scraped together seventy-five cents and bet that I wouldn't dare kiss the prettiest girl in the class, Lorena Langley. Well, seventy-five cents was a lot of money in those days and Lorena, a distant cousin, was an attractive girl. So I sneaked up to her side one day, planted a kiss on her cheek, and jumped out of the schoolroom window. News of such scandalous conduct traveled fast; when Papa heard about it, the switch came out again. Another time at Camp Hill, a classmate and I decided it would be fun to set the boys' outhouse on fire and that we probably could get away with it. We were right on the first count, wrong on the second. The principal lined up every boy in the school and, one by one, looked each of us in the eye and asked each one if he had done it. In those days before women's liberation, the girls were not even suspect. I wanted to say no, but I couldn't. Papa was informed, and his anger was the greater because he was a member of the school board and his son certainly was not setting an example of acceptable conduct in the classroom or on the school grounds. He went for the switch again. It was effective. My career as an arsonist ended abruptly, and after the Lorena Langley episode, I never again tried to play Romeo.

Our family moved from Dudleyville to Camp Hill, about eleven miles away, in 1910. Papa and Mama wanted me to be able to attend a better school. I drove the family cow to the new location, quite a responsibility for a ten-year-old, since the cow was the family's sole supplier of milk. At Camp Hill High School, which had classes from the first grade up, I enrolled in the fifth grade because I had been told in my country school that I could get a fifth reader after Christmas. One of the first problems put to me was to add two-thirds and three-fourths. We had not studied fractions at Dudleyville, but I was sure logic would sustain me. I added the two and three, then the three and four, and came up with the only possible answer: five-sevenths. Everybody laughed. With a little extra study that summer, I caught up with my classmates and went on the following term to sixth-grade arithmetic, thanks to a kind teacher named Lizzie Lockhart.

I always made good grades, but I had other interests—serving as president of the Heflin Literary Society, debating, becoming class poet, editing the school magazine, playing baseball, basketball, and tennis. During these years, we lived in a rather large old house with a big front yard and scuppernong arbors in the back. There was still no indoor plumbing, but the day we moved in I was so excited I almost turned cartwheels when I spied a telephone—yes, a telephone!—on the wall. I had never talked on the telephone, so I ran to this one, put the old-style receiver to my ear, and then—nothing. I realized that I didn't have anyone to call.

At Camp Hill High School, I met one of the three men who were to have the greatest influence on my life.* He was C. C. Mosely, the principal. Unlike anyone else I had ever met, Mosely knew there was a world outside red clay country, and he had visited much of it. He fascinated me with his stories about the great cities he had seen and the wonders they contained—tall buildings, factories, electricity, crowded railroad depots, automobiles (so many you couldn't count them), theaters, libraries. For me, this was a turning point. Aside from my Civil War veteran grandfathers, people I had known had not traveled very much, if at all. I always read a lot, but Mr. Mosely

---

*All three were educators: Mosely; George H. Denny, president of the University of Alabama; and Roscoe Pound, dean of the Harvard Law School.

was a great teacher who made the outside world seem wonder-fully alive and alluring. He made it possible to imagine a world and a life beyond eastern Alabama. He later became superin-tendent of schools for Jefferson County and Dothan.

In Camp Hill, Papa tried to fatten and sell some cattle but the venture proved to be unprofitable and he discounted it. He then wanted to try his luck as a small businessman. The recession of 1914 was coming, but no one foresaw that, least of all Papa. He and a cousin started a furniture store called McClendon and Pepper, just in time for the economic down-turn. It probably wasn't a large store, but it seemed like a lot to me and meant a great deal to Papa. It went bust. Papa tried again, buying the fanciest grocery store in Camp Hill. I learned about this during recess at school and made a beeline to the candy counter. Papa was indulgent: I ate so much candy the first day or two it's a wonder I didn't get sick. Later, Papa turned the grocery store into a restaurant with a meat market in the rear. While serving as a waiter one day, I tried to hold a tray on my outstretched arm, the way professional waiters do, and the whole tray fell, scattering food all over the floor. It seemed clear that I was not cut out for waitering, so Papa helped me set up a small pressing shop behind the meat market, where I cleaned and pressed clothes. This new vocation had a big advantage—clothes didn't leave a mess when I dropped them.

Papa was not cut out for small business, at least not at that time and in that locale. All his ventures failed. Later, he be-came town marshal of Camp Hill, winning a reputation as a fearless and dedicated law enforcement official. He risked his life once to save a Negro from being lynched by an angry mob. Years later, after the family had moved to Alexander City, the largest city in Tallapoosa County, Papa became deputy sheriff, and by all accounts a dedicated public official whose legacy to his children was a keen sense of duty. I recall when I was studying in a law office in Lafayette, someone introduced me to our congressman. "So you're the son of Wheeler Pepper," he said. I said, "Yes, sir." Continued the congressman, "Honest as Moses."

My tiny clothes-pressing business led to a new adventure. A man whose business was cleaning and blocking hats came to my shop. He was an itinerant, traveling from town to town, moving on when everyone who wanted and could afford his services ($2.50 per hat) had taken advantage of the opportunity. He talked about his travels, further whetting my fascination with the outside world I had never seen. The life of an itinerant hat cleaner sounded glamorous. So when he offered to sell his equipment for very little money, I bought it. There I was, Claude Pepper, teen age entrepreneur—hats cleaned and blocked, satisfaction guaranteed. Who could know how far and wide I might travel and the wonders I might see? After all, I had never seen Atlanta, and Birmingham just once. The only other "big city" I had visited was Waco, Texas. This was a new project, with limitless possibilities. I was excited!

I knew I would have to start off modestly, saving my money for a later assault on the big cities. So I headed first for the small cotton-mill towns around West Point, Georgia. At West Point, I took a room in a cheap motel. Before I could fall asleep, a man—a stranger—knocked on the door and said that we were to share the room. That was a custom of small-town travel in those days, so I agreed. The man seemed very nervous. He looked out the windows a lot until dark, and then he seemed startled by every sound. He didn't talk much. When I woke up the next morning, he was gone. But not very far—he had been picked up in town and charged with the murder of his wife. If it was excitement I wanted in the hat business, I was getting it. But that wasn't really what I had in mind.

A second misadventure soon followed. A man stormed to my little stand one Saturday afternoon, demanding his hat. His wife had brought it to me and he wanted either to wear it that night or not to pay out $2.50. When I couldn't deliver the hat immediately because I had put too much stiffening in it, he became irate. To calm him, I said I would buy the hat. He was pleased and walked away with money in his pocket. As for me, I had a hat that I didn't really need.

Somehow, a life cleaning and blocking hats, traveling from town to town, and encountering wife killers and irate customers quickly lost its appeal. There had to be less hazardous ways to make a living.

The hat venture occurred during the summer of 1917, after my graduation from high school. The world was at war; Woodrow Wilson, a Democrat, was in the White House. (Except for Wilson and Grover Cleveland, the Republicans had controlled the presidency since 1869, to the discomfiture of the then heavily Democratic South.) Wilson had won reelection at least partly on the slogan "He kept us out of war," but now we were being dragged into the war anyway. To eastern Alabama, the war seemed remote. But when young men—relatives and neighbors—began leaving to join the military, the war became very real and very close. Industrialized Alabama—the Birmingham area—had been producing steel and other products needed for the war effort, but in rural areas the war did not come home until the young men left home.

School systems were hard hit; teachers were few in number in the best of times, but when the war depleted the ranks further, the situation became desperate. Despite its tragic aspects, war sometimes opens up opportunities for people, and thus it was with me in the early fall of 1917. Although I had graduated from high school just the previous spring and was not quite seventeen years old, on the recommendation of a friend I was contacted by the superintendent of schools of Dothan, Alabama. He offered me sixty dollars a month to teach the fifth grade. I had taken a teachers' examination earlier and received only a second-grade certificate. Since I didn't have the money to go to college anyway, I jumped at the offer. Knowing I had a job, I bought a new suit, hat, and shoes. Somehow I had already acquired a pair of nose glasses. I set out for Dothan and a new career, two days before my seventeenth birthday.

At the end of the first semester, I was promoted to teaching high school at even bigger money—sixty-five dollars a month. But high school would be difficult: I would be older than some of my students, but the same age as most and even younger than a few. For certain, I was smaller than most—five feet seven inches tall, 115 pounds, wringing wet. One student in my class was over six feet tall and weighed about 200 pounds. When I warned him about being disorderly in class, he ignored me. I told him there was a rule I would follow in his case as in every other: after three disruptions, I would take a switch to the offender. He snickered and continued his unruly ways. Finally, I told him to remain after class. When everyone else had left, I took a switch down from the wall and said, "Now I don't like to do this, but you know what the rules are, and it's up to me to enforce them." He went on whittling with his pocket-knife. But as I approached, he looked up. His expression was one of total disbelief. "You really mean to hit me with that switch, don't you?" he said. I replied, "Yes, I do. I gave you plenty of warning. I don't know if I'll be able to finish the whipping, but I sure am going to start." Still amazed, he put his knife away, stood up, and said, "I never expected you to go through with this. Tell you what—don't whip me and I'll never give you any more trouble." I put the switch away. He was as good as his word. When I left town at the end of the year, he was the only one who came to the train to see me off.

The year of teaching was enjoyable. I organized a basketball team at the high school, only to discover that we had no uniforms or equipment. So I hit up the merchants in town and raised enough to outfit the team, which I also coached. I was busy in other ways, teaching a men's Bible class at the First Baptist Church and also serving as vice-president of the Alabama Baptist Young People's Union. This was the first time I had been on my own and I felt I had grown in knowledge and experience, but I still was determined to go to college. I returned to Camp Hill for a brief visit, then went to Birmingham to look for work, staying with an aunt, Eunice McClendon, and her family. But there were no jobs in Birmingham. Tennessee Coal and Iron Company in Ensley, Alabama, was hiring, however, so I applied there and soon I was a steelworker, riding from my boardinghouse in Bessamer to the plant gate every morning, then walking half a mile into the mill, where we changed clothes and went to work. I straightened rails, lifting one end of a 273-pound billet with a co-worker, twelve hours a day, seven days a week. There was no union. Anyone who complained about the hours was told to get out.

Well, I didn't want to join the ranks of the unemployed, but I did hope for better things. One day I learned of a vacancy in the superintendent's office, applied, and was told to report the following morning. I was given a pencil, a pad, and a desk. I noticed a buzzing sound, but not knowing what it was, did nothing. Soon the superintendent yelled, "Why in the hell don't you come in here when I buzz you?" I rushed in and opened my pad; he dictated and I wrote. "Don't you take shorthand?" he screamed. I had to say no. "Then how in the hell did you get in here?" I explained that I had applied for a vacant job and been told to report in the morning. Fortunately, he calmed down and asked me my name and where I was from and why I had come to Ensley. I told him I wanted to go to college in the fall and needed money. "Well," he said, "You look like a decent young fellow. But you're not a secretary. Maybe I can help you. What kind of job do you want down in the yard?" I told him I'd like to operate an acetylene machine, which cut the faulty end off steel billets. I did that job the rest of the time I was there. When I was in the Senate, the superintendent visited me. "Just wanted to see my old secretary," he said, and we both had a good laugh.

What I really wanted to do at summer's end was go to the University of Alabama. The money I had earned just wasn't enough, even though I, of course, planned to work part-time as a student. I had been offered a scholarship at Howard College, a Baptist institution in Birmingham, and so had a friend, Shaffer Gregory, the son of a Baptist minister. Mama had made sure I would be able to choose. Our family had a good friend in the banking business named E. L. Andrews, president of the Bank of Camp Hill. He enjoyed helping young people get a decent start in life. To him, there was no better investment than one in a deserving human being. When Mama told Mr. Andrews that I might need some money if I decided to go to the university, he said he would see to it that we got a loan. "Lena," he said to Mama, "I'm going to see that boy through." But in early September, Shaffer Gregory and I showed up at tiny Howard College. We found a room where we could stay together, and then we sat up most of the night talking. At length we agreed: we both wanted to go to the university. In the morning, we went to the president of Howard College, thanked him for the scholarships, and told him of our decision. He was gracious and wished us well. We boarded a train and headed for Tuscaloosa and the University of Alabama, a major and—as the passage of time has proved—correct decision. Mr. Andrews was as good as his word. He arranged a loan of several hundred dollars.

The small-town banker's willingness to gamble on a poor youth's future made a lasting impression on me. Reflecting on my life to this point, I thought how typical this act was. In 1936, after my first election to the Senate, Camp Hill staged a

"Claude Pepper Day" replete with parade, speeches, and good food, a fete arranged by my boyhood friend Horace Smith. In my remarks, I had an opportunity to thank Mr. Andrews for the contribution he made to my education and thus to my career. Camp Hill and eastern Alabama were like that. People always helped people as best they could. Your problems were not yours alone. If a family ran out of food, those with a little extra would share. If the wind blew a farmer's fence down, the neighbors would help him put it back up. If a little child got lost, everyone would join in the search. Bankers were supposed to have hearts of steel, and in later years I encountered some who did, but in small communities where the rule had always been to help each other, bankers played by the rule, too—to the very limits of prudence. People ask me why in my public life people's health, their handicaps, and their right to be treated fairly at any age have always been my greatest concerns. Considering my formative years, it would be strange if the situation were otherwise.

In September 1918, I turned eighteen years of age. That added another variable to my life. The military soon would be accepting eighteen-year-olds, since the United States had entered World War I in the belief it had to choose between war and seeing the German imperial army conquer all of Europe and Great Britain. But until I was called, I intended to feast in the wondrous groves of academe. Tuscaloosa was a delightful Southern city, big by my standards, but what most impressed me were the professors with their knowledge, their lively wit, their sophistication, and their eagerness to make learning the pleasurable pursuit it should be. And books! All my life I had had problems finding enough books to read. Now there were more right at hand than I thought existed in the entire world. I read histories, biographies, Shakespeare, Dickens.

During World War I, the draft age was twenty-one to thirty-one. But in 1918, Congress passed a law requiring all men eighteen to forty-five to register by September 12 of that year. Congress also authorized the army to use the facilities (dorms, classrooms, marching areas) of most of the colleges and universities of the nation and allowed students eighteen, nineteen, and twenty years of age to volunteer—which, after passing the required physical examination, I did. With others in this age group, I was inducted on October 7, 1918. We were all allowed to stay in school until summoned to active duty.

In banter with journalists, I often have made the claim that while in the army I suffered imprisonment for the sake of freedom of the press. Late one afternoon as we finished drill on the parade grounds, all three battalions were ordered to line up. An adjutant stepped out and directed that all those whose names he was about to call should take a position standing beside him. He did not say why. When I heard my name, I took my position, curious to know what was happening. Were we to be sent to officers' training school? A glance at the twelve to fifteen whose names had been called disabused me of that notion. Soon an officer marched us to the headquarters of Major E. O. C. Ord, a regular army officer in command of the Alabama Student Army Training Corps. Gruffly, Major Ord said, "I want to ask each of you two questions: your name, and whether you are a member of the executive board of this stinking sheet on the campus called the *Crimson and White* [the college newspaper]." All of us answered yes. "You are all under arrest and confined to quarters until further orders," the major declared. Shocked and confused, we were taken to our rooms and placed under guard.

Later we learned that the newspaper had published articles critical of Major Ord for shutting down the campus supply stores. One such article appeared under the headline: OPEN UP THE SUPPLY STORES, MAJOR ORD, YOU AIN'T NO KAISER. Another article criticized battalion officers for dating nurses from the

state mental asylum near the university. Our confinement continued for a full week, even including three days after the armistice was signed, ending the war. I had to peek out of my
room window in order to see any of the Armistice Day parade.
Our families, hearing we were imprisoned but not being told
why, were frantic. They thought we might have done something horrible for which we might be shot. At long last the
army discovered that the offending articles had been written
by members of the editorial board who were not members of
the Student Army Training Corps, and we were released.

To me, the most immediate benefit of being in the army
was financial; all expenses were taken care of. Of course, I was
in a situation that could lead to my being killed, but like most
eighteen-year-olds I didn't worry much about it. With studies
and military drills, the hours were long, yet no longer than I
had put in the previous summer, working twelve-hour days,
seven days a week at the steel mill. My army career, however,
was destined to be brief. The armistice signing came on November 11, 1918, little more than a month after my induction,
and, on December 12, I was given a sixty-dollar bonus and
discharged. The money carried me through Christmas. That
same month I received a "bonus" of another sort—a trip to
Birmingham to participate in the three-mile race as a member
of the university's cross-country track team.

In early 1919, I returned to the University of Alabama. I had
to find work and there wasn't much available. I landed a part-
time job at a power plant, where I rolled coal and ashes from
four until seven every morning. (One of my co-workers was a
tall youth named John Sparkman, who would later serve beside
me in the U.S. Senate and who would be the Democratic nominee for vice-president of the United States in 1952.) The early
hours left me bleary-eyed when I arrived for classes, but somehow my grades were all A's anyway.

Hazing was fairly severe at the university in those days. I

remember having to sit on two pillows while studying for final examinations because of beatings I had taken from bed slats wielded by sophomores and upperclassmen. We freshmen were required to wear green caps and were called "rats." Sophomores made the "rats" perform all sorts of errands, and a favorite form of torture was to force freshmen to make speeches in the mess hall at the close of dinner hour for the amusement of upperclassmen. I was frequently chosen to perform, having a stronger voice and more of a talent for speech making than most of my brother rats. Thus I caught the attention of a man called Cherry Rowe, head of the Student Boarding Association. One day toward the end of my freshman year, Rowe called out to me as I was walking across campus. "Hey, Rat Pepper," he shouted. "Come here." Now what? I thought. Will he beat me? Send me on a silly errand? Force me to make a fool of myself singing or dancing? But I was in for a surprise. "How would you like to be secretary-treasurer of the Student Boarding Association?" he asked. I could hardly say fine quickly enough. Years later, I would say that if the president were to offer to appoint me ambassador to the Court of St. James, I would not be nearly so exhilarated as I was by this offer, which meant that I would be paid for running the mess hall instead of rolling ashes early every morning.

That topped my freshman year, but there were other memorable experiences. One highlights the simplicity of life in America in the early decades of the twentieth century. Joe Sewell, a baseball star at the University of Alabama, went on to play with the Cleveland Indians. He helped the Indians win the World Series that year—and three weeks later, he was back on campus! Can you imagine that of any of the multimillionaire major leaguers of today? Before his World Series heroics, Joe served as my headwaiter at the mess hall. Aside from baseball, Joe was best known for his voice, which could compete successfully against a bullhorn. Every morning, Joe would stand in front of Woods Hall, where his fellow athlete-waiters lived, and call them out in a voice that I feared would shatter windowpanes.

I ran the mess hall from the fall of 1919 until the spring of 1921, the year of my graduation. I also was a member of the debate team, an activity that took me outside the state of Alabama for the first time since my trip to Texas in 1904. We debated Vanderbilt University in Tennessee and competed in both the Southern Oratorical Contest at the University of North Carolina, and the Conference of Midwest Colleges and Universities at the University of Missouri in Columbia. At graduation I was elected to Phi Beta Kappa, and I remained a member of the Reserve Officers' Training Corps, largely for economic reasons. This exposed me to mock battlefield conditions at Fort Monroe and Camp Eustis in Virginia, where we fired sixteen-inch guns. At one of the camps I was exposed to something else—jaundice.

In the spring of 1921, I became involved in campus politics in a major way. I had been elected to a number of offices in high school, but at the university I decided to go for the big one, student body president. And I lost. This was the first manifestation of a phenomenon that was to become a pattern of my life—defeats that led to greater triumphs later on. Had I won, I would have returned to Alabama the following year. Now I was free to marshal enough credits to graduate that summer and then in the fall do what I really wanted to do—go to Harvard Law School. During my brief army service, I had incurred a disability. Now I was told that I was entitled to government-subsidized vocational training. Well, the vocation I wanted was the one Papa must have had in mind when he chose my middle name, Denson, after eastern Alabama's great lawyer and judge. And the law school I wanted was the one I judged to be the best: Harvard. To go to Harvard was now miraculously within my reach. Amazing! When government lends a hand, possibilities can be limitless. That is my philosophy, and my experience. That hand extends even to former cotton pickers and plowboys from rural Alabama.

I traveled to Boston by boat from Savannah, Georgia, after taking a train from Camp Hill. In Savannah, I noticed a tall young man about my age, drinking a Coca-Cola. I ordered one, too, and decided to strike up a conversation. "My name's Pepper and I'm from Camp Hill, Alabama," I announced. He responded, "Well, my name's Walker, and I'm from Atlanta, Georgia." Thus began a friendship that was to last from that day forward. Wallace Haynes Walker also was headed for Harvard Law School; we became roommates and inseparable companions for three years. In fact, when government red tape delayed my benefit checks for several months, I would have had to drop out of school had it not been for Walker. His family was wealthy, so he could lend me the money I needed until finally a half dozen or so checks arrived at once and I was able to pay him back. We remained close friends for sixty-five years—until he passed away in 1986.

I am grateful that Fate allowed me to return the favor to Walker. Years later when I was a U.S. senator, Walker telephoned to inform me that his position as an attorney in the Department of Justice was being abolished. He had two sons studying at Harvard, and if he lost his job he would have to take them out of school. I immediately made an appointment to see Attorney General Robert Jackson and told him how Walker, when he knew nothing about me, had nonetheless lent me money that enabled me to stay in law school. I asked Jackson to try to find some way to keep Walker employed so that his sons would have the same opportunity their father had made possible for me. Jackson, who was to become a distinguished Supreme Court justice and the chief prosecutor of Nazi war criminals at the Nuremberg trials, smiled and said, "I will take care of your friend Walker."

Harvard had a profound impact on me. It opened my eyes

to the great nation beyond the South; to me, it was an entirely new world. Like many a Southerner, I came north with a chip on my shoulder. I knew all about the Civil War, having heard firsthand from my grandfathers about Yankee treachery and having read every book I could lay my hands on. When those Harvard Yankees started arguments over which side was right and which side was wrong, I would be ready. It was the least to be expected from the grandson of two Confederate veterans and the son of a man who proudly bore the name of a heroic Confederate general. But to my dismay, nobody so much as mentioned the Civil War. All my life I had listened to and participated in discussions about the War between the States, and now at last I was in a position to hoist the Southern banner in Yankee territory. But nobody was interested. What was still a bitter pill in the vanquished South was, by 1921, a closed chapter in the victorious North, which had moved on to other matters. I was all primed to defend—but no one attacked.

During the Red-baiting years of Senator Joe McCarthy, Richard Nixon, and others, Harvard did not escape the broad brush. In the campaign of 1950 in which I lost my Senate seat, the fact that I had been graduated from Harvard Law School certainly was not a plus. In one of those snide guilt-by-association remarks at which the late senator from Wisconsin and the unscrupulous future president excelled, my opponent boasted of having studied under the yellow and black colors of the University of Florida whereas I had learned the law under the crimson of Harvard, an innuendo as contemptible as it is unanswerable. The truth is that Harvard's official color, crimson, far predated the association of red and pink colors with communism. Also, the truth is that Harvard did not provide me with a political philosophy of right, left, or middle. I had formed my own by the time I enrolled there. What Harvard Law School tried to influence was the thinking process, not the thoughts; the whole idea was to make students think, not to impose a leftish ideology upon them.

The great contribution of Harvard Law School to my life and career was its faculty of brilliant men. (There were no women professors, indeed no women students. There was one black in the class, which was unusual for that time and a shock to us Southerners, who had never before sat in a classroom with a black.) The great Roscoe Pound was dean and the professors included Beale, Felix Frankfurter, Samuel Williston, Austin W. Scott, Edward H. Warren, Zachariah Chafee, and Francis B. Sayre (Woodrow Wilson's son-in-law). The text for almost every course I took was written by the professor teaching it, and vigor and a freshness of approach were characteristic of all the classes.

The students were almost as stimulating as the professors. James M. Landis,* who later became dean of the law school and also had a long and distinguished career in government, led the class in grades during my second and third years. One class behind me was Thomas Corcoran, who became famous as "Tommy the Cork," the leader of Franklin D. Roosevelt's brain trust. Phi Beta Kappa keys were so commonplace that I didn't even get around to buying the one I earned at Alabama until near the end of my last year.

Harvard taught me the difference between a broad and narrow mind; it freed me from many prejudices. Whatever and whoever I became, I would have been only a part of without Harvard Law School. I did not make the *Law Review*, a goal I cherished greatly, but I did become president of the Beale Law

---

*Landis was involved in one of the great ironies of my political life. When I was in the Senate, Ernest Graham, a prominent Floridian who ran unsuccessfully for governor, asked my help in getting his son Phil into Harvard Law School. Phil Graham, who later became publisher of the *Washington Post*, had done poorly in an examination and had been denied admission. His father assured me that Phil had a fine mind and would do well if admitted. I called James Landis, by then the dean, and on my say-so he agreed to give young Graham a chance. Graham was so successful that he became president of the *Law Review* and a clerk for Supreme Court Justice Felix Frankfurter. In 1950, Phil Graham, although often acknowledging my key role in getting him into Harvard Law, was a staunch supporter of my opponent, who had been his roommate at the University of Florida.

Club and got to the semifinals of the Ames Moot Court Competition. I graduated in the top third of the class, and at commencement was both proud and grateful—to my parents, who could have used my help but instead encouraged me to obtain the best education possible. I was also grateful to my government, to which I felt I owed a lifelong obligation.

Now that I had a law degree, what could I do with it? Offers had come in from various big-city law firms, which then, as now, coveted Harvard Law graduates. Should I join a major firm, make some money, and then try to do something in politics? I was deeply interested in politics, both because it offered opportunities to do things that mattered and because it seemed I had always been in politics. All my life I had been elected to some position or other in school, at the University of Alabama, at Harvard Law, in my church. In Cambridge, I had plunged into my first genuine political campaign, a 1924 Senate race involving Henry Cabot Lodge, Sr., who had prevented the United States from joining the League of Nations, thereby mortally wounding that organization and making World War II inevitable. So strongly did I feel about the need for the League of Nations (later I was equally avid about the United Nations) that I went into Boston, joined the Democratic Speakers Bureau, and campaigned on behalf of Lodge's opponent, a man named Gaston.* Three of my speeches were delivered in Irish neighborhoods in Boston, where my Alabama accent must have sounded as strange to the Irish as their brogues did to me. I was driven in a Winton Six automobile to certain street intersections, where I would stand on the backseat of the car and speak to the crowd in front of me. The

---

*At Camp Hill High School, while reciting a poem, I could not remember the fourth verse. I repeated the third. The words of the fourth still did not come to me, so I recited the third verse again. The class roared with laughter. I told my teacher I would never again speak to an audience. My speeches for Gaston were only a few of the many breaches of my childhood vow.

receptions were so good that the campaign managers decided to send me to Lexington and Concord, where I was a flop. Those two historic towns were rock-ribbed Republican, heavily in favor of Lodge; as soon as the voters realized they were listening to a Southern Democrat, they evaporated. I didn't help Gaston much, and neither did anyone else. Lodge, whose grandson Henry Cabot Lodge, Jr., would serve alongside me in the Senate, won easily.

What Lincoln said of the presidency—"The taste is in my mouth a bit"—was true of me with regard to politics in general. My early nibble in the Massachusetts senate race left me anticipating a full bite later on, and perhaps the full course over the long run. While I mulled over such thoughts, the Boston newspapers reported that Governor W. W. Brendon of Alabama would be visiting the city. Who better to advise an embryo politician? I went to his hotel and telephoned him from the lobby; he said he would be glad to see me. I had known the governor when he was the judge of Tuscaloosa County and I was a student at the University of Alabama. "Well, Pepper," he said, "whatcha gonna do after you leave here?" I replied, "Governor, that's just the reason I came to see you. I don't know." I told him I was leaning toward accepting an offer from a law firm in Birmingham—Martin, Thompson, and Turner. "Is that the firm of the Alabama Power Company?" he asked. "Yes, sir," I replied. "I believe it is." He looked me in the eye. "Stay away from utility firms if you're figuring on ever getting into politics." It was good advice, for utilities were regarded as fleecers of the public in those days and they became even more unpopular during the Depression years when I actually was running for public office.

My career situation remained unresolved. I didn't know where to go or what to do, but Fate intervened again. Dickey Ames, secretary of Harvard Law School, summoned me to his office one day in the spring just prior to graduation and told me to go to the Copley Plaza Hotel in Boston that afternoon to meet with the president of the University of Arkansas, J. C. Futrell. I said I'd be glad to, but what did President Futrell want to see me about? Said Ames, "He's looking for someone to teach at the University of Arkansas Law School, and I've recommended you." I said to Ames, "Well, I sure do thank you, but I have no desire to teach. I plan to practice law." Ames had already arranged the appointment, so I agreed to go. But at the Copley Plaza, no one named Futrell was registered. I started to leave when a graduate student whom I knew and who may also have been interviewed spotted me. He pointed to a man sitting behind a palm in the lobby; it was Futrell. I had come within seconds of missing him altogether. We chatted, and he urged me to come to Arkansas. I had to ask him where the university was located, and he said in the Ozark mountains. Then I had to ask him where the Ozark mountains were. Futrell was persuasive. I decided that maybe a year in academe would give me a chance to get my thoughts together and decide what I wanted to do with my life. I accepted. After leaving Futrell, I looked for a map to see if I could locate Fayetteville, Arkansas, and the Ozark mountains.

Before taking up my new life in Arkansas, I had to attend to some urgent personal business. My family had moved to Alexander City, Alabama, and I went there for a short visit. From Alexander City I traveled to Montgomery to take the Alabama State Bar examination, and then I checked into a veterans' hospital in New Orleans, on the banks of the Mississippi river, for a double hernia operation. The surgery was not pleasant, but I more vividly remember the weather. As I lay on my back for three weeks, the only defense I had against the hot, sticky summer weather was one small fan, which I had bought myself.

I learned a great lesson in that hospital. A fellow patient was a British sailor who had fallen on a broken bottle and cut all the tendons of his right forearm. He came to visit me nearly every day. One day, beaming with happiness, he came to my room and said, "Look here, Pepper, look here." I looked, and all I could see was that the middle finger on his right hand was moving, ever so slightly, back and forth. And that was the reason for his joy. I thought to myself, Happiness is relative. One of the happiest men I know is one who can move his finger, just a little.

Soon it was on to Fayetteville. I was confident I was doing the right thing, since Providence has always been better at working out the details of my life than I have. Now it had decreed that I would go to Arkansas. What next? The possibilities were limitless. Would I marry an Arkansas girl and settle there for life? Would I become a state legislator, then speaker, then state senator, governor, and U.S. senator from Arkansas? Or would I wind up in private practice there? It was also possible that I wouldn't care for Arkansas at all and that I would return to Alabama after a year, which was all the time I had agreed to stay.

As it happened, none of the above took place. Although I fell mildly in love with a daughter of President Futrell, my feelings were unrequited. And the closest I came to Arkansas politics was to teach a law student named J. William Fulbright,* who later became a U.S. senator from Arkansas and who has remained my warm friend. Even though my stay was brief, I loved Arkansas, its university, and its people. The law school dean, J. S. Waterman, an able lawyer and a fine gentle-

---

*Had I been returned to the Senate in 1950, I would have become chairman of the Foreign Relations Committee, a post that went instead to my former student Fulbright. The pattern of my defeats held: had I not lost, I never would have headed the House Select Committee on Aging or the House Rules Committee. In both those positions, I was able to do a great deal more for many more people than I ever could have done in Senate Foreign Relations.

man, took me under his wing, and we used to take long walks in the early evening to the home of his friends in the country. In the spring, I got to know the state better, visiting many communities to which I had been invited to deliver commencement addresses. Academic life was pleasant, and I never regretted having partaken of it. But something, politics, gnawed at me. After a year, I left the academic world for a world more turbulent, law cum politics. Fate had pointed me in a new direction—to Florida, "The Land of the Future."

Certainly it was the land of *my* future.

2

A Political Odyssey Begins

Fate is stronger than anything I have known.

—EURIPIDES

For more than six decades, Florida has been my home. For more than four decades, Irene Mildred Webster Pepper was my wife. Neither of these associations was planned by me. But I have no doubt that both were part of an arrangement drafted by a force much abler than I to plot out a rewarding and useful life for one Claude Denson Pepper of Camp Hill, Alabama. Had Fate not directed me to Florida, it is unlikely that I would ever have met Mildred, without whom I cannot imagine what my life would have been like. Yet, left to my own devices, I never gave a serious thought to moving to that state, which now is the repository of countless memories, dear friends, more honors than I deserve, a record of public service, and along the way, defeats and disappointments—which, in keeping with a lifelong pattern, led to opportunities for greater accomplishment than would have been possible had I always won.

The instrument that Fate, or Destiny, or Providence, used

to lure me to Florida was a young law school student who took classes from me at the University of Arkansas. Donald Trumbo came from a wealthy family that owned banks and other property in and around Muskogee, Oklahoma. As an undergraduate, Trumbo was an indifferent student, but in law school he became serious about his studies and often consulted with me about them. We became close friends. During the Christmas holiday period in 1924, my new friend had the good sense to marry a lovely young woman named Juanita Bass. He did not, however, confide these intentions to his authoritarian father, A. C. Trumbo, who was so outraged at this display of independence that he refused to pay his son's law school expenses. This forced the new bridegroom to take a job in a small family-owned bank in a dusty little town in Oklahoma. Disconsolate, Donald Trumbo wrote to me, asking that I intercede on his behalf. I wrote a long letter to his father, praising Donald's progress in law school, urging him to enable the son to continue in the direction of what could be a promising career. Not long after, Donald Trumbo joyfully returned to law school. His father's resolve had melted partly as a result of my letter, but more because he had come to realize what a charming new daughter-in-law he had acquired.

In any event, family harmony was restored. Almost every weekend, the father visited the young couple in Fayetteville, and I was always invited to join the three of them for dinner. A. C. Trumbo spoke frequently of his involvement with a syndicate that owned more than a million acres of Florida land near a small town called Perry, in Taylor County below Tallahassee on Florida's west coast, and stretching down to Homosassa in aptly named Citrus County. I clearly recall the father's enthusiasm over the venture and about Florida's future. "Florida is the El Dorado of the future," he would cry. "Florida is the golden age of the future; I want my son to share in Florida's future." At one of these dinners, the father urged me to

34

accompany Donald and his bride to Florida, tutor the son in law, and perhaps open a small law firm some day with Donald as my associate. In return, the father would provide me with a law library of my choosing. While I was still mulling this proposal, A. C. Trumbo told Donald and me of an important meeting to be held in Chicago in June 1925 at which the Hoover Syndicate, in which the senior Trumbo was a large investor, would become the Florida West Coast Development Company, a real estate corporation. The father could not make it to this crucial meeting: Would Donald and I represent him and his substantial interests? Gladly, I said. Donald agreed.

We boarded a train, I wearing a white summer suit. When we got to Chicago, it was snowing. I felt—and I'm sure looked—ludicrous. But my luggage had been lost during the trip and there was nothing I could do about my curious costume. As I strode along Michigan Avenue in my ice cream suit in the middle of a snowstorm, I provided a number of Chicagoans with a good laugh, I'm sure. Eventually, my bags arrived and I was able to change into more appropriate attire.

The quirks of Fate continued. I was introduced to a Judge W. B. Davis, who was no longer a judge but a Florida lawyer in private practice. When I heard where he was from, I told him that I was seriously considering locating in Florida. "Well," said Davis, "I'm looking for a man because I do the work in Perry of this syndicate, which is soon to become the Florida West Coast Development Company." Then he said, "You went to Harvard. Did you know a student named Woodrow Wilson?" I remembered Wilson (not the former president), who had lived near me on Cambridge Street. Davis sent a wire and quickly received a return wire from Wilson containing a satisfactory recommendation. He offered me the position on the spot. Since I already was under heavy pressure from Trumbo to go to Florida, I accepted on the condition that Donald Trumbo could go with me and perhaps help out until he could obtain his law degree. Soon a large delegation of Floridians, led by Governor John W. Martin, arrived in Chicago to celebrate the formation of the West Coast Development Company and I met many people from Perry who later became my best friends.

This was a new and promising venture, one that had found me, not the reverse. From Chicago, I traveled to Alexander City, visited with my family, and borrowed $300 from the local bank. On June 30, 1925, again resplendent in my white suit—in harmony with the weather this time but covered with soot and cinders from the open-coach train—I arrived in Perry to begin a new life in Florida. The pay was not good. After earning $2,500 for my year at the University of Arkansas Law School, I received $125 for my first month in Perry. But the direction was clearly up, and fast: the second month I was paid $150; the third, $175; and in the fourth month, I became a partner. Since I lived with Judge Davis, I managed nicely and the new law firm of Davis and Pepper prospered. With my escalating affluence, I was able at last to help my parents and my siblings, eventually sending my sister and two brothers to college. (In 1930, after I had moved from Perry to Tallahassee, I brought the entire family down to live with me.)

With a population of about 2,500, Perry was (and is) the county seat of Taylor County. It is about fifty-five miles south of Tallahassee, and for years it has been a rich source of timber. During the Civil War, it was a haven for Southern males who fled into its swamplands rather than be drafted into the Confederate army. When I arrived in 1925 there was still a residue of violence in the behavior of the county's residents, as reflected in the fact that I participated in at least twenty-five murder trials, one of which achieved a degree of fame in Florida and national legal annals.

The case involved a farmer named J. W. Buchanan, known as Buck Buchanan. In December 1927, the sheriff of Taylor County approached Judge Davis and me at a picnic, telling us that Buck Buchanan had shot and killed two revenue officers and that he wished us to represent him at trial. We visited with Buchanan at the jail. He told us he was not well-to-do, that he owned only a small farm, and that he could pay us no more than $750. We took the case. Buchanan was found guilty of killing one revenue officer as the man stood with one foot planted on the front porch of the farmhouse, vowing to enter in search of liquor despite Buchanan's objections. The jury recommended mercy, which meant a life sentence instead of death, but Buchanan refused an offer of the state's attorney to drop a second murder charge if he would not appeal the life sentence. Saying he would rather be dead than spend the rest of his life in prison, Buchanan appealed the life sentence, but the Florida Supreme Court upheld it. Just as his second murder trial was to begin, a string of killings occurred, inciting public outcries. This time the verdict was the same—guilty—but there was no recommendation of mercy. Buchanan had killed the second agent with a shotgun blast as the man ran back to a corner of the yard after seeing Buchanan kill his partner with a pistol. Unless we could win an appeal, the killer would be electrocuted. Again the Florida Supreme Court upheld the sentence, and the governor issued a death warrant.

At this point Judge Davis became ill and the entire burden of the case fell on me. I sought a writ of habeas corpus, arguing that of the two equal sentences, the one imposed first—life imprisonment—would have to be served first. The writ was denied, but by then the death warrant had expired and the governor had to issue another. Again I went to court, arguing that only a person of official status could execute the death penalty under common law and that the executioner was an appointee of the commissioners of state institutions, not of the governor and not elected by the people. Thus, the death warrant was invalid under the Florida constitution because the executioner had no "official status." That argument went to the

Fifth Circuit Court of Appeals and won some support, but not enough. Again, however, the death warrant had expired. In all, five death warrants were ruled out by technicalities or passage of time, and Buck Buchanan still lived.

I do not wish to convey the notion that I felt a double murder should go unpunished. Buchanan deserved a life sentence, but not, in my opinion, execution. The victims had come to his home during the Prohibition era, and Buchanan had agreed they could search the house, but not until he had alerted his wife who would otherwise become excited and suffer "spells." Suspecting that Buck would simply get rid of any liquor before admitting them, the revenue officers said no. According to his story, Buchanan stood in the doorway while one agent put one foot on his porch, fired a shot in the air, and then pointed a pistol at the farmer—who shot first. The murders were brutal, especially that of the second, fleeing agent, but not premeditated, and thus not punishable by death.

The years passed, and Buchanan lingered on in his death cell. After I had been in the Senate a number of years focusing on more cosmic matters, I received a letter written with a blunt pencil on a cheap, lined piece of paper torn from a tablet. It was from J. W. Buchanan and said: "Dear Mr. Pepper. I am now sixty-five years of age. I want to know if I ain't entitled to an old age pension." Not long after that, he died of atherosclerosis and high blood pressure, more than a decade after he had been condemned to death.

After nearly three years in law practice, I decided that if I were to achieve my childhood ambition to become a United States senator, it was time to start. The route I planned to follow was the usual one for an ambitious young politician: first win election to the state house of representatives, then move up to the state senate, become the senate leader, then run for attorney general, then governor, and then for the United States Senate.

As happened so often in my life, my plan did not work out. Another, better one, did.

Phase One did go according to the book. Since settling in Perry, I had made many friends and become fairly well-known in legal circles as well as in the Kiwanis Club, Chamber of Commerce, other social and civic organizations, and the First Baptist Church. It was generally known that politics had always fascinated me and that someday I would become involved. W. T. Hendry was the incumbent member of the state house of representatives from Taylor County, serving his third term. I studied him and his record carefully, concluding that although he was an able lawyer, he was not a very good politician. The year was 1928, and Florida allowed second-choice voting at the time. After filing against Hendry, I went to another candidate who appeared to have some support and asked that he persuade his followers to list me as their second choice. I would ask my supporters to return the favor.

I enjoyed campaigning, visiting all the small towns, meeting new people. But I probably could not have won without the second-choice votes and without a valuable tip I received from a Taylor County judge, John O. Culpepper. As I was campaigning one day, the judge told me to read a certain page in the journal that recorded the votes of members of the legislature on various issues. That's all he said. As soon as I could obtain a copy, I turned to the page indicated by Judge Culpepper. It told of a vote on a bill requiring "dipping" of cattle, a hot issue in northern Florida. Farmers would be required to have their cattle dipped in a disinfectant to kill ticks. It was a time-consuming and expensive requirement, though no doubt beneficial to the cattle. I looked at the roll call. The names of members who had voted aye on the bill were listed in one column, those voting nay in another. Hendry's name did not appear in either column, and I immediately realized that Judge Culpepper had handed me a campaign issue. On a matter of great importance, Taylor County's representative hadn't bothered to vote.

At subsequent rallies, I would hold up the legislative journal and tell the audience I had opened it to the page that recorded the vote on the dipping bill. Then I would say: "Well, let's have a look. Did Representative Hendry vote aye? No, I don't see his name among the ayes. He must have voted nay. I'm looking now in those listings—*E*, *F*, *G*, *H*—well, what do you know? There is no Hendry listed as voting nay either. I'm afraid this means that the voters of Taylor County were not represented at all when this important matter came before the state house of representatives. No matter what your point of view, don't you think Taylor County deserves a voice?" I let them deduce on their own that I was anxious to be that voice. Thus at age twenty-seven I made my debut in electoral politics, and it was a successful one.

While I was in the legislature, I realized I had some ability as an orator. I had made campaign speeches in the 1924 Massachusetts Senate race and had spoken a great deal in Arkansas, at commencements and the like, but in the Florida legislature there were daily opportunities to stand up and speak, and I took advantage of them. By word of mouth, I acquired a local reputation as a speaker worth listening to, and frequently members and staff workers would ask me when I planned to speak on the floor of the house so they could be there to hear me.

I was best known for the first bill I introduced, a bill that was the first step, legislatively, reflecting my concern for the elderly. It provided that elderly people could fish with a rod and reel or hook and line without having to pay a license fee. It sounds like a small matter today; it was not small then. There was no Social Security system; most older people had very little money, virtually none to spend on "luxuries." I wanted them to enjoy the fun of fishing without having to pay out precious dollars. When the bill became law, elderly people all over Florida were elated, and I achieved my first recognition as a public official willing to become involved in the concerns of older people, a too-often neglected segment of society. I was not yet thirty when the bill won the approval of the legislature, so my concern for the elderly long preceded my joining their ranks.

But politics is fickle. The favorable recognition I had won was quickly overtaken. Florida today is such a cosmopolitan state that many of its residents don't consider themselves Southerners at all. That was not the case in 1929 and 1930. Like the rest of the South, Florida then was fiercely dedicated to segregation and white supremacy. Negroes were consigned to "the back of the bus," denied admittance to restaurants and hotels, and banned from drinking at "whites only" water fountains and using "whites only" toilet facilities. They also frequently were lynched. For a Negro to run for public office was unthinkable. Few even tried to vote, and those few who did often were turned away because they could not pay a poll tax. Some who could pay didn't bother, not wanting to face harassment from whites when they showed up at the polls. Such a climate was ideal for a demagogue from Saint Petersburg, an émigré from Georgia, to introduce a resolution that would enable members of the Florida legislature to reaffirm their commitment to white supremacy.

Illinois had done what neither Florida nor any other Southern state would do for decades to come: it had elected a Negro to the U.S. House of Representatives. When the wife of President Herbert Hoover held a traditional tea at the White House for members' wives, she faced a dilemma. Should she invite the wife of the black congressman, or exclude her because of her color? It was a no-win situation. The South would be furious if a black woman were allowed to sully the White House. Yet if she were left out, the vanguard of civil rights activism would be outraged. Mrs. Hoover chose the proper course—she invited *all* wives of House members. This act, the Saint Petersburg representative insisted, deserved the condemnation of the Florida state legislature. Accordingly, he introduced a resolution castigating the First Lady for weakening the tradition of segregation and endangering the concept of white supremacy, for encouraging the notion of racial equality and "polluting the stream of Southern citizenship." By no means was I then as liberal on race as I since have become, but this resolution was more than I could take. I was one of thirteen legislators who voted against it, and in the journal of the house I made the only explanation of a vote I offered during my term. I said, "I am a Southerner and a Democrat like my ancestors before me, but I consider this resolution out of place as an act of this body." The statement hardly reflects raw courage, but my vote suggests at least the stirrings of a sense of racial justice. It would have been easy to support the resolution; there was no black vote to offend, and an aye vote would have reaffirmed to the white Florida majority that I was "one of them."

This was my first conspicuous vote on a civil rights matter, and it contributed substantially to my defeat when I sought another term in 1930. Another factor was the improved quality of my opposition. Alton Wentworth was from a prominent and well-regarded Taylor County family. He and the vote on the Hoover resolution combined to cost me my seat. And that was one of the best things that ever happened to me in public life. Had I won, my course would have been clear: speaker of the house, state senator, president of the senate, attorney general, governor, and then what I really coveted, United States senator. That was a circuitous route. In losing, I dejectedly concluded that my political career could well be over, and it had barely begun. But a more direct route opened up for me, one that I could not then foresee. Six years later, and without all the intervening stops, I followed that route and became a United

States senator. Ironically (irony has lurked in so many corners of my life) I became a senator in 1936 after, and largely because, I lost a Senate race in 1934.

In the practice of law in northern Florida, I came to know many other lawyers, one of whom was to have a major impact on my life. He was Curtis L. Waller of Tallahassee. We quickly became such close friends that when I was elected to the legislature, Waller and his wife insisted that I live with them, rent-free, during the session. After my defeat in 1930, Judge Davis sensed that I had been exhilarated by the political atmosphere of the capital and assumed, correctly, that Perry now seemed a little dull to me. Also, economic conditions were poor there. Besides, he was ailing and wanted to ease up. He urged me to continue my career on a larger, more visible stage, either in Tallahassee or Miami. I was urged also to come to Tallahassee by Justice James B. Whitfield, the patriarch and former chief justice of the Florida Supreme Court, whom I had come to know during my legislative days. Often he told me: "Mr. Pepper, I want you to move to Tallahassee. Florida needs you and this is the capital of Florida. Tallahassee will offer you an opportunity to serve Florida." So later in 1930 I moved to Tallahassee and helped form a new law firm, Waller and Pepper. Donald Trumbo had returned to Arkansas to earn his law degree; the firm of Davis and Pepper was dissolved. A year or two later, Judge Davis, a kindly man and able lawyer who had opened the door to my Florida career, passed away.

In Florida, as everywhere in the nation, 1930 was a very rocky year. The stock market had crashed in 1929; now banks were failing, farms were being foreclosed, unemployment was high and rising. Small businesses, desperate for credit, could not obtain any. Many folded. With more and more people out of work, markets for manufacturers and consumer goods shrank. People looked to government to help, but President Hoover, convinced that prosperity was "just around the corner," did next to nothing. Congress, much of which shared the president's inexplicable optimism, tried to alleviate conditions but often simply made matters worse.*

In Tallahassee, I had become closely associated with a group of young men, fifteen to twenty of us in all, many members of the legislature or reputable lobbyists. We argued back and forth about the American system, why it was failing, what should be done about it. In no sense was this an anti-American underground or a band of subversives; we were, in fact, primarily a social group, almost like a fraternity. We celebrated each other's birthdays, shared each other's miseries, and exulted in each other's triumphs. When we were serious, we thought and talked about the mess the country was in. Most of us agreed the federal government would have to step in and do more. Some advocated redistribution of wealth. We were all fully conscious of the cry for "states' rights," heard more often in the South than elsewhere, but we knew it was a code phrase for racism and that, race aside, conditions were desperate and the national government was the only hope for an attack on starvation, poverty, unemployment, lack of education, poor housing, and other ills that beset our society. We were unfocused and vague, having no well-thought-out agenda. If wanting something done about problems affecting millions of lives is "liberal," then we were all liberals.

Two years earlier, when I was a member of the Florida Democratic Central Committee, I had received a letter from a wealthy New Yorker. He just had been elected but not yet inaugurated as governor of the state, despite the debacle suffered by the national ticket when Hoover crushed another New York governor and Catholic named Al Smith, for whom I had

---

*The Hawley-Smoot Tariff Act of 1930 is a prime example. It brought the U.S. tariff to its highest point in history, and the retaliatory tariffs of foreign nations caused a sharp decline in U.S. foreign trade.

campaigned. Franklin D. Roosevelt's letter, which went to 500 Democrats in all parts of the country, asked for opinions on what the future of the party should be. I knew something about this Roosevelt—that he had campaigned on a platform promising activism and programs to relieve human suffering. Though we could not have sprung from more different backgrounds, Roosevelt and I were ideological soul mates. I had sent back a quick reply, saying that the Democratic Party should be the nation's liberal party and that Franklin D. Roosevelt should lead it. Now, two years later, Governor Roosevelt was proving himself an innovative leader, establishing on a state level many of the New Deal programs he would institute nationwide as the successor to the befuddled Hoover. His daring had attracted national attention. Other states were studying and often imitating New York's response to the Depression. In 1932, the nation's voters decided they wanted to try this type of leadership on the country as a whole: they overwhelmingly elected Franklin D. Roosevelt as president of the United States. It will not surprise the reader to learn that I campaigned enthusiastically for Roosevelt. What I—and no doubt many others—had urged in 1928, a liberal, FDR-led party, was now a reality.

Roosevelt's first hundred days in office, I am convinced, saved this country from collapse and preserved our form of government. The bank holiday, the National Recovery Act, the Works Progress Administration (WPA), Public Works Administration (PWA), the Agricultural Adjustment Administration—each met a specific national need, but together they engendered a new American spirit. People who thought their country was going down the drain quickly realized that it need not. They took their cue from the man in the White House, who cheerfully called on them to gather around their radios for some reassuring "fire-side chats." His calm, confident voice insisted that "the only thing we have to fear is fear itself." Roosevelt was like a mechanic giving a jump-start to an automobile with a near-dead battery. His pictures showed a jaunty, smiling president (most Americans were not even aware he was disabled), a welcome contrast to the glum, starchy Hoover. FDR clearly believed in the future, and Americans who had doubted there would be one came to believe in him.

My own political fires, banked but by no means extinguished by the brevity of my legislative experience, again began to glow. There was something in the air. A president was running the country the way I felt it should be run. I had been a New Dealer before there was a New Deal. Now we had a caring federal government that worried not about the Rockefellers and the Du Ponts but about elderly indigents, poverty, people's health and housing, and even about former plowboys. This was a federal government that I should be a part of. But how?

In talks with Claude Lee, Jim Clements, Dan Chappell, Curtis Waller, and others of my "band of brothers," I floated a trial balloon: Florida would elect a United States senator in 1934. "I'm giving some thought to running." They didn't laugh. They knew how much I ached to become a senator. And we all knew my credentials were slender. But fresh breezes were blowing in America, and a fellow who caught the right one might be able to ride it all the way to Washington. Our tightly knit group agreed that if I should decide to make the race, everyone would work his heart out to see that I was elected.

The incumbent was Park Trammell, the state's junior senator and a giant in Florida politics. Trammell had actually followed the political route I had outlined for myself and which I was now trying to short-circuit. He had been mayor of Lakeland, a member of the Florida house, state senator, president of the state senate, attorney general, then governor, and for nearly seventeen years a United States senator from Florida. Senator Trammell was thought to be somewhat tired. He was accused of being lazy and unproductive for his state and constituents. Drew Pearson had reported in his widely syndicated column that Trammell slept in his Senate office, which did not sit well with many voters. I thought he might be vulnerable to a challenge from someone younger, more energetic, less jaded from decades of holding public office. My only political experience—a single term in the Florida house—would be supplemented by tireless campaigning, a New Deal platform, concern for ordinary people, and some ability to keep an audience awake.

After further talks with Lee, Clements, Chappell, and others, and after gaining the enthusiastic approval of my law partner, Waller, I decided to file. But for several months I kept my intentions secret. A lot of people in Florida had never heard of Claude Pepper, and that had to be remedied. Today, an expensive "media buy" would accomplish that. In 1933, I decided to get around the state and be heard. That would cost money, and I had little. It occurred to me that the Tallahassee Kiwanis Club, of which I was a member, might be willing to pay half my expenses for a trip around Florida if I would urge other Kiwanis clubs to participate in the state convention to be held that year in Tallahassee. The club agreed, so I set out, speaking to Kiwanis clubs, meeting new people, sounding out politicians. My contacts were encouraging. "Well, Park has been up there awhile" was an often-voiced sentiment. "He hasn't done much for the state. You're young and aggressive. Maybe the people won't care if you've held office or not." They all knew I would be a decided underdog, but only a few thought victory was impossible. So I announced, with the New Deal as my platform and the slogan "Claude Pepper will give Florida vigorous and aggressive representation in the United States Senate."

Back in Tallahassee, my friends were raring to go. They liked my New Deal platform and my repeated references to its cornerstone as "the welfare of the common man." When word reached Senator Trammell in Washington, it evoked this un-flattering response: "Who is this Pepper? I never heard of him."

My campaign manager was a brilliant Florida newspaper ed-itor named Oscar Johnson, whose major failing was a then-com-mon affliction among journalists, a fondness for liquor.* That did not keep him from running an effective campaign. He did practically everything, including scheduling. He sent me around the state with a sound wagon, a truck with two large amplifiers, one facing forward, the other rearward. Thus my voice could be heard in an area of two blocks or more. We would drive into a park or stop in front of a small city hall, play some music, and then someone would announce that Claude Pepper, can-didate for the U.S. Senate, would speak there at a certain time. I made hundreds of speeches in cities, towns, and villages. Newspaper coverage was extensive—writers and editors liked the idea of a David and Goliath political battle. My opponent who had never heard of me began to worry. My public record was scanty, and it had a chink in it—my vote against the res-olution that had condemned Mrs. Hoover for inviting the black congressman's wife to the White House. Senator Trammell, exploiting his patronage powers, sent deputy U.S. marshals and deputy collectors of internal revenue, all his appointees,** over the state, distributing handbills. The fliers quoted the resolu-tion describing Mrs. Hoover's act as a breach of the doctrine of white supremacy and the separation of black from white. In large letters at the end were the words: CLAUDE PEPPER VOTED AGAINST IT. Then it directed doubters to the page of the house journal that would confirm this perfidy.

---

*My own craving for tobacco was cured during this campaign. My doctor advised me to quit smoking. That night I smoked a full pack of cigarettes, and two more the following day. Then I told myself I wouldn't smoke "for a while." Every time my impulse was to smoke, I said, "Not now. Some other time." Temptation is more readily deferred than overcome. I never smoked again.

**They are now under civil service, barred from campaigning.

Despite these efforts, the race tightened. Concerned, Trammell sought out James A. Farley, then Democratic national chairman, and gained his endorsement. He also called in his chits with organized labor, which prompted me to visit William Greene, legendary president of the American Federation of Labor, to plead my own cause. Greene praised my platform and my energetic campaign, but said the AFL would support all incumbents, including Senator Trammell, whose votes had backed labor's interests. He said he hoped the AFL could support me in a future race. My only hope was to convince the rank and file to reject the choice of their leaders, and this I tried to do. With my sound wagon and populist theme, I continued to roll around the state. The crowds were good, some of the newspapers had begun to refer to me as a "spellbinder," and the momentum seemed to be building.

Primary election day arrived at last. When the votes were counted, Senator Park Trammel was flabbergasted to learn that he had been forced into a runoff by a former state legislator who couldn't even get himself reelected to that body. Trammell led me by only 1,925 votes, and the state party establishment was in shock. It rallied behind the incumbent and was able to boost his margin in the runoff to 4,050 votes; some of them later proved to have been bought or stolen. In defeat, I felt strangely serene. My showing convinced me that the lad who had written "United States Senator" alongside his name many years ago in Camp Hill, Alabama, would realize his dream. Perhaps soon.

The 1934 election left a bitter taste and generated an enormous wave of goodwill toward the loser. When the vote totals were published, it became clear that the Trammell forces had beaten me with what was known as the "hot vote" in the Tampa area. Eleven precincts in West Tampa and Ibo City were populated by naturalized Spaniards and Italians, who ordinarily would not vote but who did when powerful, monied interests paid the poll tax for them. These interests also bribed officials in charge of the polling places, got the sheriff and county commissioners to go along, and persuaded the governor to look the other way. Thus in the runoff, I received about 400 votes from the eleven "hot" precincts. My opponent's total was more than 6,500, a number larger than his winning margin. The rest of the state was indignant to learn that a United States Senate election had been decided by the "hot vote" around Tampa. From all parts of Florida, irate citizens wrote, telephoned, or came to my law office in Tallahassee, urging me to challenge the election. Realizing that such a challenge would take years to resolve, deepen enmities within the party, and very possibly not overturn the result, I refused, congratulating Senator Trammell on his victory and promising him my support. Overnight, I became the favorite for the governorship in 1936 or for a Senate vacancy should one occur.

As it happened, two vacancies occurred. Early in 1936, Park Trammell died. Five weeks later, Florida's senior senator, Duncan Fletcher, also died in office. Because of an unwritten code that one senator should be from the northern part of the state, the other from the south, I filed for election to Senator Fletcher's seat. With memory of the stolen 1934 election still fresh, Floridians apparently felt that I had earned a Senate seat. No one filed to run against me.

Few people realize their lifelong ambitions. I was among the lucky ones. At age thirteen I had written it, now I was living it. I was Claude Pepper, United States Senator.

I must return briefly to a day five years earlier. While chatting with friends at the state capitol in Tallahassee, I was dazzled by a woman in a bright yellow dress emerging from the governor's office. I could not take my eyes off her. "Why that's the prettiest girl I've ever seen," I remarked to my friends, some of whom, fortunately, knew her. They introduced us. Her name was Mildred Webster, she lived in Saint Petersburg and was in

Tallahassee working for the state legislature. I can still see her—sparkling blue eyes, short reddish brown hair, creamy complexion, beautiful smile, perfect figure. Never in my life had I been so speedily and so totally smitten. On the spot, I invited her to accompany me to the Speaker's Ball, the major social event of the legislative session, and to my surprise and delight she accepted. When I called for her, she was wearing a beaded dress and her eyes sparkled as brightly as the beads. I had not dated a great deal, and there had been only one or two flirtations in my life. Perhaps I was subconsciously waiting for the perfect mate, which is what Mildred eventually became.

We went together on and off for about five years, during which Mildred helped in the 1934 and 1936 Senate campaigns, impressing me not just with her enthusiasm but with her political sagacity and overall efficiency as well. We would have seen each other much more often during those five years but for the fact that Mildred lived and worked for periods of time in New York City and Miami.

In 1936, I was in Washington preparing for the opening of Congress and managed to get up to New York on the weekend. Obviously, things had gotten serious and Mildred and I talked about marriage without reaching a definite decision. Later that same year, Jim Farley invited the two Florida senators, Charles O. Andrews and myself, and Governor Fred P. Cohn to New York to urge all of us to help FDR carry Florida in the 1936 presidential election and to support his programs after he was reelected. So I got to see Mildred again.*

As always, I was at home with Mama and Papa and the rest of my family for Christmas in 1936. Mildred, too, had come to Florida for the holidays, staying with her family in Saint Pe-

---

*On this trip, I also bought $750 worth of clothes, on credit. Included were a top hat, derby, tails, and tuxedo, essential for my new life in Washington and, as it turned out, useful as well for my wedding.

tersburg. On December 27, I visited her there and found her recovering from flu, but well enough to join me for an intimate dinner for two at the Chatterbox Restaurant. This time we did more than talk about marriage—we became engaged right there in the restaurant. Later, I would always say that I caught her in a weakened condition from her bout with the flu. In any event, our engagement had been very slow in coming, which may account for the speed of the events that followed. Mildred wanted a formal wedding, with our families and friends present, in the First Methodist Church of Saint Petersburg. Moreover, she wanted it to take place at 11:00 A.M. on December 29, barely thirty-six hours after we had become engaged.

The wedding did take place just as and when she wanted it. Somehow in those few hours Mildred bought her wedding dress, ordered formal clothes for the wedding party to be delivered in Saint Petersburg, and arranged for the church, the minister, the flowers, everything. How she managed all this I have never been able to comprehend. In addition to her beauty, she was incredibly efficient. Somehow or other, most of my Senate staff, in Florida for the holidays, made it to the wedding. I shall never forget my friend and law school classmate, Charles Murchison, who drove overnight from Jacksonville to be with us. Jim Clements, my top aide and old friend, with his brother Allen gave us a lovely wedding reception at Fort Myers. Then Jim drove us to Coral Gables where we spent the night in the bridal suite at the Biltmore. The following morning we flew via Pan American clipper to Havana, in those pre-Castro days a delightful resort city. I had never been in such a whirlwind. And I had never known such happiness.

We met some fine people in Havana, including some vegetable plantation owners with whom I discussed the friction between them and Florida growers. One plantation owner named Silvio Gardulio took a fancy to Mildred and said he wanted to give her a horse as a wedding gift, a fine gesture we thought little more about. After two days we flew back to Miami, then on to Jacksonville for another reception, given by Helen and Charles Murchison. From there we flew to Washington and yet another reception, given by Senator Joseph Guffey of Pennsylvania. We rented a suite at the Wardman Park Hotel and one day Mildred picked up the telephone and heard the caller say, "There's a horse down here for you." We had been getting many such calls as wedding gifts were delivered and Mildred would always say, "Send it up." From force of habit, she said it again. Silvio Gardulio had meant it when he said he wanted to give Mildred a horse—by request of the hotel management, we hurried downstairs and there met Merwale out of Coronado by Prince of Wales. At the Wardman Park's insistence, we stabled Merwale elsewhere. On a site near the present Watergate complex, we kept her for many years, riding her on weekends. She gave Mildred much pleasure.

Mildred was perfectly suited for the life of a senator's wife in Washington. She quickly acquired many close friends, especially Mamie Borah, wife of the Republican maverick, William E. Borah of Idaho. Mildred was described in print as "one of the most beautiful women in Washington" and as the capital's "most sincere hostess." She was active in the United Services Organization and the Salvation Army and was president of the Women's National Democratic Club. Most important to me, she was at my side whenever I needed her, which was often, and I tried to be equally supportive of her. Like any married couple, we had small arguments and disagreements from time to time, a good many of them involving my continued closeness to my family. But we were deeply devoted to each other, and nothing ever changed that. I could not have been more fortunate in my choice of a mate. There is a void in my life since she left, a void that can never be filled.

3

The Third Term—"I Was a Little Helpful"

*Let us contemplate our forefathers, and poster-
ity, and resolve to maintain the rights be-
queathed to us from the former, for the sake of
the latter.*

—SAMUEL ADAMS

I recorded the following in my diary on Sunday, January 3,
1937:

> Mildred and I arrived from our honeymoon 1 A.M. or
> thereabout and to Wardman Park to the bedroom suite
> we had obtained until our apartment was ready. So
> here we are, a young bride and groom and young
> Senator and Senatress in the Capital. We have lots of
> hard work. No doubt many heartaches ahead of us;
> but I hope our stay shall be as long as we like it and
> we shall be able to do a good job and at the same

54

time find our lives here stimulating and challenging.
No more thrilling time to be here.

It was the fourth year of the Roosevelt presidency. In an appeal to voters that would be echoed forty-four years later, without attribution, by Ronald Reagan, FDR in 1936 had asked Americans if they were better off than they had been four years earlier. The answer, a resounding yes, launched Roosevelt on his second term. In defeating an able but thoroughly out-gunned Republican, Alf Landon, the president had lost only two states. Without question, the country was better off. The unemployment rate had fallen from 23.6 percent in 1932 to 16.9 percent in 1936. A Social Security system, then a modest old-age pension plan, was in place. The New Deal alphabet agencies (NRA, CCC, PWA, WPA, AAA, FHA, RFC,* and many more) were, for the most part, functioning effectively. But America was not really prosperous. Poverty and hunger were widespread. Even though the Civilian Conservation Corps and the Works Progress Administration had helped reduce unemployment, millions of young men were stealing rides on or in boxcars, which took them from where they could not find work to other places where there also was no work. Only 10 percent of the nation's farms had electricity, though another alphabet agency, the Rural Electrification Agency (REA), would increase that figure to 90 percent by the time Roosevelt left the White House. The Tennessee Valley Authority, the most imaginative approach ever to harnessing nature for the benefit of millions of people, was well underway.

Still, there was unease in the land. Roosevelt's enemies—most of the press and virtually all of that class he labeled "economic royalists"—called him a dictator and railed that his actions were unconstitutional. The federal budget deficit, a

---

*Actually formed during the Hoover administration.

piddling amount by today's standards, offered a nice target for attack, especially since FDR had campaigned in 1932 on a pledge to balance the budget. The president could ignore the editorial writers and he had long since stopped trying to win over the wealthy. But there was a far more powerful threat to the success and even continuance of the New Deal: the Supreme Court of the United States. I took my seat in the Senate just in time to be caught up in a historic imbroglio between the executive and the judicial branches. It became known as Roosevelt's "court packing" plan. It alarmed millions, alienated even devoted New Dealers, and seemed to give substance to the charge that the president was a power-grabbing would-be dictator who, if successful in neutralizing the Court, would move next against the Congress.

In my diary for Friday, February 5, 1937: "President's extraordinary message to Congress on reorganization of the judiciary—the most far-reaching act of the New Deal. Dictatorship comes when executive, legislative and judicial power in one hand. What about this! Yet it may be the means of preventing some action of more permanent harm." Dilemma-time had arrived too soon for my tastes. Here I was, at thirty-six the third youngest member of the Senate,* an avowed FDR supporter who had campaigned on a New Deal platform, being forced early on either to split with my president or to submerge my convictions and, as Speaker of the House Sam Rayburn would later advise, get along by going along. The country was in an uproar. My old friend, L. B. McLeod, forecast that the people "will begin to leave the president on this." I was receiving a quick—too quick—lesson in how political Washington works. When the Florida delegation called on Jim Farley on behalf of a Florida job-seeker, Farley, I wrote in my diary, "put me on the spot about the President's judiciary bill. That's the most perplexing decision I am going to have to make. I don't like

*Rush Holt was thirty; Henry Cabot Lodge, Jr., thirty-four.

the smell of the whole thing but the decision is a bad one in any event."

For someone who has never held public office, it seems much simpler than it is just to do the right thing. It isn't easy because there are power trade-offs. Even one's ability to function can be impaired. For example, while my arm was being twisted on the court packing bill, I had need of the names of Department of Agriculture employees in Florida. The department told me I could not have them. I mentioned this to Thomas (Tommy the Cork) Corcoran, the president's chief brain truster, and he had no trouble getting the list. "Isn't that something?" I wrote in my diary. A day or two later, Corcoran, who had been a class behind me at Harvard Law School, telephoned and asked that I not commit myself on the court bill until he could talk to me. Two days after that we had lunch together, and Tommy spoke not of "the Chief's" commitment to a principle, but of his obligation to a principal. The court packing plan was an idea of the attorney general, Homer Cummings, who had helped FDR win the nomination for vice-president in 1920. The president felt the knowledge he gained in that losing campaign had enabled him to win the presidency in 1932, so now he could not turn his back on the attorney general's proudest scheme. Had the actual situation been as crass as Corcoran described it, I would not have hesitated to announce my opposition.

What triggered the court packing plan was the Supreme Court's resistance to a number of New Deal initiatives, particularly the NRA (National Recovery Act), which it voided. The NRA was a complex piece of legislation affecting both industry and labor. Critics said it suspended the antitrust laws and put the federal government behind the right to organize labor unions. Its intent was what its name implied—to bring about national recovery—but the Court ruled that some of its provisions violated the Constitution.

To prevent further incursions on what he believed were efforts to save the country from revolution and collapse, FDR

57

proposed to add a justice to the Court whenever a sitting member reached age seventy and refused to retire. The maximum number to be added was six. The appointments would be Roosevelt's, of course, and presumably they would tilt the balance, upholding the legality of New Deal approaches and preventing further erosion of the Roosevelt revolution by "nine old men."

Realizing that I had been unimpressed by his flimsy rationale for packing the Court, Tommy the Cork arranged for me to see the president himself. On February 23, Claude Pepper, troubled freshman senator, cooled his heels while Roosevelt wound up a meeting with the secretary of war and a general named Douglas MacArthur. Finally, I was ushered into the Oval Office for my first long, one-on-one session with the president. I told him candidly that most of my constituents opposed his plan, that these were not just New Deal foes but "sturdy people" with grave objections. Roosevelt nodded understandingly, then turned his powers of persuasion on high and rapidly convinced me, not that he was right, but that he sincerely believed in his (he never mentioned the attorney general) plan. The South, he said, particularly needed the NRA to increase the purchasing power of its people. Conceding the point, I nonetheless ventured that this fact was overwhelmed by the concentration of power in his hands and the enlarged authority of Congress inevitably resulting from the weakening of the judiciary. It was the obligation of a statesman to resist encroachment by one branch of government on another, a duty as important as trying to alleviate human suffering. FDR was not moved by my eloquence. He said the judiciary reform bill was "imperative." As I reported the conversation in my diary:

> He wanted to turn the nation over to his successor intact, that he could actually do nothing in great labor disturbances but express fervent hope the conflicting parties could get together—that the nation was nearer to a powder keg than we realized; that if things were

not held in control they might blow up and then Congress would [come] to him with a plea to save the nation. He feels strongly about the situation.

The president was not above a little logrolling, promising to help me win reelection in 1938 and, in my presence, notifying the army that he wanted to see some favorable action on a Florida canal project that I had been pushing. Still, I remained undecided. For two more months, I studied the legislation, discussed it with my colleagues (in particular Senators Pat Harrison and Joe Robinson, the party leaders), and finally concluded that, with many misgivings, I could vote for it. So could a majority of Senate Democrats. But as the weeks went by, more and more of us realized that the country was ahead of us on this issue and would not allow even Roosevelt to pack the Court. By the second week in May, it was clear that the president was headed for the most humiliating defeat of his presidency. On July 22, by a vote of 70 to 20, the Senate voted to recommit the measure, which meant to kill it. Vice-President John Nance Garner had been working as hard against the measure, in secret, as Roosevelt had been working for it, and in this instance Garner was able to peel away support, layer by layer. In the end, the leadership suggested that senators vote any way they wished—the support the president needed just wasn't there. I voted to recommit, after telling the president I would do so that very morning. On this day of the first real legislative debacle of his years in the White House, I expected to find the president tense and disturbed. He was neither. When I entered his office, he was working ever so calmly on a ship model.*

My relationship with President Roosevelt was very close, my

---

*I have come to believe that the packing plan was not the power grab it seemed at the time. Roosevelt may have known he would not win. It was his way of whipping the Court in public at a time when he was deeply concerned about the country.

access to him virtually unlimited. We were, of course, ideological soul mates, and that was a factor. But an event early in my career in the Senate sealed our friendship, which I treasured and which continued until the day of his death. As a freshman senator, I was not supposed to make speeches on the floor, but rules are made to be broken. Late in the afternoon of June 17, 1937, the full Senate was arguing before packed galleries a bill to sustain the New Deal programs. The price tag was $1.5 billion. It was early in Roosevelt's second term, some of the bloom was off the rose, and senators who earlier had not dared oppose the president now regarded him as something of a lame duck, since no president had ever served more than two terms.* It was no longer political hara-kiri to stand up to FDR, especially with his powerful foes insisting that the country had gone far enough toward "socialism" and that it was time to apply the brakes. The appropriation was in danger. I had been listening to the debate and reflecting upon the needs of my state and of the nation. Finally, I decided that Senate traditions were insignificant compared to my overwhelming desire to be heard on this subject. I arose and spoke, without notes, for about forty minutes, being interrupted by conservatives challenging my statements—as is the Senate custom.

In this maiden speech, I drew a biblical analogy: we senators were now in the situation of the children of Israel when they came to Kadesh-Parnia. They hesitated when they were on the verge of entering the Promised Land and were condemned to wander in the wilderness. I said: "Mr. President, you would have thought that if ever there was a people whose confidence would be assured in the Divinity which had guided them thus far, it would have been these people. Yet they hesitated, and the resultant judgment of retribution is too well-known. All of

---

*In an interview about this time, I boldly predicted that FDR would not seek a third term.

them who were then twenty years of age or more left their bones to bleach in the wanderings of the wilderness." When a senator suggested that the children of Israel may have been better off than if they had proceeded, I replied: "Whether the results were good or not the senator will have to judge by the value which he fixes upon life here and the value which he attributes to the hereafter." There was laughter. But at the end of my speech, some more Senate traditions were shattered, though not by me. To my amazement, my colleagues gave me a standing ovation. The galleries cheered, too, and were not threatened with eviction. Numerous flattering accounts appeared in the newspapers, including an especially glowing "Washington Merry-Go-Round" column by the widely read Drew Pearson and Robert Allen.

The day after the speech, Senator Robert Wagner of New York, an intimate of the president, approached me on the floor of the Senate. He said, "Pepper, I have just been down to the White House talking to the president. He said as I was leaving, 'Bob, go over to that young fellow Pepper and tell him I liked that speech he made yesterday afternoon, and tell him to come down and see me.' " I did so, and we hit it off personally as we already had philosophically. We established a relaxed and easy relationship, and though I was careful not to abuse the privilege, I called on the president many, many times in the future.* Of course, there were advantages for both of us in a close relationship, but ours had a firmer base than mutual back scratching. My fondness for Franklin D. Roosevelt as a human being was genuine and deep, equaled only by my admiration for him as a statesman.

Roosevelt's great strength was his understanding of human

---

*Arthur Krock once wrote in the *New York Times* that he had hopes for me if I could learn to distinguish between Christ and Roosevelt. I knew the difference.

struggle, which probably derived from his own physical handicap. Until crippled for life by polio, Roosevelt was just a wealthy New York dilettante, remote from the crushing pressures faced daily by the poor, the elderly, the uneducated, and the handicapped. During his years of foredoomed efforts to regain the use of his legs, FDR had opportunity to read and think deeply for perhaps the first time in his life. He emerged from his period of recuperation physically impaired, but with a new set of values, an empathy for the great masses of men (and women) leading "lives of quiet desperation," and a determination to make as many of those lives as possible less desperate. With the special relish this overpowering personality brought to everything he did, FDR ridiculed the "economic royalists" from whom he had sprung and seemed to revel in their discomfort over the advances of forces he had loosed. He seemed to sense and gain strength from a supreme inner confidence that he would go down in history as a great president because he did what had to be done when the nation was in its greatest danger since the Civil War. He once said that after one spends a year trying to move his big toe, anything is easy.

Roosevelt had a special "treatment" for favor-seekers he had to—but hated to—turn down. On at least one occasion, I was his foil. At the insistence of backers of a Florida canal project that had been authorized in 1942, then shelved by the war, I went to FDR to see about resuming construction. There was virtually no possibility that the president would divert men, material, and money from the war effort to finish building a canal. But I started to make my pitch. FDR interrupted. He asked, "Claude, do you know anything about Robert Livingston?" I replied, "Mr. President, I know a little but not too much." He went on: "You know, Robert Livingston was the chancellor of New York who swore in President Washington. He was a great jurist and a great student of the law. He contributed much to juridical literature and legal knowledge." What could I say but "That's very interesting, Mr. President"? He said that Livingston was one of his wife's ancestors, and that in addition to being a great jurist and lawyer, he was also a great diplomat. "He was really responsible for many of the great diplomatic achievements of our nation in its early days." He went on and on. He never stopped. Livingston, I learned, was also a great statesman responsible "for many of the wise decisions our government made in those early days because of the wise counsel he gave the government." My appointment was limited to fifteen minutes, which soon expired. His appointments secretary was standing beside me, a rather strong hint that my time was up. Newsmen and photographers came pouring into the room, nearly filling it up. I made one last, desperate mention of the canal. Roosevelt said, "You see, Claude, I have this press conference here now. I can't keep all these people waiting." He extended his hand, saying, "Claude, I am always glad to see you. Come see me again." I drove back to my office, sat down, and chuckled to myself. I thought, "Well, I didn't get anything done about the canal, but I am the best-informed man on Capitol Hill about Robert Livingston."

He was just being kind. He couldn't do anything to help me, but he didn't want to say so.

Another time, Dr. George H. Denny, president of the University of Alabama and my dear friend, said he had to see the president. Could I arrange an appointment and go with him? I could and did. The president greeted us warmly and asked Dr. Denny what he could do for him. Denny said he had come to the president "in desperation," adding, "You are my last hope." Denny said the university had to have a library built on campus and had been turned down by the Public Works Administration. Apologetically, FDR said he could not help, that PWA could not fund any more projects except in extraordinary circumstances. "Of course," he added, "we will provide funds if an important building should burn down."

Denny's eyes lighted up. "Mr. President, that's my case," he exclaimed. "Our library has burned down." Startled, the president said he had read Denny's application and that it said nothing about the library burning down. Replied Denny, with a straight face, "Mr. President, the Yankees burned it down in the Civil War." Roosevelt threw back his head and roared with laughter. The visit provided the president with amusement, but Dr. Denny got nothing. FDR said he had vetoed a bill Congress had passed, reimbursing a school district in Missouri for a school building torched by Confederate cavalry raiders during the Civil War. He could not turn around and help Alabama in a similar situation. Empty-handed, we left. At least we did not have to listen to a discourse on Robert Livingston.

By late 1937, my thoughts had turned to that bane of all politicians, the next election. The partial Senate term to which I had been elected was for only two years, so in 1938 I would have to face the voters again. I felt that I was strong politically, but bitter anti-administration currents were gaining strength in Florida. Mark Wilcox, an incumbent congressman from the Fourth District of Florida, was hinting that he would run against me in the primary on an anti–New Deal platform. Wilcox made clear that he had no personal grievance against me, but he was opposed to the New Deal, as were many wealthy Floridians who would be willing to finance his campaign. In mid-October, I conferred with my former law partner, Waller, and with Jack Simmons, a business friend. Many of my supporters were arguing that anti-administration feeling was growing and that I should distance myself at least somewhat from the New Deal. After much conversation and even more solitary reflection, I decided there was only one course for me. What the federal government was doing was what I believed in. Could I oppose my own heart and soul? I told my diary after one long, searching meeting: "Decided to go full speed ahead and if necessary fight the militant anti-administration crowd without gloves."

It was necessary, as I soon learned. In late October, I spoke to civic clubs in Vero Beach, Florida, and discovered how real the growing opposition was. New Deal enemies had been crying that the country was now a dictatorship, that the Bill of Rights had been suspended, that there might not be any future elections, and that Roosevelt was positioning himself to rule the United States the way Adolf Hitler was ruling Nazi Germany. This was all hokum, and the people spreading it knew that it was, but the audiences who listened could not help wondering.

My speeches demanded specifics. The New Deal foes say the Bill of Rights has been suspended. Well now, which rights? If the president has invalidated the Bill of Rights, then we must not have a free press anymore. Then why is the press still printing all those anti-Roosevelt editorials and cartoons? Did you all go to church last Sunday, or is there no longer the freedom to worship as you please? There won't be any more elections in the country? Then why am I down here campaigning for another term in the Senate? The allegations were farfetched, and it seemed to me that ridicule was the best way to counter them. What had happened in the United States, I said, was that people wanted and needed the government's help, and now they were getting it. Of course, this meant some extension of federal power, but not enough to threaten the Constitution or the Bill of Rights or any of the principles on which this nation was founded. Wilcox was one of the chief purveyors of such nonsense, which probably added some seasoning to my own rhetoric. Whenever I would finish speaking, several folks would approach me and say they hoped Wilcox would not run and that if he did they would not vote for him. But even more comforting to me was the size of the crowds that turned out for my counterarguments. By November I was able to write in my diary: "The people are for Roosevelt and the administration."

Wilcox did not see things that way. In mid-November he announced, somewhat to my relief, that he would run against me. In my diary: "So the fight is on. The issue is the New

Deal or not—liberalism vs. reaction. I am glad the uncertainty is over, for now I know where to fight and whom. I think this campaign shall determine the political character of Florida for some time to come. I want to make the state liberal, which it has never been, and now is my chance." In 1937, my definition of "liberal," sad to say, did not include Negroes. In the Senate, an anti-lynching bill was being filibustered to death by a group of Southern senators, myself among them. It is painful today to recall that I spoke for an hour one day, for three hours the next. I am consoled, but only slightly, by the fact that this was half a century ago and by my record since that time: never again have I failed to support legislation involving civil rights. I doubt that any other member of Congress with a Southern constituency can say as much. Nonetheless, I wish this sorry chapter could be expunged from my record and, more important, from my memory.

In late November, the president scheduled a fishing holiday off the Florida coast for himself; his son, James; Harry Hopkins, his closest confidant; Interior Secretary Harold Ickes; Bob Jackson, later to become attorney general and a Supreme Court justice; and a few others, including Missy LeHand, his friend and secretary. They planned to travel to Miami by train and I was invited to go to Florida with them. Well, I was glad to get the invitation. The trip would give me an opportunity to see the president in other than an Oval Office setting. And if he was still as popular in Florida as I thought he was, my being on his special train would do no harm to my campaign. We made several stops along the way, and the crowds were huge. I watched the thousands of eager faces, all straining for a look at the president. We had dinner in his special car—James and his wife, Missy LeHand, Hopkins, Jackson, and I—and the conversation was animated:

President a marvelous man—so full of vitality and information. Said we were entering a period of next

66

three years when, if we didn't win the fight for democracy, there would be revolution. He made clear
he was going to fight . . . he will let Congress chew
on its present program for a while and if it does
nothing he will go to the radio and say "My friends"
again . . . the fight he has in him! He spoke very
seriously about the possibility of his going out to defeat reactionary senators next year, naming George,
Smith.* He thinks the Senate must come to a cloture
rule—that its present tendency to reaction may be
overcome partially by changes in personnel at next
election and by pressure from the country.

The following morning, Harry Hopkins called me to one side,
much to my surprise for Hopkins was not noted for small talk
or friendly overtures (Winston Churchill dubbed him Lord Root
of the Matter). "He likes you a lot," Hopkins said matter-of-
factly. "And he doesn't like many people."

On November 29, a Monday, a huge crowd gathered at the
railroad depot in Miami. I made my way to the president's
special car, and together we went to the rear platform where a
dozen or more photographers snapped away. Roosevelt was in
great spirits, needling the photographers, saying, "One, two,
three, let 'er go." From my diary:

I got in the car with him, sitting by his side, the mayor
on my left, James in the jump seat. A great crowd
greeted the President, lining the streets the whole
distance—mile and one-half or two miles. Never saw
such remarkable fervor and genuine enthusiasm. They
were gesturing and shouting as loud as possible. I
turned to the President and said: "Now I see, Mr.
President, where you get your inspiration and how

* Walter George of Georgia; "Cotton Ed" Smith of South Carolina.

you keep a smile on your face!" He said "Yes." The reception was much noisier than one in Jacksonville two years ago. The people are with him. At the dock, former Governor Cox of Ohio* met the President and got in the car and sat for a chat. I remembered 1920. The President told Don Mahoney his hair was graying. Party left on boat, two destroyers accompanying it.

Despite the outpouring of enthusiasm for the president, my friends insisted that I do something to defuse the growing opposition to me in the Florida business community. I released a statement to the press intended to reassure business, but the truth was that the only assurance corporate Florida wanted was that I thought Roosevelt was a menace, and this of course it did not get. FDR had told me once that he was able to appoint my good friend, Hugo Black, to the Supreme Court because I was ready to take on Black's mantle as the leading Southern liberal in the Senate. But business didn't want liberals from any region in the Senate and there was little I could do to change that. My support of wage and hour bills was enough to turn employers against me. Too bad. They could vote for Wilcox.

In December, the president called a conference of liberal senators in the White House, and we agreed to continue the fight for a decent minimum wage (twenty-five cents an hour was decent then) and an eight-hour workday (most workers were putting in ten and twelve hours per day, six days a week). The president felt strongly that the New Deal had to succeed or there would be a revolution. He spoke again of going out and

*Governor James Cox was the Democratic nominee for president in 1920. FDR was his running mate. They lost to Warren Harding and Calvin Coolidge.

68

trying to defeat "reactionaries" in Democratic primaries. He also gave my spirits a lift when he said that if asked about the Florida primary, he would respond that Pepper had the record, Wilcox did not.

My strong feelings about campaigning as an all-out New Dealer were not shared by many of my closest friends and advisers. At a meeting with twelve of them at year's end, only Mac Christie, Jim Clements, and Dot Manly thought I should campaign on the Roosevelt record and program. I didn't change my mind. I wanted to wage a straight-from-the-shoulder liberal fight against the interests and the reactionaries, for the wage and hour bill, and against the lumber industry, which opposed it.

So my course was set. But I received a most unwelcome jolt. Dave Sholtz, a former governor of Florida, let it be known he was thinking of running against me, too. Moreover, he claimed the support of Jim Farley and said he had been assured the president would take no part in the Florida primary. After my support of the administration, how could Farley back someone against me? Well, I didn't know Farley as well then as I came to know him. The best description I ever heard of him came from Charley Michaelson, a friend. "Jim Farley wouldn't steal anything but an election," he said. A lot of people, including Roosevelt, would learn later that Farley was a man who couldn't be trusted.

In any event, I continued to campaign "my way," attracting considerable national attention because I was the only Southern senator to make the minimum-wage law a campaign issue. In early 1938, *Time* magazine did a cover story about me, using my picture with my sound wagon, describing me as a "Florida Fighting Cock, a White House Weather Vane." The press concluded that if a Southern senator could win despite championing a wage and hour bill—thought to be widely unpopular throughout the South—then that would amount to a vindication of the man in the White House and prove that Roosevelt and his policies were still popular in the country.

As the campaign heated up, I felt things were going well, but a politician never likes to sit on a lead. The president had remained aloof from the campaign, and I wanted some kind of public indication that he was for me. He had promised as much when he needed my vote on the Supreme Court bill. His son Jimmy was in Florida, staying at the Palm Beach home of Joseph P. Kennedy, ambassador to the Court of St. James. I made an appointment, and Mildred and I drove to the Kennedy home. There were several people present, including Harry Hopkins. Jimmy said the president did not want to appear to be telling the people of Florida how to vote, but I had been a valued supporter of the administration, believed as the president did, and had worked hard for Florida—and, said Jimmy, "We certainly hope Senator Pepper will be reelected." Everyone present heard him. We agreed that Jimmy would invite some reporters over and repeat the statement to them. One reason this was so important to me was that Sholtz's claim to Farley's support had never been repudiated. I returned to Washington and awaited the announcement with mounting anxiety, as my diary entries reflect:

> Thursday, February 3, 1938:
> No statement.

> Friday, February 4, 1938:
> No statement from Jimmy.

> Saturday, February 5, 1938:
> Still no statement from Jimmy.

On Sunday, I was angry. After discussing with my old friend Claude Lee what I should do, I picked up the telephone and called Harry Hopkins in West Palm Beach. I had told my friends to watch for Jimmy's statement and they had good reason now to question my truthfulness, since nothing had happened. I was so mad that I told Hopkins the best thing for me to do would be to get up in the Senate and announce that I had found by experience that this was an administration that could not be depended on to keep its word.

> Monday, February 7, 1938:
>
> Jimmy Roosevelt's statement appeared in the papers to the effect that the President didn't want to be interfering in Florida politics, but I had worked hard for Florida and had stood loyally by the administration and "we hope that Senator Pepper will be returned to the Senate." The headline in newspapers all across the state was: "Roosevelt Endorses Pepper." This caused a storm from the opposition. Wilcox wisecracked that the nation was waiting with bated breath to hear what Sistie and Buzzy* had to say. But he never could laugh it off, and the statement on the whole was very helpful because it filled out the whole picture of my being a liberal and standing by that side. Also, it killed the claim of Sholtz that he was supported by the administration.

In my excitement, I sent the president a wire thanking him for Jimmy's statement, but the White House called to warn me not to involve the president in such a direct way. I had the wire recalled.

At the White House later for a conference, I stayed behind. FDR said he was willing to make a public declaration about his demarcation line between liberals and conservatives, but I

---

*The president's very young grandchildren.

felt that any further presidential push might boomerang and went on to other matters, including asking the president for a small wage increase for Joe Sears, Sr., a minor federal official. The president agreed to an increase, and then told me a story: "A beggar asked a congressman for money, and the congressman played deaf. Then the beggar doubled the request. The congressman said, 'Here, you son of a bitch, I heard you the first time.' " He laughed uproariously.

At this time I was receiving numerous visits and dinner invitations from a man who would play a pivotal role in my life and my political career. He was Edward Ball, who managed the extensive Du Pont family interests in Florida, which included a railroad, real estate, and much else. Ball, who would become totally bitter toward me in years to come, was friendly with Mildred and me at this time, often inviting us to social affairs. I assume he was resigned to my reelection and wanted to make the best of it. Ball was anything but pro–New Deal. He argued that income tax rates were too high and were retarding if not strangling business expansion, a common enough complaint among businessmen. Ball and his friends also were opposed to almost everything else I supported and probably thought they could reform me, or at least bring me somewhat closer to their ways of thinking. Another businessman whom I saw frequently was Joe Kennedy, who promised to make a substantial contribution to my campaign.

A more important endorsement, however, was that of Dr. Frances Townsend, whose Townsend Plan to provide $200-a-month pensions to the elderly was a precursor of Social Security. I was one of the earliest supporters of the Townsend Plan. I also had become a friend of Bernard Baruch, the financier and famous "adviser to presidents," with whom I often discussed national issues and my approach to them in the campaign. I spent one weekend at Hobcow Barony, Baruch's charming plantation home near Georgetown, South Carolina.

We had a delightful time driving over the fields, pausing under the shade of trees for long talks. He contributed $2,500 to my campaign.

About a month before the primary, I learned that the Farley-Sholtz tie was not entirely fantasy. A friend told me that Jim Farley was openly predicting that I would win the first primary, but would lose to Sholtz in a runoff. Then Happy Chandler, whom Farley was supporting in Kentucky, would win there and in 1940 Sholtz and Chandler would deliver their state delegations to Farley, who would be running for president! President Roosevelt, who was not then thinking about a third term, must have been annoyed by Farley's machinations, but there was little he could do. He did ask Farley to say something in my behalf when he was in Tallahassee to address the legislature, but Farley did not.

It didn't really matter. I won the primary with more than a 100,000-vote margin over Wilcox, Sholtz, and two other candidates. In the campaign, I had the pleasure of appearing in front of the headquarters of some of the big lumber and naval supply stores whose owners opposed me so bitterly, telling the employees that their bosses were fighting me because I was advocating that they be paid a minimum wage of twenty-five cents an hour. The primary victory was tantamount to election again in the one-party South, and Mildred and I were elated to know we would have six more years in the Senate.

As expected, the national press interpreted my victory as a great triumph and mandate for Roosevelt, and the president could hardly wait to get me to the White House to talk about it. My diary entry for May 18, 1938: "When I walked in, the President said: 'Claude, if you were a woman I'd kiss you.' I told him I regretted missing the thrill. He said the campaign was great. I told him I merely followed a simple game learned in childhood—follow the leader . . . said he wanted me to speak in some other states and I told him I would help all I could. He looked rested and well." Politically, I was at my pinnacle. There was some speculation that I would run for president in 1940. In my diary for Sunday, May 22, 1938: "Pepper for President clubs have been formed in West Palm Beach, St. Augustine, Wewahitchka and Fort Pierce. I have sent out wires and am going to issue a public statement to stop it now—too soon."

Immediately after the news of my overwhelming victory became known, members of the House of Representatives gathered at the clerk's desk in the House chamber. I had campaigned, in a Southern state, mind you, on the issue of a minimum wage–maximum hour bill, which had been bottled up in the House Rules Committee. The members demanded that the bill be discharged from the committee and brought to the floor for an immediate vote. Needless to say, it passed. An editorial cartoon in the *Washington Star* showed a hand sprinkling pepper over the transom of the Rules Committee door and the minimum wage–maximum hour bill coming out the bottom of the door.

America in 1938 was overwhelmingly isolationist. Ominous reports from abroad suggested at least the possibility of war, and the people of the United States wanted no part of it. World War I had ended only two decades earlier, and the prevailing attitude was that if Europeans wanted to go at it again, let them, but don't count on the United States to come to the rescue. After the overthrow of Kaiser Wilhelm in 1918, it was thought that Germany, under the Treaty of Versailles, would never be able to amass enough military power to engulf the world in another war. Many people thought that still was true, but others began to worry. Adolf Hitler had come to power after publishing *Mein Kampf,* which detailed how Germany could and should dominate Europe. Engrossed in its own economic problems, the United States paid scant attention to Hitler. In fact, at a dinner given by Mrs. Woodrow Wilson at the French embassy, I talked with a General Zauprey and came away with this summary of the general's impressions of the leader of France's historic enemy: "Hitler a great fellow."

My interest in international affairs grew rapidly at this time, in part because I had been appointed to the prestigious Senate Foreign Relations Committee, more because the goings-on in Europe were increasingly alarming. The word *pogrom*, the violent attack on Jews in Germany, came into the language. Still, there was minimal concern, even though Hitler seemed to be in the early stages of restoring Germany to strength and dominance. About this time, I learned that the Senate majority leader planned to name me a delegate to the Inter-Parliamentary Union, which would be meeting at The Hague in Holland. Mildred had been to Europe in 1935 with a student group; I had never been abroad. I felt therefore that the trip would be both a pleasant and an educational experience. Most of my time was still consumed by the wages and hours bill, a final version of which we hammered out in the Senate in June. (I felt as I imagined the framers of the Constitution did when, after much compromising, the draft was complete.) Passage by the Senate was assured, so I could turn my attention to foreign affairs.

After the Senate leadership confirmed my appointment to The Hague conference delegation, I called on the president. He told me that he planned to attempt a "purge" of some Democratic members of Congress, mentioning Walter George, Millard Tydings, and some others, mainly in the Senate, but also including Representative John Joseph O'Connor of New York, who as chairman of the House Rules Committee was bottling up New Deal legislation. The president was keenly interested in my trip, discussed the growing tension in the international situation, and asked me to report to him on my return.

As soon as my appointment was announced, Joe Kennedy

wired an invitation for Mildred and me to attend a garden party in London given by the king and queen—pretty heady stuff for a former plowboy and a one-time legislative clerk. Mildred and I were delighted. We sailed in August. Landing in southern Ireland, we traveled across the beautiful Irish countryside to attend the famous Dublin Horse Show. There we encountered Mrs. Rose Kennedy and several of her children, among them a son named John.

I wanted to meet Eamon De Valera, the prime minister who had done so much for Ireland, and arranged an interview through his office. He was most hospitable. He gave us an autographed copy of Ireland's constitution, and I told him he was one of the few men to have been the leading advocate who gained a country's freedom and then had the privilege of leading that country's new government. Not remarkable at all, he said, citing George Washington and others. But he was proud of the fact that he had taken over the police force and civil servants who had fought against him, retained them in their positions, and won their complete loyalty. De Valera was quiet, unassuming, and devoted to a united Ireland—which, half a century later, has yet to come into being. We met the U.S. consul, Irving Ives, and his wife, a sister of an up-and-coming young man I had met in Denver, Adlai Stevenson. We also visited the Irish castle where the Blarney Stone is located, and of course we both kissed it. Then we received a wire from Bernard Baruch, inviting us to join a grouse-hunting party at his leased estate at Hunt Hill near Breckin in Scotland.

In Scotland, we visited Glasgow and Glen Eagle, stopping overnight in Edinburgh. One night after dinner, the telephone rang in our hotel room. Mildred answered. She turned excitedly to me and said, "Our election is being contested at home and the Associated Press representative would like to see you downstairs." I was astonished. "Tell him I'll be right down," I said and rushed to the lobby. There I found Jesse Jones, head of the Reconstruction Finance Corporation, and Stewart McDonald, director of the Federal Housing Administration, laughing delightedly. They were also heading for the grouse hunt, and decided to have a little fun at my expense.

The Baruch mansion in the Scotch heather was adjacent to the grouse estate of the king of England. Baruch had invited a number of guests, including the lovely actress, Kitty Carlisle; Frank Kent, the syndicated columnist; Baruch's daughter and son-in-law; and several others. Never before had Mildred and I experienced such elegance. In the mornings, the guests were all driven in Rolls-Royces to the foot of the heather-covered mountain. There each guest mounted a horse led by a Scotchman to ride up to the "butts" where we shot the grouse. The butts were excavations in the ground, about ten feet square, and the fronts reached about to the chests of the hunters. Sticks in the right and left corners limited the range of the hunters, each of whom had two double-barreled hammerless shotguns. Scotchmen stood by each hunter, reloading a gun as soon as it was fired. Beaters from around the side of the mountain made noises and gestures to drive the grouse toward the butts, which were up and down the mountain in a line. After a period, a halt would be called and men with dogs would retrieve the dead grouse. At lunchtime, we would ride down the mountain on our horses and be driven to a site to which other broad-backed horses had brought large baskets of food and drink. After a luxurious lunch and a brief rest on the heather, we returned to the butts for more shooting. In late afternoon, the guests all returned to Hunt Hill for a formal cocktail party and dinner, where jokes, political talk, and animated conversation enlivened the evening.

Baruch at this time was widely thought to be a strong influence on Roosevelt. Newspapers depicted him as the wise man who sat on park benches dispensing political and financial advice. But for some months Baruch had been cooling toward

Roosevelt, in large part because the president rarely consulted him anymore. Baruch talked more about Woodrow Wilson, whom he revered, than about FDR. He also conveyed the impression that he was not overly fond of Joe Kennedy. His conversations, ranging over World War I battles and peace conferences, were stimulating and blunt: he said Colonel House, Wilson's confidant, was a traitor to him and wanted to become president himself—a situation somewhat analogous to that of Roosevelt and Farley, I thought to myself.

When bad weather curtailed the grouse shooting, I was not upset because that meant more time for talks with Baruch. He spoke of being "left out" by Roosevelt, supplanted by Corcoran, Benjamin Cohen, Felix Frankfurter, and others. He was pessimistic about world conditions and doubted that the European allies had enough resources to fight a war. But Germany, he predicted, "couldn't last long" if it started a war. He declared New Deal policy toward business as "bad and infamous" because it stifled competition and expansion. Baruch was a great man and wise counselor who at this stage of his life was being bypassed by the times.

From Scotland we traveled to London, where we had dinner one evening with Ambassador and Mrs. Joseph Kennedy. Three or four English couples were present. But that did not deter Joe Kennedy, who sat at one end of the table, from calling out to me, seated near the other end, "Claude, if I'd known your winning your election was going to make that man in the White House go crazy so nobody could tell him anything, I wouldn't have helped you." (The ambassador had contributed $2,500 to my campaign.) It struck me as highly improper for an American ambassador to criticize an American president in the presence of foreigners. But I said nothing.

Leaving London, we sailed to the Hook of Holland, from where we were driven to The Hague and joined other U.S. delegates and those from thirty nations for Inter-Parliamentary

Union meetings. Senator Alben Barkley of Kentucky addressed one of the sessions. Barkley and other Democratic senators and congressmen in The Hague were taking a dim view of reports from back home about Roosevelt's purge of conservative Democrats in Congress. "He'll wreck the party," said one. I defended the move as necessary if we were to keep the country on track toward economic recovery.

But domestic news soon began to take a backseat to signs all around us of tension and militarism. Mildred and I took a train to Heidelberg, Germany, and were startled by the number of German army officers on the train. There were foot soldiers everywhere. In Berlin, our next stop, we talked with people at the American embassy who were disturbed by the military buildup that was so obvious, so threatening, and so ignored by the West. Germany had 1,200,000 men under arms, the military attaché told us, with 250,000 more to be called up shortly. Hitler's saber-rattling oratory and his effective propaganda machine were unifying the German people and winning the reluctant admiration of worried foreigners.

In Berlin, we were reunited with a delightful couple we had met on the ship, Mr. and Mrs. Paul von Gontard. They invited us to dinner, where we were introduced to Paul's parents, Baron and Baroness von Gontard. The father was a high-ranking official of the company that produces Mercedes Benz automobiles, and the mother was a daughter of Adolphus Busch of the famous beer family. The older couple invited all four of us to their 17,000-acre country estate outside Berlin, adjoining an estate once owned by Bismarck, where I went hunting with Paul and Mildred went hunting, in a carriage, with Baron von Gontard. For the first—and last—time in my life, I killed a deer. When I looked into its eyes as an insignia of "honor" was being pinned on me, I felt only horror. In years to come I often went deer hunting in Florida, but I never killed a deer again.

Even on a weekend in the country, we could not get out

from under war clouds. A General Udet of the German Luft-waffe (Air Force) joined us in the hunt, and several times he was summoned to a telephone to take calls from government and military officials in Berlin. We and the other guests, who included the daughter and son-in-law of the baron and baron-ess, talked of the possibility of war. I posed a question: How could the Germans, without reserves of petroleum, wage a war? Simple, said the son-in-law, a businessman who lived in Hol-land, the Germans would make gasoline from coal. Anticipat-ing the future, he was buying all the weapons he could get for resale to the army. The von Gontards themselves were very much opposed to Hitler. They received radio broadcasts from Russia. If this fact had been discovered by the authorities, they would have been subject to severe punishment.

On our return to Berlin, we noticed writing on the windows of large department stores, the same writing on each. We asked what the words meant and were told that they proclaimed that the store was owned by a Jew. This was part of Hitler's anti-Jewish pogroms that ranged from outright violence to subtler discrimination. Jewish professionals, for example, were not permitted to have non-Jewish patients or clients.

In Berlin, Mildred and I met with Hugh Wilson, the U.S. ambassador to Germany, who tried to be reassuring. He praised the "order" that Hitler had brought to German society, with-out noting that individual rights had been trampled and citi-zens had been imprisoned illegally to bring it about. The National Socialist (Nazi) Congress was about to open in Nu-remberg and I determined to have a firsthand look. We went down with the ambassador on September 7. The city was so crowded we had to get a hotel an hour's train ride from Nurem-berg. My diary entry:

The place and route literally bathed in swastika flags— long red swastikas in center. The huge field—stadium—at least 120,000 people present. Everywhere one turned, uniforms—the S.A., S.S., etc. Forty thousand labor boys and 2,000 girls marched, the boys with shining spades in perfect precision. The school where leaders of this unit were being trained—the boys were stripped to the waist and the girls had on light blouses—a beautiful display of mass movement and mass emotion. Hitler stood in front seat section of open car and saluted the passing companies and made short but powerful speech. . . . [We] walked up and down street and saw crowds.

A day later:

Tens of thousands line streets of Nuremberg all day to see the sights. On to party Congress Nuremberg; sat on right of leaders' stand facing audience. Hess* presiding, Hitler's deputy—about 45, young and proud looking, friendly, easy poise. Hitler sitting in second seat right of aisle, front row, on raised platform. Hair not as black as I thought—of medium stature—hair cut rather high and close back and temples; smiled many times at remarks of speakers. Arose and shook hands with Dr. Todd, builder of autobus, when he finished—returned Nazi salute of other speakers as they finished. Chatted from time to time with Hess. Marched off platform and out through audience center aisle before anyone else when meeting adjourned about 1:30. Crowd all gave Heil Hitler and Nazi salutes. He seemed rather at ease and looked younger and fairer skinned than I thought. Tremendous

---

*The same Rudolf Hess who in 1987 hanged himself in Spandau prison four decades after his conviction as a Nazi war criminal.

crowd—25,000 at least, many men standing at attention in front of platform. Speech was on [his] record, "freedom of the press" and the new law in Germany, [designating] the state as the unit primarily to be protected.

Hitler made a convincing—judging from the reaction—defense of curtailing individual liberties for the sake of what was now all-important in Germany, the state. That night more than 100,000 SA's marched twelve abreast, goose-stepping in a frightening torchlight parade, singing the Horsvesel song.

Only the Nazi officials were allowed to ride in cars in the streets of Nuremberg. On one occasion, Hitler and all of his hierarchy met in a large building where 22,000 "brownshirts" (secret police) gathered. We sat above the stage where officialdom assembled. Behind Hitler and his chief lieutenants were numerous large standards, seemingly immobile, but I noticed one move slightly. Each standard, it turned out, was held by a Nazi soldier, relieved every few minutes by another soldier. The whole militant, martial atmosphere of this congress frightened me. Clearly, it portended ill for Europe and the world.

We left Nuremberg—gladly—and arrived in Munich. Mildred and I were taken on a tour, and we agreed that Munich was the most beautiful city we had ever seen. But the great museums and art galleries surrounded a strange memorial to the "beer hall putsch" where Hitler launched his Nazi movement.

Saw place where 16 of his men killed in "putsch" (they called it the great effort to liberate Germany). The bodies lie now in two specially-constructed monuments on one side of King's Square—8 in each monument. The coffins are bronze, side by side. At the top the words "The Last Call." Towards the bottom the name and below that "Hier." The top of each monument is open, signifying freedom. On each side of the steps leading to the interior of the monument a guard stands at stiff attention, changed each hour. Hitler was once a private in barracks here before going to the front.

Well, we were getting a thorough indoctrination in Nazism and the pervasive militarism of Hitler's Third Reich. Opinions clashed. The American consul, Roy E. B. Dower, voiced his distaste for the Hitler regime and told of much unrest being kept under cover. He warned that whatever happened, America should be guided by its own self-interest and stay out of European quarrels. He seemed to think that fear was the only ingredient of the German government's power and boldly predicted that Germany would "collapse" if it began a war and did not win it within a few weeks. Two days later, Dower brought us newspaper reports of a speech by another Hitler deputy, Hermann Göring, so violent that he would not translate the words in front of Mildred. Hitler also spoke, but in less alarmist fashion, possibly because Great Britain had warned him that if he sent troops into Czechoslovakia, as he had threatened to do, there would be war. Dower called the Hitler speech "a nice backdown."

One afternoon after Mildred and I completed a tour of the House of German Art in Munich, our guide asked us if we would like to see Herr Hitler. He said the Nazi leader came in every afternoon about four, and he put us at a table on the terrace, where tea was being served. Soon Hitler arrived with Hoffman, the Nazi photographer; they sat just two tables away from us. From my diary: "He was relatively unguarded. The three S.S.'s who accompanied him sat at next table. [Hitler] is hard to describe. He looks not unusual and yet very distinctive. Perhaps the set of his face and his eyes are the distinctive features. Hair dark brown, eyes dark blue, skin light, manner easy." We were told by the guide that no one was supposed to leave the terrace while Hitler was there, but we had to get to the American Express office before closing time to get some money for our departure by train. So after looking intently— staring, actually—at Hitler for forty-five minutes, we arose and left. As a little gesture of courtesy to Hitler, when we reached the door I turned and looked at him, bowing slightly as if to say, "Sorry, but we have to go." His eyes had followed us all the way from the table to the door. I have often wondered what he would have done if I had spoken to him. Probably nothing. This was his period of greatest success. He was enormously popular. He had not started a war, and economic conditions had markedly improved in Germany.

My diary entry for September 15 was succinct and recorded a historic event: "Chamberlain* flew to see Hitler today. Brave effort to avoid war."

From Germany we traveled to Italy where fascism was every bit as much in evidence, "though I can see they don't take to it the way the Germans do." Our ambassador, Wendell Phillips, talked at length, expressing some widely held convictions:

> He feels we should not try to determine other nations' governments for them and we should not criticize what other governments do in their own affairs so much. Yet on a great moral issue, like persecution of the Jews, clearly and definitely express our opinion. He sees it as I do: that we should mind our business and trade with everybody. Try to help the world along as best we can but don't try to solve the world's problems. That's what our forebears tried to get away from.

*British Prime Minister Neville Chamberlain.

Phillips was generally admiring of the Italian dictator, Benito Mussolini, who was making a speech that night. Mildred and I stood just across the street from him. He was greeted enthusiastically.

> He is about five feet nine or ten, weight about 190 I judge. Is strong and no appreciable stomach. He radiates health, vigor, vitality. He wasn't quite sure what to do with his hands as he stood alone out on the platform, but it is clear to see that he handles these people like a master of their psychology—he is sort of papa to them and they generally love him. He turned down my request through the embassy for an interview—probably on account of his leaving town tonight. Maybe because he is much peeved at American comment on him and his government. Maybe we'd better start letting these people have any kind of government they want.

We had intended to go from Rome to Naples and some other scenic spots in southern Italy, but the drift toward war was so strong that we decided to head back toward Paris, London, and home. We took a train to Paris.

There late one afternoon we listened to the doleful appraisals of the American ambassador to France, William Bullitt. At his post in Paris, Bullitt gave us a rather strange welcome. As soon as we entered his office, he asked, "What are you doing in Paris? Don't you know the war is about to start? I have talked to everybody in Europe today and the war is going to start Saturday." From conversations with other diplomats in Europe and State Department officials in Washington, Bullitt said he had concluded that chances of war were 95 out of 100. Hitler had scheduled another speech, and Bullitt thought he would not declare war—yet. By all means, the ambassador advised us, get out of Paris. The French government was offering free transportation out of the country to all who would go. Bullitt was prescient:

> He said France and England would not accept Hitler's ultimatum to the Czechs [demanding territory] and would stand by Czechs if they fought . . . that it would be a long war and France was reconciled to virtual destruction of Paris by air. Think of it! Said he was in State Department and at Versailles and knew Versailles Treaty contained errors and so told President Wilson; that Wilson on night before signing first draft of treaty said he would not sign it and with no one but Grayson and Mrs. Wilson seeing him he signed the next morning. Was sick. . . . We flew to London, leaving Paris 6:30, arriving 9:30. . . . President Roosevelt appealed to Hitler and Beneš,* copies to Daladier** and Chamberlain, for peace or Kellogg Pact. Chamberlain has just issued statement (12:50 A.M.) asking Hitler to settle border on basis reasonable haste and peaceful determination and not force . . . assured word given by Czechs for such settlement would be kept and guaranteed by Great Britain and France. Hitler speaks tonight, 8 to 9:30. Got extremely violent against Beneš, calling him liar, etc. Announced he would stand by his ultimatum and the required territory must be delivered to him by October 1 or by clear inference he would march. President Roosevelt's appeal obviously is being ignored by Hitler and is not even reported in German papers. Mussolini declares he will mobilize unless others dis-

*Edvard Beneš, the Czech leader.
**Édouard Daladier, premier of France.

continue mobilizing. Seems war now inevitable if the powers are not willing to let Hitler absolutely have his way in Europe. Maybe Eden* was right in taking position some time ago that dictators must be met squarely and as early as possible with force. What a strange combination of circumstances and events! An irresistible fate is forging war. Tomorrow we determine about getting off home.

Joe Kennedy, on a Tuesday, said war would begin the following Saturday. At his suggestion, I sent a cable to President Roosevelt urging that ships be made available immediately to evacuate American citizens, thus saving lives and avoiding entanglements. At dinner with Ambassador Kennedy, we listened to a broadcast speech by a weary and discouraged Chamberlain. He was still hoping for peace. So moving was his talk that everyone in our group wept a little. He made clear that he would not go to war merely because one nation attacked another, which I feared might sound like a green light to Hitler. But Chamberlain asserted strongly that Britain would definitely go to war if a nation seemed determined to rule the world by force. He appealed for calm and vowed that he would continue to "the last moment" his efforts to preserve peace.

Sumner Welles, the undersecretary of state, telephoned from Washington, asking Kennedy to talk to Chamberlain for suggestions about the president's reply to a message that at last had arrived from Hitler. Responding to Roosevelt's earlier plea, Hitler had reviewed events dating back to 1918 and said that if war came, it would not be his responsibility. From my diary:

Spy reported to Kennedy that if Germany got a few hard cracks in Czechoslovakia or by Great Britain or

---

*Anthony Eden, future foreign minister and prime minister of England.

France, the internal situation in Germany would collapse. . . . Ditches are being dug day and night in the parks for protection against air raids. Everyone possible being fitted with gas masks. Germany has now announced mobilization if demands not granted by 2 P.M. tomorrow. Horrible, ghastly war now seems to be opening its hideous jaws.

The next day there seemed to be new hope.

Wednesday, September 28:
Chamberlain made a report to the House on the situation. Toward the end of his speech, a message came from Hitler inviting Chamberlain, Daladier, and Mussolini for conference at Munich tomorrow. . . . This message was dramatically announced by Chamberlain and the House galleries burst into loud cheers and waving and handclapping . . . all felt that surely when the men meet tomorrow they will work out something which will save peace. . . . The British naval mobilization ordered by the King today goes on and ditches are being dug in the parks. Children are being evacuated from London, all fitted with gas masks, etc.

As the world awaited the Munich conference, which would forever after stigmatize Chamberlain as an appeaser, hopes for peace soared. I wrote on September 29: "Though nothing is technically settled yet the tension is relaxed and it is a foregone conclusion that they cannot fail." Looking back, my foresight seems woefully lacking, but at the time another world war was unthinkable. At Munich, agreement was reached to allow German troops to occupy the Sudeten territory until appointed commissioners determined how much Czech territory "rightfully" belonged to the Germans. It seemed fair. "The day of big rejoicing. Everybody happy. A wave of good feeling and idealism sweeps over the world. People were so near to war they knew how to appreciate peace." The next day, Chamberlain and Hitler signed an agreement that their two countries would never wage war against each other but would resolve differences through peaceful collaboration. What no one—especially Chamberlain—could know was that Hitler's "agreements" were not worth the paper they were written on. With his toehold on the Sudeten territory, he moved further into Czechoslovakia. He was secretly planning to invade France and bomb Britain.

Hitler's drive for world domination was under way.

Back in Washington, I reported on my trip to the president. He was glum, saying war had been only four hours away at the time of his message to Hitler. He wondered about Joe Kennedy: "Hasn't he got a bit high-hat?" He knew Kennedy had been bad-mouthing him, and I wouldn't deny it. In fact, I told him what Kennedy had said at dinner—that my reelection had made Roosevelt so stubborn that no one could tell him anything, that his policies were doomed to fail, and that he regretted having contributed to my campaign because Roosevelt interpreted my victory as a mandate to him. The president keenly resented the remarks of Ambassador Kennedy. He asked me if any foreigners were present when Kennedy spoke. I told him of the three or four British couples. He said, "It would have been bad enough if my ambassador had made such a statement with only Americans present, but it is inexcusable for him to make a disparaging statement about his president in the presence of foreigners." The president listened with great interest to my observation that perhaps Americans were tiring of the New Deal and that he should consider another bold initiative, such as eliminating unemployment. But his main focus now was on the deteriorating international situation. The New Deal was on hold.

Roosevelt was far ahead of the country in sensing the absolute necessity of a role for America in the war that was to come. The people wanted no U.S. role at all. The *Chicago Tribune* whipped up isolationist sentiment. A group calling itself America First signed up thousands of members and collected millions of dollars to pressure the administration and Congress to keep the United States isolated from Europe's problems. Charles Lindbergh, Father Coughlan, and Senators Burton K. Wheeler and Rush Holt attracted large crowds whenever they preached the isolationist gospel and verbally crucified Roosevelt. In January 1939, our ambassador to Germany, home for a visit, told me at a White House reception that he "deplored" the antagonism toward Germany evident in this country, even with its isolationism. Germany, he said, "merely wants a place in Eastern Europe, not Western Europe, and is no threat either to Western Europe or the United States."

President Roosevelt was so beset by the isolationists that he overreacted, in my opinion, to a report that he had said the American frontier was on the Rhine. He branded the report a lie. Republicans were saying the New Deal was dead, and even Pat Harrison, one of the Democratic leaders in the Senate, declared the party's chances of winning the 1940 presidential election "gone." In February in New York, I defended the administration in a broadcast discussion whose title indicated the direction of some of the political winds then blowing. It was: "Is the Administration Policy Leading Us into War?" Vice-President Garner cornered me in the Senate cloakroom and said that although he was personally devoted to Roosevelt (this would have been news to FDR), he thought the president had "thrown away" the party's chances to win in 1940 and that FDR had made more mistakes in fifty days than Garner had thought possible. In March 1939, even I noted solemnly in my diary:

"Democrats will lose election because times [will be] bad in 1940." In Florida a few days later, I spoke publicly in favor of Alben Barkley for president and the papers made much of it. Garner and Farley were getting their ducks in a row for their bids for the nomination, and I didn't want either.

In mid-April, I listened to a marvelous speech the president delivered at Mount Vernon and for the first time thought I detected a hint that a third-term candidacy was at least a possibility. Thus, when Jim Farley asked one of my aides if I was interested in the vice-presidency (on a Farley ticket, of course), I did not become too excited. On April 19, Tommy the Cork became the first insider to confide to me that he thought Roosevelt would run again. But it was only a hunch; he had no hard information. The following day I dropped by the Supreme Court to chat with Justice Hugo Black, my friend since Alabama days. Black brought up the subject of a Roosevelt third term and predicted the president would run. But whatever has been said and written, I am convinced that at this time Roosevelt did not want another term. In August 1939, Roosevelt told Jim Farley that he would not support a conservative for the 1940 nomination, but conceded that he could not name a liberal who could win. From my diary: "Personally, he is fed up with the job—really—and no doubt won't run again unless it is his duty. If war, he's probably in again."

More and more it appeared there would be war, although not necessarily with U.S. troop involvement. In September, Great Britain and France warned Hitler to get his troops and planes out of Poland, where they had been sent in "defense" of Germany. The world viewed the worsening situation with increasing alarm. My own father even wrote a long letter to me expressing fear that Roosevelt was "about to get us into war." On Sunday, September 3, the British gave Hitler two hours to respond to their ultimatum on Poland. Two and a quarter hours later, there had been no response, so Chamberlain announced that a state of war existed between Germany and Great Britain. France's demands had also been ignored by Hitler, so Daladier declared that France and Germany were at war. I suggested that Mussolini would "get lost" if he entered the war. The remark reached him and he asked who said it. I told reporters to tell him it was Claude Pepper of Tallahassee, Florida, and Camp Hill, Alabama.

What had been dreaded for so long—a major war in Europe—was now a reality. For Sunday, September 3, 1939, my diary reads:

> Horror of horrors . . . what shall be the end? I think Germany will lose, but who knows? Russia will stay out and let the others exhaust themselves, and emerge as the strongest power in Europe. Italy will, I believe, stay out. The Balkans will get in. I'm afraid we shall before the end have to save Great Britain and France for self-defense. We can't afford to have Germany win the war. . . . The President spoke on war situation, giving assurance he was going to do all in his power to keep us out of war. Could not ask us to be neutral in thought! Wanted to keep war from America, hoped later to get a real Neutrality law. I wired him after speech that he had comforted the people and confounded the critics.

The following day underscored how hopeless the president's task would be—the Germans sank a passenger ship with seventeen hundred passengers aboard, including several hundred Americans. "First major butchery of the helpless," I wrote. "German ruthlessness goes on."

That month the Senate easily passed the Neutrality Act, the 63 to 30 margin accurately reflecting national sentiment against U.S. participation in foreign wars. I actively supported the bill, in keeping with my evolving view that the best role for the United States was to help the democracies against the dictators, but to keep our troops at home. This was Roosevelt's view at that time as well. In late October, I met with the president on the war and other matters, and he told me flatly that he was serving his second and last term. He believed that. I worried that the conservative Garner, hard at work for himself with Southern Democrats, might win the nomination. I planned to stop him by running against and defeating him in the Georgia primary—a defeat in the South would kill Garner's candidacy. I felt confident that I, running as a Roosevelt Democrat, could defeat Garner in the South of that era. But I never found out for certain.

Neither Garner nor Farley nor anyone else was generating much excitement or support, and that simply gave impetus to more third-term talk. I began to select the Florida delegation for the 1940 convention, and it had a distinct pro-Roosevelt, or proliberal, coloration. In March 1940, Bernard Baruch called me to his hotel suite in Washington. He thought that Roosevelt could win the nomination and election if he decided to run. The following month, the National Newspaper Editors Association scheduled a debate on a third term as a highlight of its annual convention. Harold Ickes and I argued in favor against two unknowns, Glenn Frank and a newcomer to the Republican party named Wendell Willkie. Meanwhile, Garner supporters in Florida were running advertisements berating me as the would-be "political dictator of Florida" because of the pro-Roosevelt (or pro-Roosevelt's choice) delegation I was assembling.

The third-term question had come to a head and had to be settled, one way or the other. On May 12, 1940, it was. In great secrecy, Harry Hopkins asked me to meet with him. When I arrived in mid-morning, Chicago Mayor Ed Kelly and Jersey City Mayor Frank Hague, both powerful bosses of big-city

Democratic machines, were present. Hopkins gave us the first official word: FDR would accept the nomination if it was given to him "enthusiastically," if he was convinced the people really wanted him to continue in office. But if it appeared there would be a battle at the convention that he might win by only a narrow margin, he would not make the race.

It was a historic occasion. George Washington had refused to consider a third term as president, and every president for the next 140 years had followed suit. (Most did not have the option). Two factors, I am convinced, swayed Roosevelt. First and foremost was the war—he did not want to put the nation's fate in untrained hands. He knew that the outcome of the war was uncertain and that victory for the Allies was by no means assured. He knew they would have no chance without immeasurable aid from the United States and that this country could not be too squeamish about international law in providing that aid. He was aware that Jim Farley and other possible successors would not be willing to stretch the leash of legality as far as it would have to be stretched. Lawyers would be consulted and their advice followed, even at the cost of freedom in the world. FDR also believed that if Hitler prevailed in Europe, the United States would have to fight him, perhaps in the Western Hemisphere. Thus, he was determined to make an all-out effort to ensure that Hitler did not prevail. Like Lincoln, whoever was president might have to overlook or step around some legal niceties. Roosevelt knew he could and would, but he could not be certain of anyone else. Of course, he would have to have the people with him. Second, I think he realized there was no other liberal Democrat who could be elected. Under Republican rule, he was convinced, the country would revert to pre–New Deal days and ways, with programs that helped the "little people" being rolled back or abolished.

He could not leave the scene under these circumstances.

Could the president win? All four of us felt confident that he could. Obviously, there would be a great hue and cry. The charge of "dictator" would be heard again in the land. It would not be easy. Many party leaders and voters who had supported Roosevelt twice would balk at doing so a third time. Republicans would make the two-term tradition *the* issue.*

As a first step, I proposed that Paul McNutt, the governor of Indiana and a liberal who was planning to seek the nomination, be asked to declare that the entry of Roosevelt would effectively end the contest. McNutt would withdraw and suggest that the other candidates follow suit. Kelly and Hague, who controlled large blocs of delegates, agreed to meet with Farley to tell him he no longer had a chance and to get out. He probably would refuse, as would Garner. So, I suggested, why not let Senator John Bankhead of Alabama be keynote speaker, in return for which he would yield Alabama's first place in the roll call to New York. New York would then nominate FDR, and the convention would riot for Roosevelt and nominate him by acclamation. Hopkins was intrigued. He ordered that no keynoter be named without consultation with me.

We met again at Harry Hopkins's apartment the following Sunday for lunch and most of the afternoon. By that time, all of us agreed that Roosevelt should run for a third term and indeed *must* do so, and that he could be elected. We determined to try to induce the American people to reach the same conclusion and to make their wishes strongly known to the president.

As politics heated up, so did the war. Many in high political

---

*The Republicans did so in both 1940 and 1944, when Roosevelt won a fourth term. After Roosevelt was dead and they controlled Congress, the Republicans pushed through the Twenty-second Amendment, limiting presidents to two terms. Their opposition to more than two terms did not soften until 1986 when they realized that the popular president of their own party would be unable to seek a third term because of the anti-Roosevelt amendment.

office, including the president, knew that the United States would have to send troops, but it still wasn't safe to say so out loud. The Germans were rolling through France, with England the next target. And after that? It was time to provide more than moral support.

The resolution that I drafted in May 1940 to this end was the first lend-lease initiative introduced in the Congress. In informal conversations with newsmen, I had wondered out loud why we could not send some of our warplanes to England. The British could use them while their need was so desperate. Later, when planes England had ordered from our factories were built, we could use those to replace the planes we had sent overseas. The idea got into print in a small way, and several people called my office to say, "At last an idea that makes a lot of sense." We could provide planes to France, too, and replace them with ones then being built for the French. Twelve telegrams, all favorable, were on my desk when I reached my office the morning after the stories appeared. Benjamin Cohen called from the White House. "A good idea," he said. We met and drafted the first lend-lease bill in the history of the United States, or of any country for that matter. I told Cohen I would introduce the bill at noon the following day.

About ten the next morning, Cohen called. He sounded worried and asked me to call Roosevelt. I said, "Ben, I don't need the permission of the president on this." But Cohen was insistent. "He might have his reasons why he can't go along." "Well, all right," I grumbled. As Cohen hung up, dreadful tidings were announced on the radio. The Germans were almost at the English Channel, and here we in America, who might have to fight the Germans alone if England fell, were engaged in business as usual. I called Missy LeHand at the White House and told her about the resolution. She said, "It would be great if we could get that." I told her that unless the president himself asked me not to, I would go ahead and introduce it at noon. The president did not call.

My mother's family. Grandfather and
Grandmother are seated in the center. Mother is
standing between them.

The office of Dr. W. G. Carleton, who delivered
me into this world on September 8, 1900.

Our home in Dudleyville, Alabama, where I was born.

Standing on the front porch in Dudleyville. I'm on the left beside my father and mother and brother Joe. Grandfather Talbot is on the far right.

With the high school glee club at age sixteen. I am fourth
from left in the first row. Mr. Moseley, our principal, is first
on the left in the last row.

The Heflin Literary Society, of which I was a member in
1916. I am third from left in the first row. Three of my
cousins were fellow members: Roy McClendon (second
from left, first row), Bruce Talbot (third from left, second
row), and Pierce Talbot (fifth from left, second row).

Lena and J. Wheeler
Pepper, my parents.

Young Harvard graduate,
about 1925.

With my father,
in his office.

My first law office was
in this building in
Perry, Florida. I
practiced here from
1925 until 1930.

The Pepper family in 1935. Seated left to right are my
sister Sarah, Father, Mother, and my brother Frank. I am
standing in the rear with my brother Joseph.

I am standing with Frank and Joseph. Seated: Mother,
Father, Sarah, and her daughter Claudette.

Mildred Webster, the girl I married.

Our wedding in St.
Petersburg, Florida,
December 29, 1936.

The bride.

Mrs. Pepper.

In our first home in Wardman Towers Sheraton Park Hotel
in 1937.

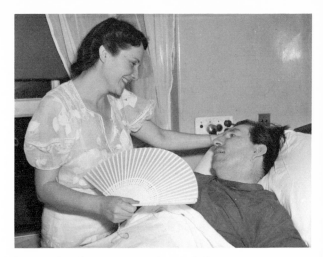

Recovering from an operation early in our marriage.

Being sworn into the U.S. Senate in January of 1937.

In the Senate tram on the way to the swearing-in ceremonies.

Senator Claude Denson Pepper.

Mildred with her parents, Thomas and Irene Webster.

Mildred with her horse Merwale.

Washington hostess.

Mildred and I at the Orange Bowl in Miami, New Year's Day, 1940. To the left is Senator Dick Russell, Mrs. E. V. Sewell, and (between us) E. V. Sewell, the Mayor of Miami.

For introducing the first Land-Lease resolution, Claude "Benedict Arnold" Pepper was hung in effigy by the Congress of American Mothers on the Capitol grounds in 1940.

With President Franklin D. Roosevelt in 1938. To the right
is Mayor Robert Williams of Miami.

Senator Pepper arriving in Miami with President Roosevelt in 1937.

Political cartoons in the early forties.

The Pepper family in Tallahassee, Florida, in 1947. First
row, left to right: Tina Pepper (Frank's wife), little
Claudette, Aunt Eunice McClendon, and Mother. I am
holding our dog, Lady. Second row: Joseph Pepper and his
wife, Ann, Sarah, her husband, Branson Willis, holding
little Branson, and Frank Pepper holding little Joseph.

On the Senate floor, I told my colleagues of the most recent German advance, warning that there was only one way for America to stay out of the war: by helping the Allies and by getting planes and battleships to them while they could still resist. Senator Arthur Vandenberg of Michigan, the Republicans' leading spokesman on foreign affairs, approached me, said he was "shocked," and shook his head in opposition and dismay. As soon as he returned to his seat, I introduced the resolution. That afternoon I informed the State Department that the resolution would be before the Senate Foreign Relations Committee the following day. The department's experts said what I was proposing was in violation of international law. "If we don't get rid of Hitler, there'll be no international law," I replied.

When the Foreign Relations Committee met, Senator Hiram Johnson of California was sitting like a stuffed frog, awaiting my arrival. My resolution was "monstrous," said Johnson. "It must be repudiated within the hour." He demanded immediate consideration. That was fine with me. Alben Barkley tried to bring me to my senses. "Claude, you're not going to get any support," he said. "I think that the country would be shocked that the Senate would consider such a resolution."

I told the committee: "This is a critical moment in history. I may be wrong, but I won't withdraw the resolution." So the vote was scheduled, after the committee took the unusual step of agreeing that all absent members would be polled. The final tally was 22 nays, 1 aye. About two weeks later, I met one evening with Ben Cohen; Walter Lippmann, the journalist and author; and Charles Marsh, the owner of eleven Southern newspapers. We drafted another version of Lend-Lease—one nearer to the final version adopted, at last, in March 1941. I introduced this second resolution, and when it came before the Senate Foreign Relations Committee, Senator Joseph Guffey of Pennsylvania joined me in support, largely because I told him I had consulted President Roosevelt about the first one.

This time the tally was 21 nays and 2 ayes. I resolved to take the issue to the floor of the Senate and to the forum of public opinion.

About three o'clock one afternoon, I went to the floor and pleaded for support. Senators simply walked out. I announced that I would speak again the following day, and when I reached the floor then, I noticed that the galleries were filling up. Also, the most extreme of the isolationist senators had gathered, and one by one they went after me hammer and tongs—Clark of Missouri, Nye of North Dakota, Walsh of Massachusetts, Wheeler of Montana, Vandenberg of Michigan. I encountered Richard Russell of Georgia in the cloakroom, and he complained, "That fool resolution of yours is taking half my time." My good friend Pat Harrison took me to one side: "This is a mistake, Claude. You're rousing up the country and agitating the Senate." "Maybe so," I replied, "but this is a critical moment in history. Maybe we should be doing things that haven't been done before."

Meanwhile, the volume of telegrams and mail pouring into the Senate and into my office particularly grew to mountainous proportions. My resolution, so "monstrous" to some senators, had struck a sympathetic cord with the people. Prominent citizens, including William Allen White, formed the Committee to Defend America by Aid to the Allies, and of course I joined. I challenged Senator Wheeler to debate the issue on his home ground in Montana. He didn't show up. Under the auspices of White's committee and later under the sponsorship of the Fight for Freedom Committee, I went all over the country, urging support for the president and calling for more aid to the Allies as our only hope to stay out of the war and still defeat Hitler. Sentiment for some kind of lend-lease legislation was substantial and building. Other committees of citizens were formed and the fight continued into 1941. The president sent me a "Dear Claude" letter saying, "You know I appreciate what you have done."

At last—in March 1941—lend-lease legislation passed the Senate and the House and was signed by the president. Friends abroad informed me that I was "awesome" in the British press. Winston Churchill expressed his gratitude for my role. Rarely had legislation so urgently needed started off with such slender prospect of enactment. In the end, it saved both Great Britain and the Soviet Union, to which its terms were later extended, from being conquered by Nazi Germany. It spared the United States from having to fight Hitler alone.

"Saturday, June 15, 1940: Paris falls. The tragedy of the blind democratic world. Unthinkable we should have thrown away the prizes of the world. The strong will survive, the weak perish, at times, at least. O beautiful gay Paris—you dead! When will you ever be resurrected?"

The fall of Paris was quickly followed by the fall of France. That began to awaken even the Senate. The president proposed compulsory military training and appointed two Republicans to his cabinet—Frank Knox as secretary of the navy, Henry Stimson as secretary of war. Incredibly, the isolationists even denounced him for that. For them the fall of France and the seemingly imminent collapse of Britain changed nothing. Senator Walsh even urged that Hitler be appeased. He argued that the Treaty of Versailles had left only one course open to Hitler, the one he had taken. In my reply to his speech, I labeled Walsh the champion of the failed policy of appeasement and I named for his benefit the real warmongers. Later I spoke on the NBC radio network on the danger that Hitler could penetrate South America, a real possibility despite the scoffs of the isolationists.

Monday, June 24, 1940:

France's terms of armistice received in the same railway car in Compiègne, just where Foch gave his terms, mean dismemberment of France, which is no longer a power in the world. Disarmed, occupied by

Germany and Italy, her coasts gone, no more use of her radio, etc., she is a vassal of Germany. What will people say about our apathy in this crucial hour? How will we explain this era to those who shall be mystified later? France destroyed and notice hardly taken of it in Congress. Britain may go the same way and it will be much the same until they strike us and then the people will be panicky and will run over all the old fossils.

On June 27, the Republican convention nominated my former debating opponent, Wendell Willkie, a utility executive, for president. Charles McNary, a Republican senator from Oregon who had run for vice-president in the 1936 Alf Landon debacle, told me, "Big business bought it for Willkie." Senator Bob Taft of Ohio and Governor Thomas E. Dewey of New York had been regarded as the leading contenders, but the businessmen backing Willkie had packed the galleries. Chants of "We Want Willkie" created the illusion of popular support, but in truth Willkie was largely unknown in the country. However, he would be a stronger candidate than either the colorless Taft or the deceitful Dewey. Roosevelt by now was convinced he had to run. No other Democrat could win.

The Democratic convention opened in July in Chicago, with the names of Roosevelt, Farley, and Garner considered certain to go before the delegates. Mayor Kelly urged me to let Florida nominate me for vice-president. The country was still so opposed to U.S. participation in the war that the president, in a preparedness speech, had inserted a phrase to the effect that "I shall not send American boys to fight European wars."

As expected, Farley refused to withdraw. He had been saying to anyone who would listen that "every member of the cabinet has told me that I'm big enough for the job but that son of a bitch," meaning FDR. Bitterness was rife over the platform, the interventionists and the isolationists refusing to give an inch. With Adlai Stevenson and others, I went to the *Chicago Daily News* office to read accounts of the raucous Democratic conventions of 1896 and 1912. Bankhead, as I had proposed, delivered the keynote address, and it was terrible. He did not even mention Roosevelt. But Barkley was named permanent chairman, and things began to happen. From my diary:

> Barkley made good speech. At mention Roosevelt's name, spontaneous demonstration. It not intended to be till end of speech . . . there was no arrangement about this demonstration. Whole [platform] committee met. Wheeler and I battled over foreign policy plank. It's strictly isolationist and I said so. Wagner resented it. Wheeler threatened to walk out of the party "if the committee lets the interventionists prevail and adopt[s] a platform as interventionist as the one the Republicans adopted at Philadelphia." I got two or three changes in—stronger plank on size of our Navy; stronger on Fifth column and stronger in endorsement of President. . . . About noon, I told Harry [Hopkins] they were letting Wheeler rewrite the platform and I called the President. He said "Damn it! I won't take that platform . . . they may want to help the Republicans, but I won't help them." . . . He said he would have to repudiate that platform and he would not accept the nomination on it. I told Wallace and he went to work on Walsh and Byrnes, and I got Kelly. Byrnes then got Wheeler and had long conference. From Governor Lehman's room, I called Secretary Hull. He was upset badly. Said such a platform increased four-fold our chances of getting into war; said he had contacted the President twice and would try to get him not to give in.

Roosevelt agreed to a few changes, but on the fundamentals he held firm and got the plank he wanted. Now the way was clear for choosing a candidate.

> Scene tense for night session on nominations. On roll call, Lister Hill of Alabama nominated Roosevelt . . . big applause and parade. Glass* nominated Jim Farley. His voice feeble and he a pathetic figure. Senator Maloney seconded Roosevelt's nomination. So did Governor Lehman of New York. Then I, from the platform, seconded Roosevelt's nomination in about 2- or 3-minute speech.** . . . Garner nominated in long, tiresome speech nobody heard. I meditated three men dead there who had been great: Farley, Garner and Glass. I slipped back and shook hands with Farley as he sat in back office listening to radio. He almost had a tear in his eye, but put up brave front. Roosevelt got 900+ votes out of 1,084. There was big demonstration. Broke up about 12 or 1. Anti-third-term resolution shouted down with loud boos. Thus, a tradition shattered. If it were ever pertinent, not applicable now.

The following day, Harry Hopkins assembled several of us who had been mentioned as possible running mates for Roosevelt. Before noon, he called me in and said the president's choice was Henry Wallace of Iowa. Well, that was that. My

---

*Senator Carter Glass of Virginia.

**I based my speech on an incident at Antietam. The soldier son of General Robert E. Lee spotted his father on a horse and moved toward him. "Son, back to your place in the line. Those people must not pass," Lee said. I related this incident, then said, "Franklin Roosevelt, tired though you may be, back to your place in the line." The president later told me this speech came across "like a cool breeze on a summer day."

expectations had not been large; I would have accepted the honor had it been offered. Immediately, I sought out Wallace, found him alone with a secretary, went over with him a speech prepared for the Iowa delegate who would nominate him. Wallace, a very spiritual character, was humble and natural. He moved swiftly to soothe and try to win over Farley and McNutt, but a storm broke out anyway. Bankhead refused to yield to Iowa, ignoring a request from the president. Instead, Alabama nominated Bankhead. From my diary:

> Jim Byrnes and I got Arkansas to yield to Iowa so it could nominate Wallace. I had talked, fortunately, to Governor Bailey of Arkansas who had agreed to go along and he controlled the delegation. Jim Farley was talking to the chairman from Arkansas just before we got hold of him. I don't know what he said . . . but Farley was not for Wallace. [There was] a host of other nominations of favorite sons and quiet declinations. This all hurt and I would not let my delegation nominate me under such circumstances. Before session began, Harry got me and said it looked as if we were in for some rough stuff and the President would not speak to the convention until Wallace nominated. We were fighting for votes hard for a good while. Finally the break came and Wallace was nominated by a good majority, and Bankhead moved it be unanimous.

The coming election had to vie with international developments for attention. Many well-known Democrats, including, of course, Farley, walked away from Roosevelt. But the bigger problem for the president was the continuing drumbeat of the isolationists. Lindbergh made a speech in which he declared his liking for order, thoroughness, and discipline, implying that he would not mind living under Hitler. He saw the war as nothing more than the usual European squabbling over territory. This remark prompted me to go to the floor of the Senate and declare Lindbergh the chief of the fifth column in the United States. I noted that a genuine American hero—General John J. Pershing—had urged that we send destroyers to England. The people of the United States would have to decide, I added, whose counsel to follow. The Senate was torn. An amendment to prohibit sending National Guard units out of the country, even to countries in the Western Hemisphere, was defeated by only one vote. I noted, "Our people and the Congress have never really made up their minds to enforce the Monroe Doctrine. . . . It has just been a name and remote generalization to the nation. Congress is not ready to defend America."

On August 9, I visited with General Pershing for a half hour:

> He's 80 but stands erect and his mind seems clear though he speaks slowly as if his false teeth impaired the fluency of his speech. He thinks the present German Army better than in the World War; that the Germans have avoided the mistakes of that war; does not rate Hitler highly as a military leader; thinks we should not think of sending troops at all to Europe but ships and planes and supplies. . . . He's now a kindly old man. He was pleased when I told him of the affection of the people for him and how they prayed for him when he was ill. He was dressed in quiet, well-tailored gray suit, glasses, thin white hair short on top and parted in the middle.

The president was moving toward supplying destroyers to Britain. On August 15, he called me to the White House to tell me he was going ahead with it. There was no chance that he could win authority from Congress to do what had to be done, so he was going ahead on the powers he believed he already had. Britain's plight worsened as Hitler launched droves of "buzz bombs"—aerial torpedoes, really—against it. Still, much of the United States could not or would not see the danger. On August 21, dozens of women who called themselves the Congress of American Mothers and who had been denouncing me for weeks hanged me in effigy in front of the Capitol, then dragged the effigy to the back of the building and on to the Supreme Court building, where they were stopped by police. So everyone would get the point, the effigy wore a sash with the name CLAUDE BENEDICT ARNOLD PEPPER.

I now have this effigy as a cherished souvenir in the Mildred and Claude Pepper Library at Florida State University in Tallahassee. I campaigned all over the nation for the ticket of Franklin D. Roosevelt and Henry Wallace. The country was still leery about entering the war, but it also was willing to continue to follow Roosevelt's leadership. My travels convinced me that for the first time in their history, Americans would elect a president to a third term. On November 5, they did just that. The election had been reduced to one overriding issue: trust.

On the last day of the year, I jotted down this note at the end of my diary:

> 1940 was a big year. The President was nominated a third time—I was a little helpful. This was my first National Convention. I got a chance to see it work from the inside. I was chairman of my delegation and spoke before the Convention. In the ensuing campaign, I got to speak in the Far West and made many new friends. Then the international situation gave me a chance to distinguish myself as the first one seeking persistently for aid to England and a straightforward and tremendous effort at national preparation.

4

"We've Got to Stand for Something"

Each generation wastes a little more of the future with greed and lust for riches.

—DONALD ROBERT PERRY MARQUIS

On June 21, 1941, a still apathetic America received a jolt. Adolf Hitler's troops invaded Russia, a country with which Germany had signed a nonaggression treaty, even though Russian leaders must have been aware of Hitler's contempt for treaties. The odds on England's short-term survivability improved; Hitler would have to wage war on two fronts now, dividing his resources. But my own view was that the conquest of Russia was, for Hitler, a necessary prelude to his final assault on the West. If Russia fell quickly, as it was widely assumed it would, then Great Britain and the United States would be the only major powers not under Hitler's boot, except for Japan, with which he had an alliance. Many American officials and commentators welcomed the German invasion. Let the Communists and the Fascists kill each other off, they urged. I thought this was short-sighted. My immediate reaction was that the West should provide weapons, ships, and planes to the Soviets, since Hitler clearly was the greater menace. No sooner had word of the invasion crackled over the news wires than I recommended that we include the Soviet Union in the provisions of the Lend-Lease Act, which had finally won congressional approval in March. But Russia was hated and feared by many Americans who could not see that it represented the best chance to stop Hitler—if it received our help. Our ambassador to Moscow, Joseph Davies, thought the Soviets would be able to resist the Nazi onslaught "for a long time." If all the enemies of Hitler worked together, I was convinced, the madman could be stopped.

In late July I had lunch at the embassy in Washington with the Soviet ambassador to the United States, Andrei Gromyko. He told me the Russians were anxious for the closest possible collaboration with the United States and Britain. I wrote in my diary: "They want bombers, pursuit planes, anti-aircraft guns, a liquid for holding ingredients together in making shells, equipment for refining gasoline. They get assurances from Welles, but not the materials asked for. Down the line below the president there is not much love of Russia and maybe no exertion to get things to her. . . . Russian military mission of high officials on way here so as to get to the top military people here."

By October, the Soviet forces were being crushed by the Nazis, who were driving straight for Moscow. The president, moving cautiously lest he get too far in front of his own parade, at last asked Congress for changes in the Neutrality Act that would allow us to send considerably more aid to Russia. I noted: "Tragic indifference still apparent in Congress. Democracy will just be saved if at all." Although some people, such as the

Congress of Mothers that hanged me in effigy, regarded me as a warmonger, my policy had not changed. It was still: Help the Allies crush Hitler, and stay out of the war. To my relief, the Senate on November 7—exactly one month before Pearl Harbor—approved the revised Neutrality Act, giving Roosevelt greater leeway in helping nations that were resisting Hitler.

With world attention focused on the battering Hitler was inflicting on the Russians and the British, Japan did not loom large in congressional concerns. But it was moving aggressively in the Pacific, adding to its empire. Japan had invaded Manchuria and China and occupied Indochina. I have recorded that in late November, Senator Tom Connally of Texas, chairman of the Senate Foreign Relations Committee, "gave out unhappy statement looking like appeasement to Japan. I gave out one rather warm the other way." On November 19, "I gave out pretty hot anti-Japan statement today to afternoon papers." It was clear that Japan was embarked on a program of conquest similar to the one Germany had launched in Europe. There were reports that the administration, its hands full, would be willing to appease Japan, I wrote, adding that "I shall fight if they do." On November 28, the president announced that whether there would be war or peace in the Pacific was up to Japan. The general expectation favored peace. Surely the Japanese would have to back down if faced with the probability of war with the United States. But the Japanese emissaries in Washington for negotiations gave no sign that Japan would give up any of the territory it had seized. They were engaged in an international charade of world-class dimensions, pretending to negotiate while, back home, the decision to attack Pearl Harbor had already been made.

On December 7, a day that FDR said would "live in infamy," Mildred and I were returning to Washington from New York when word came of the Japanese sneak attack on Pearl Harbor. The whole country was stunned. After years of living on the edge of war and never toppling into it, war had come to us. We would not know the extent of the damage at Pearl Harbor for several weeks, but we were told that 350 American soldiers died when the Japanese bombed a barracks. Many, many more Americans lay on the ocean bottom. After the initial shock came a national resolve: We hadn't wanted war, but now that we were in one the people would unite and win it. "I think we should declare war on the whole Axis while we are at it," I wrote, "since Hitler pushed Japan into this. Japan declared war on us as of 6:00 A.M. today, we learn . . . all but Senator Nye of isolationist crowd have come around now. I gave out statement, not a question of who has been right, but of unity henceforth. Joint session at 12:30 P.M. tomorrow. Well, here it is—war—war—God strengthen us all."

Congress declared war on Japan after a brief but masterful talk by the president. Already, American and British forces were under attack on Wake Island, Guam, Midway, the Philippines, Hong Kong, the Malay peninsula, and Singapore. The British had declared war on Japan before we did. On December 11, after Germany and Italy declared war on the United States, Congress declared war on them. As the year ended, Manila was being bombed, Hong Kong had fallen. The Japanese clearly were much better prepared than we. It would be a long, bloody, tragic war.

I urged total mobilization, and when some criticized that step as too extreme, I became aware that I had acquired—or had had bestowed on me by my political enemies and some of the press—an image as something of a "wild man." Often at speaking engagements, people would approach me to say how pleased and surprised they were to find me so "reasonable." Certainly I had been in the forefront on many controversial issues, such as Lend-Lease, and I had been under persistent attack by the isolationists, but I did not appreciate being thought of as unreflective. Also, I had been aware of the fact that for a period of time the FBI had me under surveillance, and I complained to the director, J. Edgar Hoover.* Hoover told me that the bureau was trying to be unobtrusively protective—that several threats against my life were in the FBI's possession. Whether this was true or whether I was suspect for having occasionally had a good word to say about Russia I never knew for certain. One of my former colleagues, who was at that time with the FBI, told me that he served in the Capitol, keeping me under general surveillance because of these threats against my life. I didn't know of his work at the time. Hoover's paranoia about Communism has since been well-documented.

As 1942 wore on, American forces were holding the Solomon islands against Japanese assaults, but the epic battle was being waged over Stalingrad. Casualties were tragically high on both sides. The Russians would not yield and the Germans would not be stopped. The Soviets increasingly complained that they were not getting enough help from the United States, and they were right. I spoke at a CIO rally in New York that was calling for a Second Front, just what Stalin was begging for. (My appearance there would be cited in future campaigns as evidence that I was a Red or at least a pinko.) In October, the Soviets claimed that the German advance on Stalingrad had been broken after some of the bitterest fighting and heaviest casualties in the history of warfare. In November, without significant help from us, the Red Army went on the offensive in the Stalingrad area. The year 1942 ended with the fighting in Europe inconclusive, but with the Soviets holding on surprisingly well. In the Pacific, the Japanese ruled, but American forces were gaining strength. At home, the nation grumbled about gasoline rationing. The Senate voted to exempt its members from rationing, with only two dissenting votes, one of them mine.

---

*Years later, George Danielson, then a colleague of mine in the House, told me that as an FBI agent in the early 1940s, he was assigned to protect me at the Capitol.

By the spring of 1943, U.S. planes were raiding Tokyo, and although no one expected the war to end soon, there was much talk about the postwar period, whether there should be a new League of Nations and whether the Soviets would cooperate with the British and Americans in striving for a lasting peace.

Meanwhile, I read some statistics that caused me grave concern. They made me wonder about the health of the American population, which had always been a subject of great interest to me as focused largely on the elderly and the poor. But our Selective Service system had discovered that young Americans were not in very good shape either. Nearly 2.5 million had been rejected for military service because they were educationally, mentally, physically, or morally deficient; another 300,000 had been turned down because they were illiterate. This was the situation in the richest country on earth, rich enough to do something about it. Well, the Congress was not much interested in legislation that did not directly affect the war effort, but I argued that this situation did—it represented a severe drain on our manpower. I was able to win a small appropriation and to borrow federal personnel to launch a study of this depressing phenomenon, which I felt reflected poorly on our society.

The Senate also established a Select Subcommittee on Wartime Health and Education within the Committee on Education and Labor. I was named chairman of the subcommittee and for three years conducted hearings. Selective Service authorities testified that 29.5 percent of potential draftees had been found unfit for service. Surgeon General Thomas Parran described improved health care as "imperative" and suggested an integrated national hospital system and prepaid medical insurance for all citizens, federally funded. Fiorello H. La Guardia, the mayor of New York City, made similar proposals.

In 1946 my subcommittee issued a report declaring that the poor health documented by Selective Service could be prevented in the future through a federal program incorporating

111

aid for hospital construction and medical insurance programs. About the same time, Senators Lister Hill and Harold Burton introduced a bill authorizing federal grants to the states for construction of hospital facilities. Passed as the Hill-Burton Act, the legislation established one of the most far-reaching and popular federal programs of the era.

I also introduced a number of bills attacked as radical at the time: to provide federally subsidized medical care, without a means test, to mothers and to children up to eighteen years of age; to involve the federal government in a massive cancer research program; and to do the same with respect to heart disease research. When introduced, these proposals had little support. They have since been incorporated into our national health research and delivery system.

Today these proposals have grown into thirteen National Institutes of Health, a National Medical Library, and a vast national research program. I was co-author of legislation setting up the National Cancer Institute in 1937. In 1967 I received the Albert and Mary Lasker Foundation award for being the principal sponsor of bills establishing five of these Institutes of Health. We still are not putting enough money into research and into battling critical diseases, nor are we providing full medical coverage to the American people, old and young. That remains one of my chief legislative objectives.

In any event, on July 21, 1943, I visited with the president, a practice I had continued but curtailed a bit because of his absorption in the war. His immersion was so nearly total that for the first time in my memory he said not a word about politics, even though there would be a presidential election the next year. There already had been speculation about a fourth-term bid, with most people assuming that if the war was still being waged, Roosevelt, health permitting, would run again. His supporters took it for granted; his enemies were resigned to it. But during our talk, he gave me no clue to his plans. One purpose of my visit had been to suggest that Tommy the Cork be named head of the Office of Economic Warfare. Corcoran was then out of the government, having run up some huge debts, which was an embarrassment to the president and also the reason Tommy had to earn more than a government salary. FDR said he would like to have Tommy back in government, but he plainly was not enthusiastic about it and gave me no hint as to what, if anything, he would do. From my diary:

> Talked about the war going very well, our having furnished all the equipment for our two million men overseas and much to our Allies, though that not so in World War I. Said he was to make early radio address. Talked about inflation and danger to war bond campaign if inflation came. Mentioned the nature of the opposition, though some honest differences of opinion in Congress. Said was keeping main eye on the war. No hint of politics for next year.

The war *was* going well. Four days after I called on the president, Mussolini "resigned." I wrote that it was "the beginning of the end of Italy in the war. Not known where Mussolini is. King takes over commands and makes Marshal Brodaglio Prime Minister and Secretary of State. Fascism cracking up."

For a long time, I had been thinking about the postwar period, hopeful that we would not lose the peace after winning the war, as had happened after World War I. I felt that the Senate might prove to be a dangerous stumbling block, and thought about proposing a constitutional amendment that would do away with the requirement of a two-thirds vote in ratifying treaties. So many senators would revert to their natural inclination—isolationism—once the fighting stopped. It would be impossible to get two-thirds of the Senate to agree that the sun rises in the east. But amending the Constitution is difficult and complex, requiring years of effort. So I decided to introduce a resolution now, committing the United States, while the fighting was still going on, to joining an international organization dedicated to preserving the peace. Since we had made the mistake of not joining the League of Nations after World War I, our Allies had every reason to believe we would turn our backs again at the end of this war. But Tom Corcoran tried to talk me out of my resolution, saying it was too soon.

While I thought about it, there was a delightful interlude. The Duke and Duchess of Windsor arrived in Washington. Mildred and I were invited to a dinner for the couple at the British embassy. I wrote to my family:

> The Duchess is rather thin. She is quite tall, has a considerable mole on the right side of her chin, and has naturally a bit of a British accent. She talked rather freely to me about the abdication of the Duke, and the Royal family and their attitude toward the Duke. She made it clear that the present Queen is quite jealous of the Duke and long has been, and naturally wasn't very much for her. The Duke, who sat across the table from her, next to Mildred, constantly looked at the Duchess, indicating that they were still very much attached to each other.
>
> The Duke is a grand gentleman. He is alert, deeply conscientious and sincere. He is doing a fine job as governor of the Bahamas and working at it just as hard as if it were a kingdom that he ruled. He agreed that if invited and he could get clearance from his government, he would come and address the Florida legislature gladly. He said that he wanted Mildred and me to come over to Nassau and visit them sometime the latter part of the year. So we had an interesting evening.

In late November, a group of senators who shared my fears about losing the peace met to talk about the elections of 1944. Senator Kenneth McKeller of Tennessee expressed fear that the Democrats would lose control of the Senate. He predicted that if that happened, "it would be 1918 all over again"—the sentiment for U.S. participation in a peace organization would no longer prevail. McKeller produced a list of several Democratic senators who were in danger of losing, and I was gratified that my name was not one of them. The president, meanwhile, met with Churchill and Chiang Kai-shek in Cairo toward the end of the year and later with Churchill and Stalin in Tehran. They agreed that once Japan was defeated, it would be stripped of all territory acquired through aggression since 1895.

Unlike the practice today, when a new presidential campaign begins as soon as the old one ends, in the 1940s electioneering did not begin until the election year. In 1944, it started in February, with Wendell Willkie barnstorming in the West, hoping to win the Republican nomination a second time, and no doubt praying for a less formidable opponent than FDR on his second time around. But he received little encouragement on this point. Vice-President Wallace, speaking in California, predicted flatly that the president would run for a fourth term. My more immediate concern was my own election, which would take place in May, not November, the Democratic primary still being the only race that counted in the one-party South. On Saint Valentine's Day, I met with the president. I was pleased to see him looking so well. He asked about my campaign, and I was hoping he would offer to help me win reelection. I was not disappointed: "He asked me to devise some occasion to write him about something and he would reply, wishing me success in my election and asking me to come in and see him immediately after my election and talk about some other matters I had been helping him with." We also discussed some

Florida needs, and I noted that "he used 'hell' two or three times, yet conversationally." The fact that I would refer at all to his using this mild expletive suggests that there was far less abusive language in the Roosevelt White House than in, say, the Nixon White House. Or the Truman White House, for that matter.

While I was in Florida visiting my family and doing a little campaigning, an event occurred in Washington that would have far-reaching repercussions on my political career. The president vetoed a new tax bill, describing it in a message for Congress as "not a tax bill but a tax relief bill providing relief not for the needy but for the greedy." The description was entirely accurate. But Democratic senators and congressmen who had supported the bill were furious at the president for figuratively stripping them in public. No one was more enraged than Senator Alben Barkley of Kentucky, the Democratic leader. He delivered a scathing speech in the Senate, criticizing the veto, the veto message, and the president. At the end of his speech, Barkley announced his resignation as majority leader, effective at a caucus he called for 10:30 the following morning. The senators, with three or four exceptions, arose and applauded. Then they filed by Barkley's seat to shake his hand while the packed galleries cheered. Vice-President Wallace, who was presiding, got up and left the moment the speech was over.

It was undoubtedly the worst day for Franklin Roosevelt in the Senate in all his years as president. FDR sent Steve Early, his press secretary, to Barkley's home to apologize, claim a misunderstanding, and urge Barkley to continue as majority leader. Early had to wait several hours on Barkley's porch before the senator came home. It was a situation without precedent—the leader of a president's own party berating him and resigning in the most public fashion.

From Florida, I kept in touch with the situation hour by hour and sometimes minute by minute through calls to my office and to my close friend, Senator Guffey of Pennsylvania. I deplored the turmoil and spectacle of a president's being scolded by a longtime supporter. But I had to admit that, in a way, the president had brought this donnybrook on himself by making Barkley the leader over the much better suited Pat Harrison, for whom I had voted. The White House had brought pressure on enough senators to enable Barkley to win by one vote. But he had been an inept leader. Therefore, the White House did not communicate with him or seek his advice as often as is usually the case. The president did not regard Barkley as strong or fully trustworthy. Barkley had never put together an effective leadership organization; the aides he hired were barely competent. He seldom anticipated the future or avoided a crisis through skillful and timely action. And he was lazy.

The Democratic caucus met as scheduled and Barkley entered the room to much cheering. He offered his resignation as majority leader, and it was accepted. Then the caucus immediately and unanimously reelected him. This was a clever ruse to remove Barkley from any obligation to the president, who had enabled him to beat Harrison but who had no role, other than that of unwilling catalyst, in Barkley's reelection. Barkley accepted his now-sanitized leadership post after being notified of his reelection by a committee of five anti-Roosevelt Democrats and one lone presidential supporter. To make FDR's dark day complete, the House by a vote of 299 to 95 overrode his veto of the tax bill.

The night before my return to Washington, I received a telephone call from Herbert Wolfe of Saint Augustine, Florida, inviting me to spend the night at his lovely home. Wolfe, a successful road builder, was a leading conservative businessman in Florida. I accepted the invitation. During the evening, Wolfe kept bringing the conversation back to the president's veto. He wanted to know what I thought of it. I told Wolfe that, as he knew, I generally supported President Roosevelt and that I thought a fair tax bill was needed. But I refused to tell him how I would vote the next day. Much later I learned that Ed Ball had persuaded Wolfe to invite me to his home and sound me out. Ball wanted the tax bill, with its special privileges to the already privileged, passed.

Early the following morning, I arrived back in Washington. I had pretty much decided how I would vote, but first I consulted with my staff and with Charles Marsh, a prominent newspaper publisher, friend, and adviser. Then I determined to vote to sustain the veto and to tell the Senate—and the Ed Balls of this world—why. From my diary: "Knew it would hurt me at home but it was my deep conviction. And I was determined to stand by it. I knew the real reason was the reactionaries against Roosevelt and said so in calm speech just after veto message read. Chamber full and galleries crowded. Got good attention after first few cries of 'vote' when I arose." Barkley did not want any discussion at all, but I insisted. No other senator spoke.

My remarks included my definition of what the Democratic party should be, as outlined in the letter I had written to Governor-elect Roosevelt in 1928, which I had inserted in the *Congressional Record*. I asserted my belief that the "welfare of the majority of the people lies in the triumph of the principles espoused by the Democratic Party. . . . I want the Democratic Party genuinely to become the Liberal Party of this Nation. I want it not to compromise upon that matter . . . we must stand for principle and not election always. We must be so firm in our allegiance to a utilitarian political philosophy that the people of this Nation shall know upon whom to call when they are convinced that that philosophy is right." The tax bill, I cried, was illiberal legislation that Democrats should oppose. "We've got to stand for something," I pleaded, to little practical effect. When the votes were counted, only fourteen members had supported the president's veto.

These proceedings in Washington were being carefully monitored from Florida. The reason was that the tax bill contained special relief for the lumber industry, which was and is very important and powerful in Florida. My vote to sustain the veto could not have surprised anyone—I had never been a supporter of corporate welfare, which I deemed this bill to be. But what really infuriated the Florida business community was my audacity in defying Barkley and speaking out in favor of the veto on the Senate floor.

I had voted to send men to war, many of whom would never come home. I didn't see anything wrong with taxing fairly heavily the war contractors who were safe at home making money.

The business leaders apparently overestimated my rhetorical powers. They feared that in speaking out, I might convince enough senators that the veto should be sustained. When this proved not to be the case, the very fact that I had tried—and I had tried—to deprive them of their special, undeserved tax privileges called for revenge. That very afternoon, a group of Florida industrialists met and in a matter of hours raised $62,000 for the beginning of a fund to oust Claude Pepper from the Senate. Since the primary of 1944 was so near at hand, they despaired of defeating me then, though they would try. In any event, I would be up for reelection again six years later, and the war chest would have plenty of time to grow. Six years is a long time to harbor a grudge, but this group was long on patience. Its leader was Ed Ball, who was noted for a very long memory. If he could not defeat me in 1944 (and he came close to succeeding), he would await the big payoff in 1950.

The ideological tide was turning rapidly in Florida in 1944. In a way, it was stranding me on the beach, for the liberal tide had long since peaked. Thousands and thousands of wealthy people from the North had retired and moved into the state, attracted by its warm climate, beauty, and pleasant conditions for living. Most of them were conservative. The issues on which I had campaigned in 1936 and 1938 had not disappeared—poverty, unemployment, health care, Social Security—but they were no longer the most pressing issues. Florida had prospered dur-

119

ing the war, with military installations and defense industries that had been established or greatly expanded. Floridians were no longer worrying about losing their jobs—there was plenty of work. The population was exploding. Instead of wondering where their next meal was coming from, people were saving money to buy new cars and boats and homes and furniture once the war ended and production shifted back to consumer goods.

When people are doing well financially, they lose sight of those who are left out. Programs such as welfare, unemployment compensation, minimum wages—my agenda—lose much of their appeal. Demagogues thrive by arguing that such programs as national health insurance and student loans are wasteful and costly, and that tax dollars earned by hard working citizens should not be spent on the "undeserving" poor. By 1944, Florida was increasingly hospitable to such reasoning. I could not ride this new wave of self-satisfaction. It would have looked like the height of hypocrisy, and that is exactly what it would have been. As Florida turned toward the right, Claude Pepper moved straight ahead. A separation of some sort, at some point, was inevitable.

Ball and his group had money. In addition to what they could raise, the American Medical Association was prepared to spend thousands of dollars to defeat me because I was an advocate of "socialized medicine," the program that partially came into being, decades later, as Medicare. But they had no candidate. After trying and failing to get a number of congressmen and former governors to run against me, they settled on Ollie Edmunds, a county judge from Duvall County. Although he didn't seem to be a very strong opponent, many of my longtime friends and supporters nonetheless thought I should mend my ways if I wanted to be certain of staying on in the Senate. The least I could do was soft-pedal issues like those I had campaigned on in the past, such as the wages and hours bill I had led to passage only two years before. "No," I said. "My record is there for all to see. I'm not ashamed of it and I'm not going to run away from it."

I campaigned the way I always had.

In 1938, I had won the primary by a 100,000-vote margin, so I wasn't really worried, even though I realized Florida had changed and would change more. In 1944, however, my margin shrank to 10,000 votes, which was much too close for comfort. The well-organized and lavishly financed effort to remove me from the Senate had fallen short. Like it or not, the corporate community would have to put up with Claude Pepper in the Senate for six more years.

With another term to look forward to, now I could turn my attention to helping keep President Roosevelt at the helm until the war—and the peace—were won.

On August 24, I spent a strange evening at the White House:

> Dinner at the White House. The President entertaining the President of Iceland. At the end of the dinner, our President spoke about Iceland and made rather clever and interesting remarks, but it was obvious that he and the President of Iceland had taken a few cocktails upstairs while the guests (all men) waited downstairs. The President drank toast to the President of Iceland. After our applause, etc., the President of Iceland, standing, gave a talk, not very clear, and drank a toast to the President. President Roosevelt joined in; then, apparently not recalling his previous toast, offered another to his guest, but few joined him.

FDR did not have a drinking problem, but I had wondered a few times after hearing his slurred speech if he had not taken to having a drink or two at the end of the day.

A few days later in Florida I received a disturbing report from my longtime friend, Ches Dishong. He had been analyzing the voting patterns from the primary election, wondering why I had lost so many counties in northern Florida, and had concluded from talking to residents that one of my opposition's shabbiest tactics—labeling me a "nigger lover"—had been effective. The northern counties, bordering Georgia, were as racist as any areas in the Deep South. White voters had been disturbed by photographs of me speaking to a Negro church meeting and by others of me shaking hands with black people at the conclusion of some of my rallies. My opponents had blown up some of these photographs, reproduced them, and distributed pamphlets and fliers all over the state, but particularly in the northern counties.

The race issue is a factor in nearly all elections today, but it is nothing like it was in earlier years, including 1944. Then there were no blacks on major league baseball teams, nor on collegiate or professional football teams. There were not even any black basketball players on college teams or in the National Basketball Association.* The armed forces had not been integrated. Companies of blacks, whose officers were usually white, fought gallantly in the war, but they were not allowed to serve alongside or socialize with white troops.** If I needed a reminder of how deep the hatred of many whites toward blacks was in that year, I received one on this trip to Florida. After hearing the report from Ches, I went to Tallahassee for a visit with the governor at the state capitol. Governor Fuller Warren was desperately trying to prevent the lynching of three Negroes who had raped and shot the wife of a white soldier in Gadsden County. In my diary, I noted:

> There was feeling against the governor for not letting the Negroes fall into white hands. The local people

*NBA rosters are now as much as 75 percent black.
**Not until 1949 did an American president, Harry S Truman, recommend integration of the armed forces.

said there had never been a trial of a Negro for the rape of a white woman (all lynched) and they didn't want a trial now. The governor called out state troops and they guarded the court house in Quincy—two companies. They said they could deliver the defendants, but not without bloodshed. Tragic situation in the South about the Negro. More conflict to come. Tragic failure of the white extremists to realize the necessity of the law handling such matters. Eventually, the federal government will step in in such cases and while there will be bloodshed a few times, the courts will eventually gain the mastery of the mob.

Well, by and large, that is what happened. Lynching is pretty much a thing of the past. Racism, unhappily, is not.

The political conventions in the summer of 1944 nominated two New York governors, past and present, for president—FDR for the Democrats and Thomas E. Dewey for the Republicans. The hue and cry over the third term was repeated with respect to the fourth, but it was considerably muted. Roosevelt in his third term had not assumed dictatorial powers, nor had he suspended the Constitution, and called off elections, as his opponents had warned that he would. The people were not readily frightened by the same kind of talk four years later. FDR had another advantage—he had guided the nation safely through its worst economic storm and to a point in World War II where that terrible struggle was being won. Americans were not in the mood to turn him out.

In campaigning for the president, I got one major rise out of Dewey.* At a rally in Seattle, I told the audience that the president would have a far better chance of getting Russia to help

---

*After losing some primaries, Wendell Willkie gave up his quest.

123

us in the war against Japan after the defeat of Germany than Dewey would. The statement was shown to Dewey, who termed it, sarcastically, "remarkable." He refused, however, to respond to it until he had seen the complete text. When I heard that, I amplified the statement. President Roosevelt, I noted, had extended diplomatic recognition to the Soviet government. He also had signed a lend-lease bill to include aid to Russia. Dewey had denounced both actions. I asked Dewey to tell the American people what he had said at the time the United States recognized the Soviet Union, and what his public statements had been when the Lend-Lease Act was amended. I never heard from Dewey again.

A month before the election, Al Smith died. He had never made peace with Roosevelt, whose success he envied. Smith had been rejected by the American electorate, who had elected his successor as governor of New York to the presidency three times and was about to make it four. I wrote: "Al Smith is dead. Was colorful figure. Was never like the liberal the President is." In fact, the president once told me that the first break between him and Smith occurred when some private-power executives came to see him [Roosevelt] when he was governor. They asked him if he planned to treat the power issue the way Governor Smith had—"talk ferociously about private power but do nothing to regulate it." Smith learned of the incident and was greatly embarrassed. The relationship began to deteriorate at that point and the rupture was complete when Roosevelt won the presidential nomination in 1932. Smith wanted that nomination for himself, to redeem his sorry performance of 1928.

Before the convention, I had an odd conversation with Alben Barkley. It appeared there would be a battle for the vice-presidential nomination, Henry Wallace having aroused considerable opposition. A couple of letters from the president praising the capabilities of Supreme Court Justice William O. Douglas and Senator Harry S Truman had been made public, forcing the president to write another letter praising Wallace. Barkley told me this breach of protocol disturbed him, but the more he talked about it the clearer it became that what really bothered Barkley was that the president had offered no encouragement to Barkley's own aspirations, thus forcing him to declare that he was not a candidate. At the same time, James Byrnes had let the press know that FDR had encouraged him to go to Chicago and get in the race for vice-president. This had Barkley seething, for the president had had no such message for him, nor for Speaker of the House Sam Rayburn, who was equally miffed. Barkley told me that he regretted to learn "that one he had served and loved all these years [FDR] had feet of clay."

I suspect that President Roosevelt was very much like the elephant who never forgets. He told me in a conversation about the convention of 1944: "We'll let Barkley be permanent chairman. He can hit hard with the gavel." It is my opinion that Barkley's wrathful performance over the tax bill veto cost him the presidency, because he could have been nominated for vice-president in 1944. Becoming angry was something of a habit with him. When some of the labor leaders at the convention told Barkley he was too old to be considered for president or vice-president, he stalked out of the convention and headed for the airport and the next flight home. Leslie Biffle, the secretary of the Senate, followed him in a taxicab, caught him at the airport, and brought him back to the convention. Biffle arranged a big ovation for Barkley that evening, but the ovation was all that the Kentucky senator received.

He could have received so much more. Alben Barkley missed the biggest boat that comes by in a politician's lifetime.

125

5

"Dump Truman"

When you strike at a king, you must kill him.

—OLIVER WENDELL HOLMES, JR.

In the early 1940s, it became clear that Franklin D. Roosevelt would not live forever. Indeed, he might not live for very long. This was difficult for the millions of people who idolized him to grasp. Roosevelt had been such a dominating figure on the national and international scenes for so long it was impossible to imagine him gone, and equally hard to envision someone else in his place. Henry A. Wallace was vice-president. He was a competent public official who could be relied on to carry out Roosevelt's domestic and foreign policies. But Wallace was too liberal for most of the party establishment. Powerful forces had made clear to Roosevelt that if he ran for a fourth term in 1944, which nearly everyone took for granted, they could not support Henry Wallace as his running mate. This was a delicate subject. The mere mention of it suggested that Roosevelt could not survive a fourth term; thus it was critical that his running mate be looked on not as a possible but as a probable presi-

126

dent. To FDR himself, party leaders framed the issue differently: Wallace, they convinced the president, would cost the Democrats one or two million votes if he were on the ticket.

Although I supported Henry Wallace, I was a realist. My gaze wandered over the Senate chamber. Not many senators had been nominated in recent years for president or vice-president by either party. But every senator was aware that the colleague whose elbow he brushed against, or the one sitting across the aisle with the opposition party, could well be the next president of the United States. When my eyes fell on certain senators, this was an unsettling thought, for the Senate is peopled by charlatans and mediocrities as well as by men (and too rarely women) of unquestioned integrity and uncommon intelligence. At this particular moment in history, there were many able Republicans—Taft, Vandenberg, Borah, Bricker, all too conservative for my tastes. On the Democratic side of the aisle sat such Senate barons as Russell, George, Connolly, Barkley, Thomas, Pittman, good senators, none of whom seemed a potentially worthy successor to Roosevelt. When my stare focused on the senator who actually would succeed FDR—Harry S Truman of Missouri—the thought of this seemingly ordinary man becoming leader of the free world, if it entered my mind at all, exited very quickly.

Pleasant enough, conscientious, and decent, Senator Truman was the leader of no significant Senate faction. Plain in appearance and manner, he was generally looked on as a plodder and political hack who owed his career to the unsavory Pendergast political machine in Missouri. It had plucked him from an obscure county judgeship and dropped him into the United States Senate, where he could not have been said to have flowered. I, as a former small businessman engaged in cleaning and blocking hats, certainly could not hold it against Truman that he was a haberdasher before entering politics. Nor did I judge him harshly for the fact that the haberdashery failed,

127

my own father having had similar difficulties. But of ninety-six senators serving during the early 1940s, Truman had to be placed among the least likely to ascend to higher office. We got along well. I liked Harry Truman. Our problems and major disagreements lay in the future.

The first evidence that this unassuming Missourian may have been the victim of untruthful packaging came in February 1941. There was more there than met the eye. Bland, go-along, get-along Harry arose in the Senate to reveal that for a month he had been traveling more than 30,000 miles to observe the work of defense contractors. He returned convinced that massive waste and fraud were rampant and urged the Senate to appoint a committee to investigate. Senator Truman stopped by my desk on his way to the well of the Senate to introduce a resolution setting up that committee. "Claude," he said, "take a look at this resolution and tell me what you think of it." I asked, "What is it, Harry?" He explained that it was a resolution to investigate the way the government was running the war as far as production and economic aspects were concerned. "If we Democrats don't investigate ourselves," I remember his saying, "the damn Republicans will investigate us." I read the resolution and commended him for it. Thereupon, Harry Truman stepped into the well of the Senate and introduced his resolution. That act, combined with shrewd maneuvering by his fellow Missourian Bob Hannegan and some fortuitous circumstances, made him president of the United States. The subject of the resolution—the Truman Investigations Committee—was timely and needed. And its author was wise enough, after being named chairman, to call the attorney general and ask for the best lawyer he knew to be general counsel of the committee. An excellent staff was assembled, which ensured the committee's success. Had Truman hired political cronies instead of real professionals, the committee would have flopped.

The Truman Committee quickly established that a mere world

war with the future of democracy at stake was insufficient reason for defense contractors to set aside their normal greed. Patriotism, it seems, was for the masses. Many businesses under contract to produce the tools of war were simultaneously plundering the American taxpayer through fraud, overcharges, and shoddy workmanship. The man from Missouri had dared to say "show me" to the powerful military-industrial complex and he had caught many people in the act. His reports enabled Harry Truman to burst free of the anonymity in which he had been cloaked. He became a national figure.

The first references to Truman in my diary note merely that he came to Florida to campaign for me in 1944 and that I was in Missouri later that year to make a few speeches for him. I wrote of Truman: "He is able, honest, modest, sincere man," a judgment I never had reason to change.

A tide was developing within the Democratic party, and one of the fascinating things about politics is that one never knows what the impact of a tide will be. Much to his surprise, this one would sweep Truman into the vice-presidency and the presidency. The more Roosevelt's health seemed to deteriorate, the more opposition to Wallace hardened. To conservatives and even many moderates, Wallace was a woolly-headed thinker with his head in the clouds, a near-Socialist too divorced from reality to defend this nation's interests in the postwar world. It was a harsh and, in my opinion, unwarranted appraisal. But it was widely held and Wallace could do little to overcome it. Roosevelt would be the nominee for president for the fourth time, unprecedented in our history. Given his track record and the fact that the people trusted him to guide the nation to victory in the war, he probably would be reelected in November.

Henry Wallace was a very able man, but he was a poor politician. Barney Hodez, general counsel for Mayor Ed Kelly of Chicago and himself a leading Democrat, once told me that

Vice-President Wallace never called the mayor or came by to pay his respects when he visited Chicago. To Wallace, that would be embracing and identifying himself with machine politics, at which Mayor Kelly was so adept. President Roosevelt, however, always kept up a warm and friendly relationship with machine politicians. He needed their votes in order to do great things for the country. That was his rationalization. But Wallace stood aloof. Shortly before the Democratic National Convention of 1944, I met with the president at the White House and asked him if he planned to support Wallace for the vice-presidential nomination in the same manner he had in 1940— by refusing to accept his own renomination until the convention had nominated Wallace. "No," Roosevelt said. "I can't do that this time." But he added, "I want to be loyal to Henry Wallace. I think he would be a good president if someone were to shoot me." I suggested that the president appoint Wallace ambassador to Russia or China or some other major country, thus avoiding a humiliating Wallace defeat at the convention, "because if you don't do for him this time what you did last time, he can't win." The president looked glum. "Well," he said, "I just can't do that this time."

Roosevelt's actuarial outlook was bleak. He was only sixty-two, but the stress he had been under for so long had clearly taken a heavy toll. Thus there was no shortage of aspirants for the vice-presidential nomination. For Southerners, the vice-presidency was the only possible route to the White House because the nation had not elected a Southerner as president since before the Civil War.* James Byrnes of South Carolina, whose career would include service in the Senate, on the Supreme Court, as "assistant president," and as secretary of state, thought he was entitled to the nomination. Senator Harry Byrd of Virginia thought he was. Neither could understand that he

*Wilson, born in Virginia, spent most of his life in New Jersey.

was unacceptable to organized labor, a powerful Democratic constituency, and to those who believed in civil rights. I am sure that neither Byrnes nor Byrd ever cast a pro-labor or pro— civil rights vote in his life. Yet each was prepared to ask for and both expected to get labor's backing as well as the support of liberal Democrats. Ambition wears blinders.

There was some support for Senator Alben Barkley of Kentucky, the Democratic leader in the Senate, and some liberal and labor backing for Senator Claude Pepper of Florida, although as long as Wallace remained in the race I would do nothing to encourage it. I was still supporting Wallace, even though I knew that without Roosevelt's insistence, he had virtually no chance to be nominated.

Byrnes, who suddenly wanted liberal approval, and who apparently discounted my own chances of being nominated, sought to enlist me in his cause. As a top assistant to the president, Byrnes had an office in the White House. One day he noticed that on the president's schedule was an appointment to see me. Byrnes telephoned, asking that I stop by his office before going in to see Roosevelt. All right, I said. I'll be glad to. Byrnes told me he would welcome my support and that he would appreciate my talking to the president about the strengths he could bring to the ticket. Of course he knew that I was committed to Wallace, but he shared the widespread assumption that Wallace would have to drop out at some point and he wanted my backing then. I was noncommittal.

When I met with the president, I told him of Byrnes's ambition and FDR was of course not surprised. He was very candid. He told me that in 1940, Secretary of State Cordell Hull was his first choice, but Hull would not accept the vice-presidential nomination. Byrnes was his second choice. But, the president said, a cardinal of the Catholic church (I understood it was Cardinal Menteline of Chicago) told him that Byrnes was unacceptable to the church. The reason for the church's opposition was not spelled out, though Roosevelt had assumed that it was based on the fact that Byrnes had been born into the Catholic church but had left it (Roosevelt thought the reason was that Byrnes had fallen in love with a girl who was not a Catholic). Unwilling to defy the church in 1940, Roosevelt was no more ready to do so in 1944. In our conversation, the name of Harry S Truman did not come up.

Unwittingly, I was in the center of a storm that would leave Roosevelt and Byrnes estranged for life. When Byrnes finally laid his cards on the table and told the president he wanted the nomination, Roosevelt, as usual, was unable to tell him he would not be considered. In his customary jovial way, the president said, "Why yes, Jimmy, I would be delighted to have you as my running mate." But FDR knew that Byrnes could not be nominated. Therefore he did not tell Byrnes that he would ask the convention to nominate him. Roosevelt did mention Byrnes's problems with organized labor, apparently telling him to "clear it with Sidney," meaning that Sidney Hillman, the powerful president of the CIO, had a veto power over the vice-presidential nomination. Byrnes leaked the remark to the press, embarrassing Roosevelt. Byrnes, with his usual assurance, which bordered on arrogance, went to Chicago and took over the Presidential Suite at the Congress Hotel, convention headquarters. As if he were the crown prince, he sent for various leading Democrats, telling them he was the president's choice. When he made that claim to a roomful of labor leaders, they didn't buy. Said one: "The president tells us he has not chosen you. He said he told you to clear it with Sidney. And Sidney Hillman says that not only did you never contact him, he isn't for you in any event." That was when the Byrnes boomlet burst. Byrnes soon resigned in a huff and returned to South Carolina, where he was later elected governor.

Richard Russell of Georgia, a powerful senator who also had

no record of support for organized labor or civil rights, wanted to be vice-president, too. His rebuff was as embarrassing as that of Jimmy Byrnes. FDR could not bring himself to tell Russell that he had no chance, so Russell actively solicited labor support. He told John L. Lewis,* the bushy-browed president of the United Mine Workers, that he would support repeal of the hated Taft-Hartley law if the UMW would throw its support to him. Word of this astonishing desperation pledge reached Harry Byrd, who had given up his own quest and was guiding a resolution of support for Russell through the Virginia Democratic Convention. Enraged, Byrd blocked the endorsement. Russell rose no higher in public life than any other Southerner of his era: chairman of a Senate committee. He and Byrd were both able, distinguished senators whose records in public life were outstanding. They could not, however, understand that in faithfully following the Southern line, opposing labor, civil rights, and liberal legislation in general, they could not at a certain stage in their lives decide they would like to become president and presto!—have the voters flock to their banners.

Much of organized labor remained faithful to Wallace and efforts were made to jam the galleries and stampede the convention for him. But the opposition was too broad and too entrenched. Labor had to consider second choices, or the convention might deadlock and nominate a compromise candidate such as House Speaker Will Bankhead of Alabama or Senator Bob Kerr of Oklahoma. As a liberal, I was acceptable, but as long as the Wallace candidacy appeared to be viable, mine had to remain moribund. In scanning the political horizon for second choices, Sidney Hillman and others looked for a Democrat with a pro-labor, pro–civil rights voting record who

---

*Lewis, four years earlier, had offered himself as FDR's running mate, but the president was not interested.

would not turn off the conservatives the way Wallace did (and perhaps I would). They hit upon Harry Truman. He didn't really offend any significant voting bloc, and he had earned a national reputation with his Truman Committee investigations.

But the one who really manipulated Truman's nomination was his fellow Missourian, Bob Hannegan. Hannegan had been appointed collector of internal revenue at Truman's insistence. Later, when Truman decided he would like to be vice-president, it was his good fortune that Hannegan had become chairman of the Democratic National Committee. As such, Hannegan ran the convention. It opened on a Sunday, and the highlight was the public release of a letter from Roosevelt to a delegate, saying that if he were a delegate to the convention, he would vote for Henry Wallace for the vice-presidential nomination. So Wallace scored first—in the headlines.

The following day, the president's special railroad car, carrying him to the west coast from which he would fly to a meeting in the Pacific with General MacArthur, stopped in Chicago. Hannegan boarded the car as it sat in the fetid stockyards. He assured the president he would do everything possible to nominate Wallace. Then he began to unveil the true Hannegan scenario. Suppose, he said, the Wallace effort falls short; the president cannot be reached by telephone. What other choice or choices would he accept? Hannegan proposed Senator Harry Truman and Supreme Court Justice William O. Douglas. Roosevelt said, "Well, that's all right if you put Douglas's name first." The next day—the record is not clear on this—Hannegan told Roosevelt either that Douglas was out camping and could not be reached, or that he was not interested in running for vice-president. The president then agreed to Hannegan's proposal that Truman's name be listed first. He did so, I am convinced, because he expected to live out his fourth term and thus didn't care too much who his running mate would be. He also knew that his own strength, not that of the vice-presidential candidate, would win the election, so he cared only about

134

avoiding someone who might cost a lot of votes, such as Henry Wallace. He was also tired. That gave Hannegan the power he needed to put over his crony Truman. Hannegan's friend would be vice-president, and I am sure it occurred to the chairman that chances were excellent that he also would be president—with all that could mean for Bob Hannegan.

There was one chance to change the course of history, to change the name of the president who would follow FDR. Nominations for vice-president would be made on a Thursday, but on Wednesday evening Wallace supporters launched a boisterous demonstration in the convention hall. It grew and grew. As chairman of the Florida delegation and a Wallace backer still, I sensed an opportunity. I stood on my chair and observed the number of state standards visible in the Wallace parade. It appeared that most states were represented. This could mean only one thing—broad support for Wallace—because chairmen would not allow their delegates to parade for a candidate they objected to strongly. Emotions ran high. I was convinced that if a vote could be taken that evening, Wallace could be nominated.

Still standing on my chair, I waved my standard to attract the attention of the convention chairman. This was the signal for a delegation chairman to win recognition to speak; his microphone would be activated. I shouted at the top of my lungs and waved my standard violently, to no avail. Frustrated, I fought my way through the aisles to the steps leading to the platform. Guarding the steps was a labor leader and friend who readily admitted me. One step below the platform I was dumbfounded to hear the chairman, Senator Samuel B. Jackson of Indiana, say rapidly, "The motion is made that the convention adjourn, all opposed say no, the convention is adjourned." A roar of disapproval thundered from the floor, but the chairman left the platform and many delegates started to leave. Thus the fate of a nation is sometimes determined.

No one will ever know if Wallace could have been nominated that night. But the party powers sensed and feared the possibility, and they could not take that chance. The following day in the lobby of my hotel, Senator Jackson walked over to me and said, "Claude, I hated to do what I had to do last night, but I saw you coming up those steps and I knew if you made the motion the convention would nominate Henry Wallace. I had strict instructions from Hannegan not to let the convention nominate the vice-president last night. So I had to adjourn the convention in your face. I hope you understand." What I understood was that, for better or worse, history was turned topsy-turvy that night in Chicago.

Henry Wallace led in the early balloting, but all signs of the hoped-for stampede had evaporated. On the second ballot, Truman gained and became the obvious alternative. Thus favorite sons, one after another, stood up and threw their support to Truman. Thanks to Bob Hannegan, word had circulated around the convention that if Roosevelt could not have Wallace, he wanted Truman. There was no need for a third ballot. Truman was the nominee.

Until all hope was gone, I remained loyal to Henry Wallace. I nominated him and worked actively in his behalf. By some accounts, this was the beginning of "bad blood" between Harry Truman and me, but I don't accept that. I had been in Wallace's corner long before Truman's name was mentioned, and although Truman has been known both to bear a grudge and to "get even," this was not that kind of a situation. Politicians know that one's word, once given, must be kept, and Truman was a seasoned politician who knew how the game was played. Knowing, however, that I had backed Wallace against him once and figuring that I might do so again, Truman understandably did not take me into his confidence the way Roosevelt had. I was one of several senators invited to an event at LaMar, Missouri, honoring Truman's election as vice-president, and of course I attended. But we were not close in the sense that Roosevelt and I were.

Just before and during the campaign of 1944, my concern for the health of the president deepened. He was haggard, his face was lined, black circles appeared under his eyes. No longer did the White House allow photographers to use klieg lights when photographing him close up. He made a radio speech from Seattle that, I noted in my diary, was the worst I ever heard him deliver. Outraged and concerned, Tommy the Cork called to blame the poor performance on the fact that his top aides were not with the president. Harold Ickes said it was essential that Roosevelt make at least three or four good campaign appearances—people were talking, the voters were beginning to suspect that he was seriously ill.

But the president proved, again, to have remarkable recuperative powers. In late summer, he went before the Teamsters' convention and delivered one of the most effective political speeches ever, relating how the Scotch blood of his terrier, Fala, had boiled at accusations that a navy cruiser, at a cost of millions, had been sent to rescue Fala when the president left the pet in the Pacific on his way back from a meeting with MacArthur. FDR outlined what he intended to do during his fourth term and wonderfully repeated over and over again the phrase "and we will do it without the help of Martin, Barton, and Fish," three obstructionist Republican congressmen. Soon his audience was reciting the three names with him. The president was in top form. A highly successful businessman and friend of mine told me that he laughed so hard at the president's speech he actually lay down and rolled on the floor. Late in the campaign, Roosevelt appeared in rainy weather before three million people, riding in an open touring car through New York City, and the question of the president's health was resolved—at least for the election. Roosevelt won a fourth term. And Harry Truman became the third man to serve as FDR's vice-president.

In my diary for Tuesday, January 30, 1945: "The President's 63rd birthday. May he long live. He is one of the giants of history with the little and large points of the great." On February 6, 1945, I noted: "The President, Churchill and Stalin are meeting somewhere in the Black Sea area: (1) military victory and (2) the peace and its permanence." This was the historic Yalta summit, and when the terms of the agreements were disclosed a bit later, I wrote that "we in short agree at long last to take our full part in European and world affairs—isolation out the window if this agreement is backed up by Congress and the country." This deeply felt sentiment was at the heart of disagreements I would have when Truman took charge of American foreign policy.

My diary entry for March 21, 1945, had an ominous ring:

> To see the President for 10:45 A.M. appointment. Saw him 12:30. Shocked when I first saw how thin he was. He is nervous and talks in sort of far off or uncertain way. I told him, when Warm Springs was mentioned, no one would leave or had left in all the history a greater monument of accomplishment than he, and his information and knowledge [were] nearest to universal of anything living, I thought. I talked about my health study, veterans, Bill Pawley, Aubrey Williams, my desire to go overseas. He prefers visitors to go alone rather than in large groups overseas. I wonder what happened to him physically. Was it just the constant pressure? Or was [it] something [sudden]?

It must have crossed my mind that I would not see this great and good man again. I think that explains my effusive and awkward tribute to his legacy. In any event, I never again saw Franklin Delano Roosevelt alive.

The war in Europe was winding down. From my diary for April 11: "Germany cracking up rapidly. Little organized resistance in northern Germany." It was unthinkable that FDR would not be onstage when the final curtain fell. I received a letter from the president, who was at Warm Springs where, I fervently hoped, he would be restored to good health. The letter was in response to one I had written to him on the proper roles of the Senate and the Executive regarding foreign policy. It read:

April 9, 1945

Dear Claude:

Yours of April 5 has been sent to me down here where I am getting a ten-day vacation, more for catching up with mail than for a rest.

I like what you say, and it is perfectly clear that fundamentally you and I mean exactly the same thing. As a matter of fact while in questions of foreign policy the President ought to do the spadework of negotiations and the original nomination of all officers, a long experience leads me to recognize that the Senate ought to be consulted both on the policy and some of the nominations. Both you and I know that as a matter of practice too much consulting would slow up both matters.

What is needed is the removal of the political point of view on the part of some Presidents and many senators. There are altogether too many instances throughout our history, some of them even recent ones, [that are] completely unnecessary. I like to feel that we have really accomplished marvels in the matter of both our domestic and foreign policies in changing the point of view of a lot of people toward more liberal trends not only here but throughout the world.

On the consummation of a treaty, I hope that the next trend of public opinion will recognize that under our own theory, nations are co-equal and therefore any treaty must represent compromises. We cannot jump to what we consider perfection if the other fellow does not go the whole way. He might think that his point of view was just as good or better than ours.

I do hope to see you one of these days soon. I will certainly do so as soon as I get back from the opening day of the San Francisco parley [the chartering of the United Nations].

Always sincerely,
FDR

The United Nations organization was his, my, and the world's hope for future peace.

From my diary for Thursday, April 12, 1945:

Off on 5:30 train for Chicago. To speak in Gary tonight. At 7 P.M. on the train . . . received a message from the railroad people that President Roosevelt died today at Warm Springs. Mildred had called the station master at Cumberland, Maryland, and he told me the dinners were cancelled and for me to return. Received two telegrams there. What a tragedy for the nation and the world. . . . The President was sitting for a portrait sketch at 1 C.W.T. [Central War Time] for a Russian artist (lady), having finished his paperwork and being ready for a late lunch. Suddenly, he put his hand to the back of his head and said "I have a terrible headache." He almost at once lapsed into unconsciousness. Arthur Prettyman, his Negro naval valet, lifted him to his bed. He never regained consciousness and died at 3:35 C.W.T. (4:35 E.W.T.).

Steve Early gave [the news] out here and notified Mrs. Roosevelt who was called from the Sulgrave Club.

Early, in her sitting room, told her the President had "slept away." Early then called Vice-President Truman at the Capitol and told him to come to the White House as quickly and as quietly as possible. He (Truman) hurried to the White House, was ushered into Mrs. Roosevelt's sitting room, and she told him the President had passed away. He asked what he could do, and she replied it was a question of what she and the family could do to help him. Mrs. Roosevelt remained composed and said she was more sorry for the people of the nation and the world than for herself and the family. Mrs. Roosevelt, Early and Admiral McIntyre, the surgeon general and the President's physician, flew to Warm Springs that night, arriving a little after midnight.

Vice-President Truman summoned the Cabinet to the Cabinet room and (also) some Senators and Representatives; also Mrs. Truman and daughter Margaret. At 7:09, Chief Justice Stone administered the oath and Harry Truman became the 32nd President. Truman and family shortly went to their apartment (rental, $120 per month). He cut off telephone calls but called his 92-year-old mother in Missouri.

In a series of radio interviews, I said that the world had lost one of the greatest and best men who ever lived and I prayed "that God would keep and bless President Truman to carry on his great work."

Despite the deterioration so evident to anyone who saw his photographs at that time, Roosevelt's death stunned the world. So many times he had seemed on the verge of breakdown only to bounce back, tilt the cigarette holder, smile that golden smile, and somehow reassure his own and friendly nations that he was in charge and all was well. Ever since he had told "my fellow

141

Americans" that the only thing they had to fear was fear itself, his very presence at the head of government conveyed a sense of security to millions. Suddenly, with the great military victory he had worked so hard to achieve now at hand, he was gone. The void was enormous. If Truman seemed inadequate to fill it—and he did—well, no mere mortal can immediately supplant a legend.

Friday, April 13, 1945:

At 1:00 President Truman came down to Biffle's office and members of the Senate and leaders of the House went in to speak to him. He was grave but smiling often and just as informal as ever. They all told him they wanted to help and he said he needed it and sometimes in serious but matter-of-fact way said pray for him. He had a drink as he always did when he lunched there as Senator or Vice-President. Free discussion about the President (whom nearly all still called Harry) addressing a joint session on Monday and length and content of his speech. He intended 5 minutes. We talked him up to 15 or 20 minutes, I think. He said he would address the Armed Services Tuesday evening next at 10 at the request of the Joint Chiefs of Staff. At the luncheon, he asked the opinion of each of us there about his speech to the joint session and said he had come down to the hill first to show he wanted to cooperate with Congress. He went out and spoke to the newspapermen and shook hands with all the Senate attachés and pages. Later he went back by the Senate Office Building and greeted old staff and some people in the corridor.

We had a dinner (informal) at our apartment—the Hugo Blacks, Thurman Arnolds, Tom Corcorans, Ben Cohen, Lister Hills—and talked. Jimmy Byrnes on his own flew back from S.C. and got into contact with Truman at once. He and Truman are close and he will attach himself very closely to the new administration. In fact, he will soon be running it. I don't know yet what his aims are, but he is able to help greatly and he greatly loves power. I wish he were more liberal. He quit President Roosevelt recently and never forgave him for his not being made Vice-President.

The following day, Saturday, the train bearing Roosevelt's body arrived in Washington. Mildred, a friend, and I went aboard to speak to Mrs. Roosevelt. She was with her daughter Anna, her son Elliott, Bernard Baruch, and President Truman. She knew then something the rest of us did not—that Lucy Mercer, the president's longtime friend, was with him when he died and Eleanor Roosevelt was not. What a sad closing chapter to a failed marriage. On April 14:

We saw the [casket] of the President put out a special car window onto a caisson drawn by 6 large and perfectly-matched white horses. The family, members of the Cabinet, the Supreme Court and special friends of White House people rode behind the body. Preceding the body were various military, naval, marine or auxiliary units—up Delaware to Constitution, down Constitution to 15th Street, then to the White House. Funeral in East Room of the White House at 4 P.M. Anthony Eden present, something over 200 present. Simple Episcopal service. The body remained there until it was carried to the train just before 10 P.M. in a hearse preceded by tank destroyers. I was one of 17 senators appointed to go to Hyde Park.

As the train made its way north, I could not help thinking about Lincoln's funeral train. Thousands of people lined the tracks in an emotional outpouring for Roosevelt that matched the one historians have described for Lincoln.

The Roosevelt estate at Hyde Park, New York, was to be FDR's final resting place. He was buried near the lovely old home and the library in a beautiful garden enclosed by a towering hemlock hedge. Three volleys were fired by cadets from West Point, after each of which Fala, the Scotch terrier, howled mournfully. The last words of the president's longtime minister, as Roosevelt was lowered into his grave, were a refrain from an old hymn: "Father in Thy gracious keeping, leave we now Thy servant sleeping." (Before a joint session of Congress in 1983 commemorating the one-hundredth anniversary of Roosevelt's birth, I concluded my tribute with this sentence: "And so we take our leave of this great and good man in the words of his old minister spoken as the president was laid to rest at Hyde Park, 'Father in Thy gracious keeping, leave we now Thy servant sleeping.' ")

The service at Hyde Park was concluded by the playing of taps, after which the family filed out, followed by the new president and then those assembled. All but overcome with emotion, I wrote that night: "The greatest of our Presidents has returned to his fathers and His Father."

I shared the worldwide feeling of goodwill toward President Truman and the anxiety for him to succeed. So much depended on him. The Russian armies were in Berlin, and the world was just beginning to absorb the extent of the German atrocities against the Jews. Soon, Europe would have to be rebuilt. The Japanese would fight on to the end, I feared. Most important, a strong United Nations organization was needed to ensure that we did not, as we had done last time, lose the peace after winning the war. Truman had his hands full. It was not a time for petty political bickering.

On April 24, 1945, a dozen days after he had taken office, I called on President Truman. "First, I assured him of my desire to help him," I wrote. After a lengthy discussion of my proposal to establish an independent agency for medical research,* the president said, "You know, Claude, I was for Roosevelt before he became president and supported him in the Senate, but now I am responsible for the unity of the country, and I suspect most of the time you will find me about in the middle of the road." I told him I did not quarrel with his taking that position but I knew he would not expect me, a senator, to quit advocating those causes in which I believed. I noted that "he smiled, put his hand on my shoulder, and said, 'That's just what I want you to do and I'll be with you whenever I can.' " I was not comforted. Truman's determination to be "in the middle of the road" fortified misgivings I felt when he addressed the joint session of Congress, vowing to continue Roosevelt's foreign policy but saying practically nothing about his domestic program. The New Deal had been on hold throughout the war. There would be much to do after the war for the sick, the elderly, the handicapped, the uneducated, and the ill-housed, yet Truman was mute on the subject.

I was concerned but not yet alarmed because the daily headlines told where the emphasis properly had to be. On April 28, Mussolini, who had taken umbrage when I warned him that he would "get lost" if he entered the war, was trapped by Italian patriots at Como and, with his young mistress, was shot and hanged by the heels. The Fascist dictator died ingloriously, promising "an empire" to his executioner and crying "no, no" as the order to fire rang out. Hitler's death with his mistress, Eva Braun, soon followed in the Berlin bunker where his dreams of world conquest had turned into nightmares. In 1941, Hitler had looked through a telescope at the spires of the Kremlin; now the Soviet flag flew over Berlin. The only monuments there

* This became the National Institutes of Health.

would ever be to Hitler were millions of graves of his countrymen and others, cities and nations devastated, six million Jews tortured and killed. On May 8, what was left of the "thousand year" Third Reich surrendered unconditionally. Soon the pincers would close on the Japanese.

Only one month into his presidency, Harry Truman awakened the fears of liberals in the Democratic party. Cy Bevan, the national committeeman from Michigan, wrote to me, stressing that the Democrats could not carry his state without the support of liberals and minority groups, toward whom the administration had made absolutely no overtures. He emphasized that no matter how Truman felt about Henry Wallace, there was still a strong Wallace following in the country, and the president should make peace with the man who might have been president. Bevan's letter took on added significance when Jim Sheppard of Los Angeles, head of finances for the Democratic party in eight western states, dined with me in Washington. Sheppard said he wanted to begin immediately to organize a move that would land me the vice-presidential nomination in 1948. Clearly, Truman would not take Wallace on his ticket. Therefore, he would need another liberal to keep the party's left from defecting, probably to a Wallace-led third party. I, as a liberal Southerner, could be "put over," said Sheppard, who added that he could raise some money for staff to advance my cause. Well, there was a certain logic to what he said; Truman would need a running mate more liberal than he. But it was a long time to 1948. And despite what happened in 1944, presidential nominees usually have a free hand in choosing someone for the number two spot on the ticket.

How beleaguered liberalism was in those days is reflected by my work in the Senate. My preoccupation was with a bill to establish a Fair Employment Practices Commission. But Southerners did not want fair employment practices to apply to the Negro! And they were joined by many Northerners in not

146

wanting the provisions to apply to women! I failed to liberalize
the bill in committee and voted against it. But I made clear
that if an attempt were made to filibuster it to death on the
Senate floor, I would vote for cloture (mandating an end to the
filibuster) because some kind of an FEPC was better than no
FEPC at all.

In June, the House passed an anti-poll-tax bill. Imagine! As
late as 1945, hundreds of thousands of United States citizens
were denied their franchise if they could not afford to pay a
two-dollar tax—and many could not. I issued a public statement commending the House and calling on the Senate to pass
the bill speedily, pointing out that the measure went right to
the very root of democracy in our nation. The right to vote had
been bought by the sacrifice of patriots from the beginning of
this country and defended by succeeding generations. It had
no price tag on it until white Southerners hit upon the poll tax
as a way to keep Negroes away from the polls. There was irony
in my enthusiasm for the House action because for years I had
argued for the anti-poll-tax bill on the ground that a poll tax
was unconstitutional anyway.* My Florida colleague, Senator
Spessard Holland, a strong conservative, refused to support my
position but initiated a constitutional amendment to outlaw the
poll tax. The Supreme Court settled matters by ruling that the
poll tax was unconstitutional, as I had argued. In 1945, Senator
George Norris of Nebraska and I tried to get through the Senate a bill giving equal rights to women, but it was filibustered
to death.

An encounter that would lead to a major milestone in my
festering feud with Truman occurred in June 1945. General
Dwight D. Eisenhower came home from the war and addressed a joint session of Congress. From my diary:

*I received splendid support for my position from Virginia Durr, sister of
the first Mrs. Hugo Black and an Alabama congresswoman.

He spoke in a low, rather soft, quick conversational tone which was not heard generally by the galleries. He is about 5 ft. 11 in. tall and judged semi-bald, trim figure, broad open face, brown or tan hair, wide and easy smile, good voice. You instinctively like him and note his quick, decisive manner and mind. He is also a diplomat of great parts as his whole speech devoted to praising nearly everyone disclosed. That quality was one of his chief attributes. There was good applause but there was something lacking in the emotion of it, I thought. It did not seem he stirred the audience. He favorably impressed it and pleased it, but he did not lift it up. [But] it was his day and he deserved it.

Neither of us could know that events were under way that would place the two of us at the center of a political explosion, from which Ike would walk away unscathed but from which I would have extensive wounds that would take a very long time to heal.

The longer Truman was in office, the greater my misgivings about him. Liberals who had served honorably and well under FDR were finding themselves removed from cabinet and agency posts to make way for more conservative Truman appointees. Of course, I grant to any president the right to choose his own team. But when he does, he reveals himself with greater clarity than he does with his own rhetoric. Truman was not only placing himself in the middle of the road, but with some appointments a bit to the right of center. At dinner one night at the home of Frances Perkins, the secretary of labor, Attorney General Francis Biddle called me aside. Steve Early had telephoned that day, said Biddle, and told him the president wanted his resignation within twenty-four hours. Biddle told Early he wanted that message to come straight from the president if that really was his wish, but Truman had said at the White House he could not tell Biddle personally because of the good job he had done. Then why oust him? Truman wanted Tom Clark of Texas as attorney general, and that was curtains for Biddle, an able lawyer and a man of breadth and compassion, who later served with distinction as judge of the international court trying the Nazi war criminals at Nuremberg. Objections to Clark were not ideological—he was liberal enough—but he wasn't the sort to say no to the president, something a president needs in an attorney general.

In any event, the pattern was set. Marriner Eccles, who had guided the Federal Reserve Board during the depths of the Depression, was removed and most other cabinet members either resigned or were fired. Truman was flying his own flag, as he was entitled to, but those of us who wanted the Roosevelt legacy preserved and extended viewed these developments with increasing alarm. My diary entry for July 4: "The political crowd is now in the saddle and they are beginning to ride herd. It will jeopardize the fate of this administration. My opinion is the last liberal in the cabinet will soon be gone, [except for] Wallace.* I think when they go, Wallace should go. He is not one of this crowd. Neither am I." The following day I lunched with Wallace. We were told that Secretary of the Treasury Henry Morgenthau had resigned, that Ickes would go s n, and Wallace would be the only Roosevelt liberal remaining. I pointed out to Wallace that this would present him with a problem— he would be a sitting duck—and he agreed.

What to do? The breach between the president and me was widening. I had told him I would continue to pursue matters that concerned me, and he agreed that I should. What was needed was a liberal domestic agenda, which Truman obviously was not about to provide. Senator Harley Kilgore of

---

*Wallace had been appointed secretary of commerce by FDR.

West Virginia and I drew up a list of senators to invite to a luncheon where we would draw up a comprehensive, liberal legislative program. Seventeen of us met and reached general agreement on an agenda that focused on the needs of the people—affordable health care, better housing, loans for education, jobs, decent wages, and reasonable working hours. It was hardly a radical program, but word got around that we had met and Truman seemed to resent us as a rump group established to obstruct his agenda. We had no such intent, and he had no agenda anyway. Alben Barkley, the Senate majority leader, also was miffed that he had no part in the meeting. Well, there was a leadership vacuum that we attempted to fill. The president should have been grateful. He was all but completely absorbed by international concerns—winding down the war with Japan, winning congressional approval for the United Nations charter, learning how to deal with Stalin, and one other matter.

From my diary for Monday, August 6, 1945: "President Truman announces atomic bomb loosed on Japan equal in power to 20,000 tons of TNT or the load of 2,000 B-29s. The discovery and the product have great possibilities for peace." A day later: "Much interest in the atomic bomb everywhere. Everyone hopeful it will shorten the war." On August 8: "Learned on the golf course that Russia had declared war on Japan. This, with the atomic bomb, our vast superiority on the sea and in the air should end war soon, it would seem. Truman didn't say so, but understand that it was agreed at Yalta that Russia should enter the war. I know in reason President Roosevelt had an understanding to that effect with Stalin." On Monday, August 13, I visited the president at 12:45 P.M., briefing him on a trip to war-torn Europe I was about to undertake and presenting him with a copy of a fifteen-point program formulated by Kilgore and me. Then I left for New York. At 7 P.M., as noted in my diary, "the President gave out official statement that the Japs had accepted our terms and surrendered . . . peace at long last—can we realize it?—peace again in man's custody! But at such a price!"

Considering that when he became president he did not even know there was such a thing as an atomic bomb or a Manhattan Project to develop one, Harry Truman had been a fairly quick study.* Horrible as it was, the bomb probably shortened the war and perhaps saved millions of lives, but I could not overcome some misgivings about our using it. Had we done all we could to let the Japanese know what we had and what it could do? Was it necessary to drop a second bomb while the Japanese were still trying to comprehend the devastation wreaked by the first? Such thoughts would bother many people later on, but in August 1945 practically every mind was fastened on just one joyful fact: The war was over!

It was time for me to sail to Europe. Mildred and her sister Marie saw me off in New York on the *Queen Elizabeth*, making her first commercial voyage after service in the war. I left an America that was dancing in the streets to visit a Europe and a Great Britain that in many areas had been reduced to rubble. Now I like to celebrate as well as the next fellow, but my trip had been long planned and was of considerable importance. The American public takes a generally dim view of the so-called congressional junket. It holds that senators and congressmen love to visit exotic places, sun themselves at the beaches, dine at three-star restaurants, and, of course, bill the taxpayers. It does happen, and if the press gets wind of it there is adverse publicity aplenty. But most travel by members of the House

---

*The Soviets knew about the Manhattan Project, even though the vice-president of the United States did not. In 1985 in Ottawa I noted to the Soviet chairman of a delegation to the Inter-Parliamentary Union that when Truman, as president, told Stalin at Potsdam about a major explosion, Stalin said nothing. "Did he know?" I asked. The reply: "We knew about the Manhattan Project."

and Senate has a valid purpose. More often than not, the trips are arduous, educational, and essential to informed legislating. For example, when I heard Hitler speak at the Nuremberg Congress in 1938, I realized that he portended grave danger to freedom and liberty in the world. This experience led me to introduce the first lend-lease legislation in 1940 and to lead the fight for American aid to the Allies in the hope that we could help defeat Hitler without entering the war ourselves.

My postwar trip was no less serious in purpose and no less fruitful in terms of acquired perspective. I visited nineteen countries and interviewed dozens of world leaders, including Churchill, Stalin, Tito, de Gaulle, and Anthony Eden. I went because as a member of the Senate Foreign Relations Committee I would be required to vote on enormous outlays of taxpayers' dollars for rebuilding nations. I would also be called on to help form and guide U.S. foreign policy. To meet this responsibility, I wanted to see the needs firsthand and to meet the foreign leaders who would be using wisely, or wasting, money from the United States. Most important of all, I had believed since my law school days at Harvard that although we won World War I, we lost the peace, and the price for that was a cruel one—millions of lives, unbelievable devastation, billions of dollars. I was in a position to influence the course of my country. I wanted the knowledge that would enable me to cast wise votes and offer intelligent counsel.

My immersion in foreign affairs consumed the rest of 1945. I did not return until near year's end, ignoring entreaties from some of my strong labor supporters that domestic matters required my attention. My prolonged absence from the Senate at least halted the rift between the president and me, though *rift* may be too strong a word. Despite our differences on domestic policy, I gave no thought to opposing Truman's nomination in 1948. My feeling was not that Truman should be "dumped" but that he could be nudged toward more liberal policies by such initiatives as the one Senator Kilgore and I took, drafting a legislative agenda that would continue and expand the New Deal.

In 1946, President Truman proclaimed what came to be known as the Truman Doctrine. It was intended to prevent Greece and Turkey from being taken over by Soviet-directed Communist governments, an objective I fully supported. But I opposed the doctrine itself, opening the door to "soft on communism" charges from political opponents who knew better. They could not resist flailing me with a political bludgeon that I had handed to them. My opposition to the Truman Doctrine was rooted in my conviction that the United Nations had to succeed and that it could not if one of the major signatories undercut it. That is exactly what I feared the doctrine would do. It called for sending American troops to Greece and Turkey, and then for massive infusions of economic aid to restore the shattered economies of both nations. Both Greece and Turkey would be more pro-West and more pro-democracy as a result of the Truman Doctrine.

But wait! True, the United States had joined the United Nations, averting a repetition of our abandonment of the League of Nations after World War I. But how effective could the UN be if we, instead of working through it, went around it? We were repeating the history that helped undermine the League of Nations: Europe's leading countries bypassed the league to solve the continent's problems through the Lacano Pact, an agreement totally outside the League of Nations. Of course, Greece and Turkey needed help and obviously the United States would provide the lion's share even if we went through the UN. No other nation was on a firm financial footing. But why slap a fledgling organization in the face by going off on our own? We could at least try to make this a multi-nation UN venture. We were in a position to be magnanimous—no one else had "the bomb" and no other major power was unscarred by air raids and invasions.

I knew my position was politically risky, but the stakes were future peace. I was convinced that the Truman Doctrine would strangle the UN in its cradle, fuel United States–Soviet antagonisms, and leave the world without an effective instrument for settling disagreements among nations. Perhaps I was as naive as critics then and since have said I was. On the contrary, who can say for certain that the postwar world would not have had fewer wars, hot and cold, had the United Nations been given the full big-power support it never received? As debate over the Truman Doctrine raged, the secretary-general of the United Nations, Trygve Lie, met with Senator James M. Murray and me at the Carlton Hotel in Washington. He was alarmed over the impact that unilateral action by the United States would have on the UN. I recall clearly the startling comment he made as we departed: "One more action like this [the Truman Doctrine] and the United Nations will be dead."

In the Foreign Relations Committee and on the Senate floor I led the fight against the Truman Doctrine, not endearing myself to its chief advocate, the president of the United States. Over and over, I noted that treaties enacted outside the League of Nations had doomed that organization and probably made World War II inevitable. Were we prepared now to risk scuttling the United Nations, thereby increasing the likelihood of World War III? The UN, I conceded, might not turn out to be all its founders believed and hoped. But it deserved a chance.

When it became clear that the Truman Doctrine would win congressional approval, I pushed for an amendment providing that if the United Nations should adopt a resolution that our troops be recalled from Greece and Turkey, we would honor that resolution. That was an important concession, and the president and the Senate went along with it. It spared the United Nations a complete humiliation. But the Truman administration never seized the opportunity to make the UN the force for peace that it could have been. A bit later the Marshall Plan to rehabilitate Western Europe was unveiled, and again the United States was to act unilaterally. The Soviets were not asked to join.

In my meeting with Stalin in September 1945, the Soviet dictator told me that more than six months earlier he had asked the United States for a loan or a grant of $6 billion and that he had not even had the courtesy of a reply. On my return, I mentioned this incident on the Senate floor and asked the State Department for a status report. The department replied that it thought such a request had been received, but that it had been lost. No one, of course, believed that, least of all Stalin. Also, when the first meeting to set up the Marshall Plan was held in Paris, Soviet Foreign Minister V. M. Molotov showed up with a staff of one hundred. After a week, it was clear to him that the Soviet Union would not be a beneficiary of the plan, so he and his entourage departed. It is undeniable that of all the nations that warred against Hitler, the Soviet Union suffered the most. Even President Reagan has agreed, having described the destruction as being "as if everything in the United States east of Chicago was devastated." But the Soviets received no help under the Marshall Plan. A slogan in support of the plan— To stop communism in Europe—more accurately described its purpose than the official explanation—To help our allies recover from the blows inflicted by Hitler.

So the Marshall Plan and the Truman Doctrine both ignored the UN, with foreseeable damage to its reputation. Both programs were, of course, stunning successes, so my opposition in hindsight seems even more wrongheaded than it did to my critics at the time. I am aware, as I was in 1946, of Soviet intransigence, of its violations of the Yalta agreements, and of its brutal occupation of much of Eastern Europe. Truman faced formidable political problems from Republicans always anxious to shout "soft on communism" at any effort to ease U.S.-Soviet antagonisms and to bring about U.S.-Soviet collaboration. But with the continuation of civilization at risk, it is essential that a forceful leader ignore the babble and try something that just might work. History—and humankind—demand no less.

As the months and then the years slipped by, labor and liberal Democrats became increasingly disenchanted with Truman. He had seized the steel mills to end a strike that was perfectly legal, although costly and disruptive. Courts declared the seizure was beyond the president's powers. Although his popularity had soared early in his administration, topping even Roosevelt's, by the end of 1947 Harry Truman was in deep trouble politically. Republicans, frozen out of the White House since Herbert Hoover's glum departure in 1933, saw hope after taking it on the chin four times from Franklin Roosevelt. Truman's policies were more popular than he was, a situation antithetical to that of Ronald Reagan forty years later. Truman simply had not titillated the country as Roosevelt had. As election year 1948 arrived, I noted in my diary for January 1: "The New Year will be full of problems. I doubt whether the Democrats under all circumstances can win—especially if Eisenhower is the Republican nominee." It seemed certain that Henry Wallace, fired from his post as secretary of commerce at the bitter insistence of Byrnes, then secretary of state, would oppose Truman from the left, and Southern conservatives were already threatening to bolt if the party platform took a bold (for those days) stand on civil rights.

In Miami on January 3, a delegation of Democrats called on me to ask how they could get Wallace delegates' names on the ballot. They also wanted to know if they would have to change their registration in order to vote for Wallace if he ran as a third-party candidate. I hoped there would not be a third party, if only for selfish reasons. Should large numbers of voters drop their Democratic registration, how would that affect me if I ran as a Democrat for another Senate term in 1950? Could I get them to change back? A day later, I learned, as noted in my diary, that "the Southerners speak of another sort of secession on account of the President's 10-point civil rights program." On February 9, in typical fashion, Truman let them know how intimidated he was: "The President says he will stand firm on the civil rights issue." I admired Truman for his forthrightness.

On February 12, I took a delegation of Florida officials to the White House and the president gave us a foretaste of the feisty, fighting underdog campaign he would wage: He told us that the Congress was "not interested in the little man and the public, but in the big profiteers like the big oil companies." He said flatly that he was in favor of wage and price controls. I announced my support of Truman for the nomination, much to the consternation of the Wallace camp and of many of my own supporters. The latter wanted me to recant and then make a deal with the Truman people. It would go like this: Truman would choose me to run for vice-president. He would promise that the party platform would be "decent," meaning relatively liberal. In return, I would persuade Wallace to stay out of the race for president in 1948. The scenario had considerable support from organized labor and from several prominent liberal Democrats, many of whom had concluded, as I had, that despite his failings, Truman had the power of incumbency and probably would be nominated and we might as well get behind him. Otherwise, what none of us wanted might happen: a Republican would win the election and roll back all the social progress achieved in sixteen years of Democratic rule.

There nonetheless was plenty to worry about. Truman's approval rating continued to plummet. And in a special congressional election in February in New York, a Wallace-supported candidate won, to almost universal astonishment. Some Democrats hoped Truman would see the handwriting on the wall and decide not to seek a full four-year term. The president responded to this sentiment, again in Trumanesque fashion.

157

On March 8, he made it official. He would seek the Democratic party's nomination for president of the United States. "Most comments of Democrats very cautious," I wrote.

From my March 23 entry: "The political opposition to Pres. Truman daily grows, yet Sen. Hatch quotes the Pres. as determined to fight out the matter whatever the results." That same day, the Senate passed the Greece-Turkey aid bill, which I argued against, warning that "we are on our way to war" through a policy of unilateral actions bypassing the United Nations. The "war" I foresaw and warned of began soon enough; fortunately it was a cold war. I publicly suggested a meeting between Stalin and Truman to reduce tensions that could very quickly heat up that cold war. No such meeting took place.

On April 2, the Senate voted 77 to 10 to override a Truman veto of a tax bill. I was one of the seventy-seven. The House overrode the veto by an equally lopsided margin. Rarely had a Congress been so willing to rebuke and humiliate a president. It was perfectly safe politically to do so. "The sooner the President goes, the better," I wrote. Two days later my entry was: "More support for Eisenhower for Pres." A Kansas Democrat who would be a delegate to the convention announced that he wanted to support a ticket of Eisenhower and Pepper. Truman, he said, was "out." In May, I lunched with Chester Bowles, a prominent liberal Democrat who thought Truman's foreign policy was misdirected and was preventing progress toward genuine peace. Bowles said the president must be "displaced." The yearning for a Democratic ticket headed by Eisenhower had become common place in the public prints, and the general's silence—he would not say whether he was a Democrat or a Republican or neither—encouraged the "anybody but Truman" factions.

Truman seemed to be floundering. He seized the nation's railroads to head off a strike, solidifying labor opposition. He also made a monstrous proposal: that all striking railroad workers be drafted into the armed forces where they would be subjected to "unlimited punishment" for their refusal to work. Incredibly, this notion, better suited to a dictatorship than a democracy, cleared a Senate committee. When it was taken before the full Senate, Senator Robert Taft and I, who had little in common ideologically, hit the floor at the same time. Taft* was a conservative Republican from Ohio, but it was difficult to tell which of us was more outraged by this draconian proposal from Truman. We aroused enough concern to delay action. After the session, I assembled most of the labor leaders in my apartment to organize a drive against the bill. We were able to block consideration of the measure until the Senate came to its senses and dropped it from the legislative calendar. At a glum dinner in mid-May with the Hugo Blacks, Lister Hills, and Tom Corcorans, not a word favorable to Truman was heard. And the Democratic National Convention was but a few weeks away.

Strangely, in light of what we now know about Eisenhower, the Republicans were not wooing this war hero with anything like the intensity of a growing number of Democrats.** Thomas E. Dewey, the governor of New York who had lost to Roosevelt in 1944, and Harold Stassen, the governor of Minnesota, were battling in Republican primaries. The thought of Dewey as president was abhorrent to me. Of all the politicians I have known, Dewey was the most like Richard Nixon, with the large exception that he probably was not a criminal. But he was as manipulative, as hypocritical, as "tricky," if you will. Stassen, difficult as it is to believe after his foolish ten or more campaigns for the presidency, was a fresh face in 1948, but after I heard him in a debate with Dewey, I wrote: "Stassen is a phony

---

*Although Taft and I were at opposite poles on most issues, we had a good relationship. When William White was writing a biography, *The Taft Story,* Taft told the author he could call him off the Senate floor anytime "except when Claude Pepper is speaking."

**Years later it became known that at the Potsdam Conference, Truman told Eisenhower that if Ike would run as a Democrat, he would step aside.

and I believe not too intellectual." Another entry after Dewey defeated Stassen in the Oregon primary shows how unprescient I was about Stassen's durability: "Dewey wins over Stassen in Oregon. Good riddance to Stassen."

On June 1, a group of Southern senators huddled, weighing a move to draft Eisenhower for the Democratic nomination. Four days later, I was approached by a politico who claimed to be familiar with Eisenhower's thinking. He told me Eisenhower would run and suggested that "a committee go and see him—not over two." The public phase of the preconvention maneuvering was all going Eisenhower's way, but behind the scenes, the Truman people were buttonholing delegates, telling them they wanted early pledges of support, assuring them that the president would "remember" those who committed to him now. At this stage, Truman had no opposition in lining up delegates who, after all, would choose the nominee. Eisenhower could hardly compete for delegates without offering at least private assurances that he would run. And this he was unwilling to do. (Any "private" assurances he might have made would not have remained private for very long.)

In the Gallup poll, Truman's approval rating fell to 26 percent.* It appeared suicidal for the Democrats to nominate him. A number of prominent Democrats came to that conclusion, among them Eleanor and James Roosevelt; Mayor William O'Dwyer of New York; Jake Arvey, the powerful national committeeman from Illinois; numerous members of Congress; and many political pundits and publishers. Their concern, which I fully shared, was that Thomas E. Dewey would be elected president and, with his big-money supporters cheering him on, would begin the dismantling of the New Deal whose continuance meant so much to the so-called little men and women of

---

*About the same rate of approval given to Richard Nixon in 1974, when the House Judiciary Committee was voting articles of impeachment against him.

the country. The Republicans were blaring the slogan "It's time for a change," and with the uninspiring Truman as the alternative, more and more voters seemed to agree.

But why Eisenhower? First and foremost, he could win. For months, prominent Democrats had been urging him to run and he had not said one word to discourage them. Maybe our hopes were father to the thought, but we believed that if Eisenhower could not embrace the Democratic philosophy he would have found a way to let us know. He never did. The small, usually two-person delegations we sent to sound him out all returned with the identical message. It was: "Fellows, he will not raise a finger to get the nomination, but he will accept it if we give it to him." One of the emissaries was Olin Johnston, the senator from South Carolina. Senators Lister Hill and John Sparkman of Alabama were part of the pro-Eisenhower group that I also joined, hoping to prevent a Dewey presidency and in the process to salvage a domestic social program tilted toward the have-nots for one of the few times in our history. So universally admired was Eisenhower that both Southern conservatives resisting Truman's civil rights program and party liberals who wanted to strengthen it turned to the war hero as their savior. In truth, neither faction knew where Eisenhower stood on anything. But he projected integrity, humanity, and a spirit of fairness. With that as a base, we could work out the details later. Now that the aura of the postwar Eisenhower has faded, now that there is a record of his eight years as a Republican president, it must be difficult for anyone not there at the time to comprehend why we desperate Democrats turned to him. The word *desperate* probably answers the question.

The next move was mine. With Eisenhower still leaving our emissaries convinced that he would accept the nomination if we handed it to him, I went to the Philadelphia convention site a couple of days early. I "controlled" half of the sixteen-member Florida delegation because I had persuaded those delegates to commit to Eisenhower. Two days before the conven-

161

tion opened, reporters asked me who was going to be nominated. I said I didn't know who would be nominated, but that I knew two men whose names would be placed in nomination. Who? they asked, and I replied, President Truman and General Eisenhower. Who, they wanted to know, would nominate Eisenhower? He would be nominated by members of the Florida delegation if by nobody else, I said. The word spread like wildfire. Headlines the next day electrified the delegates and I dare say much of the nation by the prospect of a Truman-Eisenhower battle for the nomination. Most of the speculation was that the general, despite Truman's hold on the party apparatus, would win.

The ink was hardly dry when, on the morning of July 9, my Washington staff reached me in Philadelphia. A telegram had just been delivered to the office, and it was from General Eisenhower. In the strongest terms, he said he would not accept the nomination under any circumstances. Eisenhower insisted he was reiterating previous public disclaimers. But that simply was not true. Until that telegram reached my office, Dwight Eisenhower had never said or even indicated that he would reject a draft. He could have said, as General Sherman did, that if nominated he would not run and if elected he would not serve. But he said nothing, and his silence was taken as assent by many sincere and well-intentioned people, myself included. The telegram read:

SENATOR CLAUDE PEPPER:

THIS IS PERSONAL FOR YOU. THE PUBLIC PRESS REPORTS THAT YOU MAY BE CONSIDERING, IN SPITE OF MY RECENT STATEMENT, THE PRESENTATION OF MY NAME TO THE DEMOCRATIC NATIONAL CONVENTION FOR NOMINATION TO THE OFFICE OF THE PRESIDENCY. IF THESE REPORTS ARE CORRECT, I RESPECTFULLY AND EARNESTLY REQUEST AND URGE THAT YOU

DROP SUCH INTENTION BECAUSE I ASSURE YOU THAT TO CARRY IT OUT WOULD RESULT IN ACUTE EMBARRASSMENT TO ALL CONCERNED AS WELL AS CONFUSION IN THE MINDS OF MANY OF OUR CITIZENS. MY DECISION, WHICH HAS TWICE BEEN MADE PUBLIC, IS BASED UPON MY SINCERE CONVICTION AS TO THE BEST INTERESTS OF OUR COUNTRY. UNDER NO CONDITION WILL I BE IN THE POSITION OF REPUDIATING OR EVEN SEEMING TO SWERVE FROM THE LETTER OR SPIRIT OF MY PRIOR ANNOUNCEMENTS. I WILL NOT VIOLATE MY OWN CONCEPTION OF MY APPROPRIATE SPHERE OF DUTY. NO MATTER UNDER WHAT TERMS, CONDITIONS, OR PREMISES A PROPOSAL MIGHT BE COUCHED I WOULD REFUSE TO ACCEPT THE NOMINATION. I KEENLY REALIZE THAT YOUR REPORTED STATEMENTS NOT ONLY DO ME HIGH PERSONAL HONOR BUT IMPLY THE GREATEST POSSIBLE CONFIDENCE IN ME. I VENTURE TO INVOKE THE AID OF THAT CONFIDENCE IN ASKING YOU TO ACCEPT MY REFUSAL AS FINAL AND COMPLETE, WHICH IT EMPHATICALLY IS.

DWIGHT D. EISENHOWER

Not many are aware of how un-Ike-like the general's performance that week had been. After absorbing the full impact of the telegram, I conferred with my closest aide, Jim Clements, and with Lister Hill. I decided to call Jake Arvey, a party boss and the pro-Eisenhower national committeeman from Illinois. Arvey said he and Mayor O'Dwyer knew the gist of the telegram I had received from Eisenhower. Arvey told me a strange tale. Three days before Ike sent the telegram, I had given an interview urging a nonpartisan draft of Eisenhower. The following day, Wednesday, July 7, the interview was published, and Arvey and O'Dwyer read it and then called on the general.

He was "buoyed up" about running, Arvey told me; he gave the pair "great encouragement." Arvey and O'Dwyer went home very hopeful and told many people that they were pretty well convinced that Eisenhower would run. But the following day, Thursday, Eisenhower telephoned both men to say he had acted "on impulse" the day before and that he was in no position to run or to accept the nomination. This was indeed strange behavior for a commander who had led great armies to great victories. There is no record that he ever did that "on impulse." It defied my understanding that he could be impulsive on such an important matter as seeking election to the highest office in the land.

Judging from the sequence of events and the way they played out, I have to assume that Ike decided to run and that cooler heads—perhaps General Marshall's—prevailed. For a general to try to depose his wartime commander in chief would certainly have rubbed Marshall the wrong way, but this is sheer speculation on my part. Something, however, must have kept Eisenhower coy for several months, exhilarated for one day, and entirely out of the race twenty-four hours after that. I assume, too, that Ike recalled Truman's offer at the time of the Potsdam Conference to step aside for him—that having refused such a proposal it was ungallant at best then to go head-to-head against his former commander in chief. Eisenhower may also have realized he would be more comfortable as a Republican, although he had never voted, and that he could probably win nomination as a Republican sometime in the future. On that he was, of course, correct.

In any event, Eisenhower was out of the picture. Now what? From my diary:

> Arvey . . . said he and the mayor [O'Dwyer] thought we must get behind Truman. Said he knew Truman would lose since he was running behind local tickets [in the polls] but it would be a Truman defeat, not a

party defeat. I urged we get behind a real liberal who
could revive party, but he felt Truman only hope now
and read Jim [Clements] a paraphrased statement by
him and O'Dwyer. I urged they withhold statement
to give us time to confer on presidential candidate or
vice-president candidate or platform.

But O'Dwyer refused. Next I called Eisenhower, but he was
out and his office would not take the responsibility of giving
me permission to release his telegram. After conferring with a
lawyer, I released it anyway, and the story, of course, dominated the headlines.

The Truman opposition, I noted, was "discouraged." But I
was not quite ready to give up. "Now see we must go ahead
behind some liberal and better candidate," I wrote. Some support was building for Supreme Court Justice William O. Douglas, a brilliant man and a liberal who had served as chairman of
the Securities and Exchange Commission, compiling a fine record. "Several spoke to me about presenting my name," I also
wrote. On the following day, Saturday, a number of Democratic congressmen and a couple of liberal columnists came to
our room for breakfast. After a long discussion, Representative
William Ritchie of Nebraska agreed to lead a movement in my
behalf as the liberal candidate for president.

No sooner had this group left than another one arrived, headed
by prominent labor leaders, including Jack Kroll, head of the
AFL Political Action Committee; Dave McDonald, president
of the United Steel Workers; and many others. Other state party
leaders came, and someone telephoned Jimmy Roosevelt to tell
him a number of liberal Democrats were rallying behind me.
He said he was pleased and would help. Leon Henderson, the
former head of the Office of Price Administration, appeared
and said that I would be president today "if things had gone
as they should have in Chicago [when Truman was picked to
run with Roosevelt]." Jimmy Roosevelt, then a congressman

PEPPER

from California, said he could get me some delegates from that
state if I could demonstrate some real Southern support. Given
my position on civil rights, that would not be easy, but I went
to work on it. So many people were coming to my rooms that
I had to switch hotels to make room for them, people from
New Hampshire to California, Montana to Florida. Douglas had
yet to make his intentions clear. There was some debate as to
which of us would make the better candidate. It became later
and later and finally the Douglas camp sent word that he would
announce his decision by eleven o'clock the following morning. Finally, a large number of labor delegates and liberals filled
a large room to overflowing and agreed that I should be the
candidate to oppose President Truman.

For a day and a half, a constant stream of people poured into
my rooms. Then the numbers began to dwindle. My supporters—the people who did not want Harry Truman—slowly began to realize they were going to get him anyway. As Truman
himself said later, no one could defeat a sitting president who
wanted to be renominated. Some examples: President Hoover
was thoroughly discredited in 1932, but the Republican party
renominated him. In 1912, President Taft was very unpopular,
but the Republicans felt they had to renominate him, even
though they knew that with former President Theodore Roosevelt running as a Progressive, Taft had no chance to win.*
As I relive my own experience in 1948 through scribblings in
my diary, it all sounds exciting and important, and of course it
was. But it was destined to come to naught. I did not have the
power of incumbency. Nor could I do in hours what Truman
had been doing for months—tie up delegates. Although friends
insisted that my name go before the convention, and although
I was convinced I had more delegates than anyone but Tru-

*In 1976, Republicans probably preferred Ronald Reagan, but incumbent
Gerald Ford was nominated. In 1968, with the proliferation of primaries,
Lyndon Johnson could have been denied renomination, which is probably
why he did not run.

man, I withdrew before the balloting began. Truman won about 1,000 of some 1,100 delegate votes, chose Alben Barkley as his running mate, and set out to do what hardly anyone thought he could do—win the election.

After the nominations, I was the third person to speak to President Truman on the platform and I assured him of my support. I campaigned all across the country for him, and if this seems hypocritical or opportunistic or both, it's the way politics is and ought to be: fight to the end, but when the votes have been counted, unite behind the winner. I had no trouble backing Truman against Dewey and against the splinter parties led by Strom Thurmond on the right and Henry Wallace on the left.

Through the years, there have been reports that I backed Eisenhower for the nomination knowing he would refuse, at which point I could step in and seek the nomination for myself. Not true. I never had such a notion. I tried to "dump Truman" because I thought he would go down, taking with him all the programs and the causes I believed in and wanted to see preserved. My own brief flirtation with the presidency was impractical, but not entirely fanciful. Until my defeat in the Senate campaign of 1950, there were people who thought, and in some cases feared, that I could become president, as attested by House Speaker Tip O'Neill. In a conversation with Joseph P. Kennedy after my losing race, O'Neill asked, "Why did you oppose Claude Pepper?* You helped him earlier and I thought you and he were friends." Kennedy replied, "I did help him earlier and we were friends, but I thought Claude Pepper had a chance to be the Democratic nominee for president and I thought he was too liberal. The best way to keep him from being nominated for president was to defeat him for reelection to the Senate." I regret—but cannot fault—his logic.

*Kennedy contributed $125,000 or $150,000 to my opponent; he contributed a similar amount that year to Richard Nixon's Senate race.

And what about the "king" whom I had struck and failed to kill? It is a fact that two years after being considered for president, I was out of public life entirely. The person who defeated me in the Florida Democratic primary of 1950 was George Smathers, who told *Time* magazine in 1983 that he ran against me, his political patron, because Truman told him he wanted "someone to beat that son of a bitch, Claude Pepper." It seems odd that Smathers would wait thirty-three years to tell this story. To my face, Truman always insisted that he did not hold my support of Eisenhower in 1948 against me, and he even raised a little money for me in 1950. That year I also spoke with President Truman at a reception in Washington. We shook hands and he said, "Claude, I want you to come down to see me next week and tell me how I can help you in your campaign." The following week I wrote down some of the things Roosevelt had done for me and told the president I would be pleased if he could do the same. He read the list and said, "I'll see what I can do to help." Then he added, "You know, you have an advantage over me. Roosevelt never raised his finger to help me. Now in addition to your own strength you have me here to help you."

None of Truman's intimates still living in 1983 had ever heard the story Smathers told, and Margaret Truman in her biography of her father, *Harry S Truman* (William Morrow and Company, New York, 1975), makes numerous unflattering references to me, but nothing that would support the Smathers version. On several occasions, President Truman went out of his way to express regret over my defeat.* So either the Smathers story is untrue, or Truman was totally unprincipled and hypocritical. I find it impossible to think of him that way.

---

*The Washington press corps in fact interpreted my defeat as a setback for Truman because I conducted a pro-Roosevelt–Truman campaign. Smathers's campaign was primarily anti-Pepper, secondarily anti-Truman.

6

Rubbing Significant Elbows

*We should not pretend to understand the world
only by the intellect; we apprehend it just as
much by feeling.*
—CARL GUSTAV JUNG

As 1950, the last year of my second full term in the Senate,
drew near, it was obvious that a lavishly financed, all-out effort
to defeat me for reelection was cresting in Florida. Ed Ball had
begun marshaling campaign dollars and strategy almost from
the moment I had been narrowly renominated in 1944. But
Ball and big business had thrown everything in their arsenal at
me before and still come up short. Now, however, they had an
ally—McCarthyism. To say that I underestimated this insidi-
ous force does not begin to state the case. Nothing in my private or public life had prepared me to understand this malady.
Despite sixteen years in the sometimes sordid world of politics,
I could not comprehend the depths to which human beings
would sink in order to destroy individuals who did not share
their point of view. I was naive. There is no other word for it.

Turning back now to 1945 and 1946, I can readily see that I fed the McCarthyite beast some of the raw meat on which it thrives. In the latter year, I attended a Henry Wallace rally at Madison Square Garden in New York City. I went at the request of the Democratic National Committee, but who knew that? With many other figures from the worlds of politics and entertainment, I sat on the stage and was included in a number of photographs. In one, reprinted time and again during the campaign of 1950, I appeared next to Paul Robeson, the controversial and deservedly famous singer who was not only black but who would later admit that he was a member of the Communist party. The guilt-by-association cult in Florida had its smoking gun.

More difficult for that group to justify (as if McCarthyites ever felt it necessary to justify anything) was the exploitation of my postwar trip to Europe in 1945, one of the most serious, demanding, and satisfying undertakings of my career. My political enemies considered the event to be a Communist brainwashing administered to me by the evil dictator and foremost Communist of them all, Joseph Stalin. Forgotten as the campaign year approached was the fact that for four grueling months I traveled to nineteen countries and visited with a dozen heads of state in addition to Stalin. The trip was preparation of the most rigorous sort for the responsibility I expected to shoulder if reelected in 1950—the chairmanship of the Senate Foreign Relations Committee. And even if that never happened, as indeed it did not, I still had four more years to serve as a member of that committee. I felt an obligation to equip myself so that I might vote intelligently on matters of transcendent importance to shaping the kind of world we would live in after history's most devastating war. International understanding was the need. I felt I could advance this understanding by shaking the hands, looking into the eyes, and hearing the aspirations of foreign leaders. I embarked from New York aglow with hope for world peace, not suspecting I was handing Ed Ball a political weapon with which to bludgeon me down the road.

Landing in London, I first visited Parliament, by chance encountering the great wartime leader Winston Churchill in a corridor. We had met briefly before in Washington. I extended my hand and Churchill, who had been put out to pasture by the British electorate, shook it indulgently. For a Southerner weaned on friendship and hospitality, this would not do. So I told Churchill that if he could run for office in America, he would carry Florida anytime. He managed a smile. But he struck me as the typical Tory, without the wholesome warmth of other British politicians I had met. Labor had won the most recent election, so Churchill was out, looking in, and obviously not pleased. I moved on to an appointment with the new foreign secretary, Ernest Bevan, a solid, strong, and earnest man who had come up the hard way. Bevan was much pleasanter than Churchill, candidly admitting that the Labor party victory had surprised him. He said Churchill had helped bring himself down with his bitter denunciations of the Labor party, campaigning in much the same way he had in 1906, and the voters were offended. Churchill was still a British imperialist—in the House of Commons he demanded of the government whether it intended to keep Hong Kong and whether it would keep or "give away" the British colonies, as if these were the matters of greatest moment. I was more impressed by the lesser known— and much less remembered—Clement Attlee, the Labor party leader who had succeeded Churchill as prime minister. Attlee clearly had a social conscience and I noted of him in my diary: "Will do well."

I visited with Anthony Eden, the former foreign secretary (and future prime minister), at his lovely home sixty miles south of London and met with other officials at the Foreign Affairs Office as well as with Sir Stafford Cripps, president of the British Board of Trade. Afterward I was informed that if I could extend my London stay, I would receive an audience with Churchill, so of course I did, our chance encounter having been completely unsatisfying.

Our meeting was set for 5:30 P.M. the following day. He was ten minutes late and full of apologies. We sat in the small living room of a flat owned by his daughter and son-in-law where he and Mrs. Churchill were staying, No. 10 Downing Street no longer being available to them. He wore a gray suit with a light stripe and a black bow tie. I confided these impressions to my diary:

> He is remarkably youthful, face round, eyes blue, hair thin but rather red. He is not as stout as I thought he was. Began by complimenting my article on Lend-Lease (which appeared in a London newspaper) and launched into a talk on Lend-Lease. Said Stalin had advisers and no doubt others in this country whom he had to consider. Said he (Stalin) was most pleasant and human man [who liked] humor; that once at Tehran when he (Churchill) toasted "the great Proletariat"—Stalin toasted "the Carlton Club"* . . . it was clearly understood Stalin would come in the Japan war when the German war was over; that he had stated in the House that Stalin promised him he would come in within 3 months after German war ended and he did exactly 3 months later; that the Russians always like to do a little better than they say.
>
> He had noticed that President Roosevelt had sort of a far away look at Yalta and mentioned it as having a religious aspect, but he was in full possession of his faculties. Made no statement respecting his attitude towards President Roosevelt but spoke warmly of his

*An exclusive London social club.

constant good humor and joking at Newfoundland and in the earlier days; said at Yalta it all seemed to be pressing on him. Remarking about Russian toasts, said he was quite able to keep up and smilingly said he was somewhat practiced in such a matter. I told him I understood that was one of his many virtues, which he laughingly repeated. He offered me a whiskey and soda which I took when I sat down. He asked me to serve myself, which I did, and he fixed one for himself. He asked whether I thought his defeat was a good thing or a bad thing for him, saying some thought it was a good thing. I told him many agreed that the Labor government could do much more in requiring sacrifice of the people than his government.

Then I suggested he not follow so actively the House of Commons matters but write because for the next few months or years forces which were inevitable would be operating. Moreover, I said, there might be a time when the world desperately needed a strong voice again. He said at once: "I shall never hold office again." And he said he was not going to write now. He speaks rather rapidly and his sentences and words come easily but he stammers in the most intriguing way. His son, Randolph, came in—handsome, pleasant. Then, Mrs. Churchill, quite gray but her hair neatly done and very gracious. It was time for them to go to the theater and he had to change his clothes. I had been with him 45 minutes.

P.S. Churchill had great praise for Marshall and Eisenhower.

Next stop—Paris. I found it rather shabby and the people depressed. French politics was in turmoil. Leon Blum, the head of the Socialist party, told me he would never join up with the

Communists because they take direction from Moscow. Blum, then seventy-three "but alert of body and most alert in mind and spirit," I noted, said that all the principal French political parties are liberal.* At the American embassy, officials were convinced that the United States would have to help the Western European nations to keep them from lapsing into communism and that France would be the bulwark of a revitalized Europe.

From Paris I traveled to Germany. The devastation I saw in Hamburg and Frankfurt was shocking. The same was true of Cologne. A vast section of Hamburg was called "the dead city" because not a single house had been left standing and nearly a half million people were living in cellars.

Frankfurt—another casualty of Hitler's madness—was headquarters for General Eisenhower, with whom I visited for an hour. I found him "a most engaging man, very able, quick, direct and democratic. He is a rare man, our best interpretation of American democracy. I told him that Churchill had said he was the most selfless man he had ever known, and he made no comment. He talked favorably about the Russians and our improving relations with them." Ike seemed to think that one of the problems with the Russians was their lack of experience in dealing with Western democracies, and their lack of self-confidence. When I suggested that he do everything possible to send unneeded doctors back to the States, he started issuing such an order in my presence. I was most impressed with Eisenhower and his chief of staff, General Beadle Smith.

At lunch with General Smith, I prodded him to tell me something about the true relationship between Eisenhower and General Douglas MacArthur, about which there were many rumors. Smith grinned. Then he thought of an anecdote which

---

*In 1950, my visit with the Socialist Blum, like my interview with Stalin, would be recalled by my political foes.

he said "sums it up." When MacArthur was serving as commander in the Philippines, he was honored one night at a banquet. One of the speakers, a Filipino, lauded MacArthur and expressed hope that his tenure in the Philippines would be a long one. But then he added that if MacArthur should be transferred to another post, the military and the people of the Philippines would be pleased to work with MacArthur's "able assistant," Dwight Eisenhower. MacArthur listened glumly as the speaker continued with more praise for Eisenhower, "and two weeks later," Beadle Smith laughed, "MacArthur ordered Eisenhower back to the States."

After this delightful interlude, I resumed the mission that had brought me to Germany—discovering what the German people would need. From Frankfurt I went to Berlin, but everywhere the answer was the same: food. I drove through the ruined capital of the Third Reich, "mile after mile," I wrote, "of wreckage and ruin. In the old Berlin area in the heart of the city, not a building not destroyed, the Tiergarten looking like a cyclone had gone through it. Palaces, everything broken into ruins. The Brandenburg gates were still standing," as was the Victory Column commemorating the German victory in the Franco-Prussian War, "but atop it is a French flag." I spent hours in the Reichschancellery—Hitler's home and executive offices—and even entered the air raid shelters below Hitler's apartment. My sense of the horrors committed by and in the name of this Fascist sharpened as I inspected the premises where he had lived and worked his evil. My solemn conviction was that Germany's capacity to make war must be destroyed.

From Berlin, I flew to Moscow aboard a crowded Russian plane. Passengers, myself included, sat in bucket seats, and there were no seat belts. The pilots flew at treetop level. It was an experience I would not willingly repeat, but we made it, and the American taxpayers were among the beneficiaries (the Soviet government allowed us to fly free of charge). Ambassador Averell Harriman greeted us with a buffet supper at the United States embassy, a large and comfortable residence where I stayed. After supper, I met with Anastas I. Mikoyan, who was in charge of trade and commerce, and we discussed possibilities for increased trade between our two countries. Because everything said had to be translated, it was slow and heavy going, and no conclusions were reached.

My attitude at that time, reflected in my diary, was that though living in peaceful collaboration with the Soviets might be difficult, it was something we had to work at, and work at hard. The alternative was unthinkable. A small delegation from the U.S. House of Representatives was with me in Moscow, and I sternly rebuked a staff member for his preformed anti-Soviet conclusions, an attitude that reflected, I feared, the views of some of the House members. Not knowing much of Russian history—invasions and wars down through the centuries—they were intolerant of the suspicious, almost paranoid attitude they encountered in Moscow. Allowances had to be made. But they were not, on this small stage nor on the larger one that determined the course of history.

On the evening of Friday, September 14, 1945, I was admitted to the Kremlin for an audience with Stalin, the "man of steel" who had survived purges, imprisonment, and even the disfavor of Lenin to rise to power in the largest and most feared Communist country in the world. Once in absolute command, Stalin had conducted purges of his own, killing and imprisoning hundreds of thousands of his enemies as he brutally consolidated his power. Could America deal with such a monster? There was only one answer: It had to.

So it was that Claude Pepper of Tallahassee, Florida, formerly of Camp Hill, Alabama, came face-to-face with the Georgian who, with a former haberdasher from Missouri, held the fate of the world in his hands. It was an experience I would not have foregone even if I had suspected the twisted use Ed

Ball and friends would make of it when I sought reelection to the Senate.

I was ushered into a large office, which was not Stalin's working office. I had been informed that no one was allowed to learn where he lived. A Russian interpreter sat at the end of a large table, with Stalin to his right and Andrei Vyshinsky, then deputy foreign minister, to Stalin's right. I sat immediately opposite Stalin, with George Kennan, the acting ambassador,* to my left.

I studied the Soviet dictator carefully. He was about five feet seven inches tall, slightly stout, his dark hair streaked with gray and combed back in a pompadour. His mustache sat heavily on a strong, square face. He wore a dark gray tunic that came up to his chin, with sleeves that were too long for his arms. A red stripe ran up his trouser leg and over the tunic he wore a plain, old army jacket. His complexion was gray, the face expressionless except when he smiled. Then he looked like a little Santa Claus.

After expressing appreciation for the audience, I told Stalin that I had been a friend of President Roosevelt. He did not respond. Then I stressed that I had not come in an official capacity and that I did not represent my government. I said, "I am forty-five years old and a member of the Foreign Relations Committee of the Senate of the United States, which has a very large role in the formulation of our foreign policy." When my remark about my age was translated, the Soviet dictator, who was then sixty-six years old, remarked, "I envy you."

Asked what his nation's objectives would be in domestic and foreign policy in the next few years, Stalin replied at considerable length. Over and over again, he stressed that the Soviet Union had suffered incalculable damages in World War II, that

---

*Ambassador Harriman had been ordered to fly to Berlin to meet with General Eisenhower.

all its energies and resources would be required to restore the industrial strength of the country and to raise the standard of living of its people. He described severe damage to the Soviet Union's transportation system, to its industry, and to its production facilities. His command of production figures was precise. He could reel off the figures for coal production, current and prewar. At one point, Vyshinsky, his interpreter, told me the figure for steel production, but Stalin, in Russian, contradicted him. "I said pig iron," he grumbled. He talked further about the devastation his country had suffered, adding that he had appealed to the United States for help. Specifically, Stalin said, he had requested a loan of $6 billion, but six months later he had not yet received a reply. Of his foreign policy, Stalin said it would focus on collaboration with other nations to keep the world at peace.

Critics of my trip to Moscow (those who did not call me a Communist included me in the term "fellow travelers") always assumed that I took everything Stalin said at face value. I did not. But this was not the time or place to be cynical or accusatory. I wanted to hear him out. There would be ample opportunity later to determine if he kept his promises, which, unfortunately for the world, he did not always do.

That he had requested such a huge loan from the United States surprised me, although I assumed all along that the United States would try to help the Soviet Union, just as it would its other wartime allies. I told Stalin that such a large amount of money would not likely be made available without strong assurance that the funds would actually be used for repairing war damage and not for continued heavy war production. Stalin smiled again and replied that considering the extent of its devastation, worse than any other country suffered, the Soviet Union could not possibly devote money it might obtain in loans to war production. "It would be suicide for us," he said. Already, four million men had been demobilized, and an equal number would be released soon, reducing the Red Army to one-third of its wartime strength.*

I asked Stalin if he felt that U.S.-Soviet collaboration was proceeding satisfactorily. He replied that the common interest of the two countries had brought them "very close together" during the war and said the Soviet Union was greatly indebted to the United States for the help it had provided. But he noted that the tie that held us together—the need to defeat Nazi Germany—no longer existed and that a new basis must be found for close relationships in the future. That will not be easy to find, he conceded, adding, to my astonishment, "Christ said seek and ye shall find." Why was this infidel quoting Christ? I asked myself. Once more I pressed for Stalin's view on efforts by the United States to find a basis for continued collaboration. "They are trying," he observed.

When the conversation turned to the British, I remembered that Churchill had admired Stalin's sense of humor. I decided to test it. Assuring him that he would find continuity in Great Britain's foreign policy despite the defeat of the Conservatives, I asked Stalin if he had heard of Churchill's remark about Labor Foreign Minister Ernest Bevan's foreign policy speech to the House of Commons. The British wartime leader had listened, and when the speech was over had remarked, "How fat Anthony Eden has grown." (Eden was foreign minister in Churchill's Conservative government.) Stalin laughed delightedly, a deep, mellow laugh.

Relating impressions from my visit to Germany, I told Stalin that I feared Germany could rise again and suggested that perhaps the Ruhr could be internationalized. The Soviet leader seized on that. The Ruhr was the most important considera-

*When Kennan and I reported the Stalin interview to the State Department, officials were amazed by this information. "We have been trying for months to find that out," they told us. It pays sometimes to keep talking to people.

tion, he said. Take it away and Germany, which derived 85 percent of its war production from the Ruhr, would be unable to make war again.

Stalin's greatest show of emotion was prompted when I asked him what future policy should be with respect to Germany and Japan. He brought his clenched fist down on the table. We must be "severe" with them, he said. We had been too soft with Germany after World War I, allowing her to grow strong again industrially and militarily and once more lead the world to war. He expressed fear that we would allow Japan to rebuild its strength and warned that if we did so there would be another war in the future. He was hopeful about peace, he said, but realistic as well. The United Nations, he felt, would be helpful but no guarantor of peace.

"With what message should I leave the Soviet Union?" I asked. Stalin hesitated, then said, "Just judge the Soviet Union objectively. Do not either praise us or scold us. Just know us and judge us as we are and base your estimate of us on facts and not rumors." After a surprisingly weak handshake, Stalin said farewell. He turned to Kennan and praised him for the quality of his translation. In English, Vyshinsky concurred. "Damn good," he said.

After Kennan and I had completed our report of the meeting to the State Department, I flew off to Cairo to write about it for the *New York Times* and the North American Newspaper Alliance. I was wary enough of Soviet censorship to postpone my writing until I had left the country. The Newspaper Alliance paid me $1,000 for my report.

The meeting with Stalin was a highlight of my public life, even though amid intense anti-Communist fervor it became a political liability of the first order. Stalin had not turned me into a Communist. He hadn't even tried. He said nothing at all about the "superiority" of the Soviet system. He did not berate capitalism. He seemed to understand that each of us had his beliefs, that each would adhere to them, and that we should go on from there to chart areas of agreement. As a member of the Senate Foreign Relations Committee, I felt that I was fulfilling my obligation to the Senate and to the American people. In my next campaign, however, the political climate would be so loathsome because of McCarthyism that this important meeting would be cited as evidence that I was either a Communist or so sympathetic to communism that I had no place in American public life. Had I foreseen such a consequence, I would have been troubled. But my meeting with Stalin would have taken place just as it did.

After Stalin and Churchill, the other world leaders I visited paled in comparison, but only because their smaller, less powerful countries gave them much more limited parts on the world scene. Many played significant and substantial roles in the immediate postwar period and in the years that followed. One who impressed me was the twenty-five-year-old shah of Iran, Reza Mohammad Pahlavi. The Russians and British had taken turns occupying Iran. The shah's father, known as Reza Shah, had been forced to abdicate. He died in exile, a fate that also would befall the son, whose flight would lead to the Iranian hostage crisis and have an impact on the U.S. presidential election of 1980. In Baghdad, I had a conversation with the prime minister that could well have taken place in 1985 instead of 1945. He professed friendship toward the United States, then launched a harangue against our assumed support of Zionism, followed by a bitter attack against the "aggressive designs of the Jews" against the entire Moslem world. At a press conference I held in Baghdad, every question concerned Zionism.

I examined the other side of that coin as well. Escorted by officials of the Jewish Agency, I visited Tel Aviv and a number of small Jewish settlements and farms. The state of Israel would not come into being for two more years, but I found the Jewish settlers in what was then Palestine working hard, making the infertile land produce crops. They worked in open fields surrounded by Arabs armed with rifles. In Jerusalem, again the only topic of conversation was the prospect of a Jewish homeland in Palestine.

Since the revelation of the Holocaust, world opinion had shifted to the point that Jews were more hopeful and Arabs more fearful than either had ever been before. In Bethlehem, Arabs were polite to me, but they were worried about American support—at that time unofficial—for carving the state of Israel out of Palestine. In Beirut, then such a beautiful city—the Paris of the Middle East—Bayard Dodge, president of American University, and officials of the U.S. embassy advised me to assure the Arabs that no Jewish state in Palestine was contemplated, advice that I fortunately did not heed. In Damascus, the president of Syria wanted the United States to help get the French and the British out of his country. I had to tell him what he already knew—that neither was willing to go before the other. The Middle East was a fascinating but sorely troubled spot on the globe then, and it has become more so since.

The most colorful of my encounters was with King Ibn-Saud of Saudi Arabia, who sent his lavishly appointed private plane to fly me to Jidda. Ibn-Saud worked in a complex of tents that included a cluster for his three wives and numerous concubines. I was assigned a tent of my own and given an Arab costume in which to dress. A military guard of honor was drawn up in front of the king's very large tent (with Persian carpets on the floor, of course), and a special guard unit in sheikh's costumes, with rifles and swords, formed a large semicircle in front. Ibn-Saud, a huge monarch (about six feet four inches, 220 pounds), greeted me with outstretched hand. He wore a large cloak made of dark brown camel hair, a white smock underneath it, and no shoes! A red turban was topped by a black and gold headpiece, all of which made him seem even taller.

I was informed that the king wanted me to be his guest at dinner (eight courses). Still dressed in my Arab getup, I was admitted to an after-dinner audience with the king. He proved to be concerned about little besides Russia. Unless the United States took a firm stand, he warned, the Soviets would soon be in control of Northern Europe and of China, not through war but by exporting communism. He was disdainful of the British, who were punishing Saudi Arabia, he said, for its increasingly warm relationship with the United States. The British were always undercutting the United States in the Middle East, he said, a strange stance given all that the United States had done to prevent England's conquest by Germany. I was aware of British efforts to prevent U.S. airlines from gaining landing rights in the Middle East, and from Cairo I sent a long cable to President Truman, suggesting that the United States and Britain reconcile their differences or the influence of both would wane in the Middle East and give way to some other power (we both knew which power I meant) in this critical area. Then I flew off for important visits to two key nations, Turkey and Greece. Soon President Truman and I would arrive at different conclusions as to what U.S. policy toward Turkey and Greece should be.*

Naples, Rome, and the Vatican were next on my itinerary, followed by Vienna and Belgrade, where I met the legendary

---

*An amusing sidelight from my stay with Ibn-Saud: General Ben Giles, commanding officer of the U.S. Air Force in the Middle East, related that when the king was hoping to expedite completion of a U.S. air base at Dahren, he offered Giles "the company of one of the ladies of my court." Giles, a married man, declined. Ibn-Saud asked his wife's age and learning that she was along in years, said, "Oh, I mean a young lady." Giles again said no. For years after my trip, I would relate the Giles story and embellish it, saying that when I was escorted to my tent near Jidda, I was asked how I wished my tent flap left. Teasing my wife Mildred, I would say that I ordered the flap left ajar, quickly adding that "if anything but the desert air ever came into my tent, I never knew it." I was never certain whether Mildred believed me.

Marshal Tito, whose resistance to Nazism is one of the inspiring stories of World War II. Tito was a fine physical specimen, not tall (about five feet eight, 180 pounds), very well proportioned and athletic-looking. His struggles on the field of battle had not deprived him of his sense of humor. He put me at ease by relating an amusing anecdote: while posing for a photograph with Churchill, he warned the British leader to sit at his right or risk charges of being to the left of a Communist. His laughter was hearty. A huge police dog named Tiger lay at Tito's feet while we talked, drank cold wine, and ate cold food.

Tito asked me to talk frankly, and I took him at his word. The United States could not help Yugoslavia economically or even recognize his government unless the essentials of democracy were established in the country. My information, I told Tito, was that there was no freedom of the press, people were taken forcibly from their homes by secret police, and opposition parties had no voice. He needed economic assistance urgently, and I advised him to seek help from both Russia and the United States, but for the latter to be of help, Tito would first have to convince President Truman and the American people that his government met minimum democratic requirements. To my relief and somewhat to my surprise, he took my blunt talk in good spirit, then told me his version of what he was accomplishing along these lines, which wasn't much.

I also visited Bucharest and Prague, shoring up my conviction that Eastern Europe had all the stability of a bowl of gelatin. Several of the countries, including Yugoslavia, were planning elections, and various factions were striving for power. In most of the region, the Russians were roundly hated and deeply distrusted, but they were an overpowering fact of life, on the scene and unwilling to pull back. For years, right-wing critics of agreements reached by Roosevelt and Truman have complained that we "let" the Soviets gain a foothold in Eastern Europe. The facts, which are not always of interest to the right wing, are that the Russian troops got there on their own and that it would have taken World War III to dislodge them. At dinner in Prague, Jan Masaryk, then the foreign minister, told me that Churchill had become "very arrogant" as he saw the Russians asserting claims that reinforced his earlier fears that they would try to control Eastern Europe. Masaryk said he did not enjoy having "to play my flute" for the Russians, but noted that the Red Army had liberated his country from the Germans and that Czechoslovakia was geographically proximate to Russia. Thus, he would have to cooperate.* He did not think the Soviets intended conquest, nor did he believe they would try to communize Europe. I cite these views long after we know what really happened to demonstrate a point: Matters are not always as clear when they are happening as they are with benefit of hindsight.

On November 7, I visited the Czech president, Edvard Beneš, who had just learned that President Truman had appealed to Stalin and obtained an agreement for withdrawal of Soviet and American troops from Czechoslovakia by December 1. Beneš, like Masaryk, was grateful to Russia for liberating his country from the Nazis, and he was equally convinced that the Soviets were not planning any wars of conquest. Beneš underscored the necessity of U.S.-Soviet collaboration and said flatly that Czechoslovakia would remain democratic.** Emotionally, Beneš recalled that he had been convinced since 1934 that Hitler would try to annex Czechoslovakia and then wage war throughout Europe. He tried to convince Britain and France. Until Hitler made his move in June 1938, Beneš said he was certain that Britain and France would help the Czechs to resist the Nazis. On June 8, they informed him they would not. Had they stood with Czechoslovakia then, Beneš said, Russia and Poland would

---

*The "cooperation" was one-way. When Masaryk proved insufficiently compliant, the Soviets pushed him to his death from a balcony.

**Beneš had been assured by the Soviets that if they could "guide" foreign policy, they would not interfere with domestic policy. The promise was not kept.

have rallied to the cause and a failed Hitler would have been overthrown. In my diary I wrote: "What a price was exacted by appeasement!"

But all that was history. Hitler had not been overthrown, and now in 1945 many of his generals were about to be tried as war criminals at Nuremberg, Germany. My friend, Supreme Court Justice Robert Jackson, who was to preside, invited me to attend, and I saw a rogues' gallery that probably exceeded in depravity any assembled in all history—Jodl, Keitel, Streicher, Raeder, Kesselring, Speer, Hess, Göring, Doenitz. By accident, I entered a room where Göring was conferring with defense counsel. The Nazi Luftwaffe general arose, bowed graciously, and sat down. Soon he would escape the executioner by biting into a cyanide capsule someone had managed to slip to him.

Easily the most imperious and least forthcoming of the heads of state whom I interviewed was General Charles de Gaulle, who received me in Paris. Although his country had been overrun by and forced to surrender to the Germans, de Gaulle regarded himself a world leader of stature no less than that of Truman, Churchill, and Stalin. In fact, he was frequently disdainful of all of them, as he had been of President Roosevelt. The French nation, de Gaulle believed, was entitled to a world role equal to that of the victorious allies. Anything less and he would brood and sulk. Apparently he was in his anti-American mode when I encountered him, for he volunteered little that was new or informative. Our discussion was so unproductive that I made no notes and simply recorded in my diary the fact that we had met.

From Paris I flew to London in General Eisenhower's plane.*

---

*On board, I was introduced to other passengers, including Kay Summersby, Eisenhower's celebrated driver in WWII. I had a very pleasant talk with her.

There I conferred with an old friend from Illinois, Adlai Stevenson, then the acting head of the U.S. delegation to the United Nations Organization Preparatory Commission. Stevenson was caught up in a minor imbroglio over reports circulated by the British that the United States did not want UN headquarters to be in the United States. The postwar British seemed to enjoy making mischief for their old ally for some reason or other. Stevenson set forth our official position: We were not seeking the headquarters, but we would welcome it. This was a relief to me. No one was more committed than I to a strong American involvement in the United Nations. I also had lunch with Andrei Gromyko, then—as he remained until 1946—the Soviet ambassador to the United States. He complained, as Stalin had, about the lack of action by the United States on the Soviet bid for a $6 billion loan.

On December 13, I was back on U.S. soil for the first time in four months. I hope I have made clear that I regarded my firsthand view of postwar Europe and my face-to-face meetings with world leaders as invaluable preparation for one who would have a voice in the postwar foreign policy of the United States. Thus I was heartened three days after my return when Joseph E. Davies, our former ambassador to Moscow, told me at a party that he had named President Roosevelt, General Eisenhower, and Senator Claude Pepper as the three Americans who had done the most for U.S.-Soviet relations. An organization planning to make an award had asked for such nominations.

I cite this accolade and its estimable source as we move on now to vastly different assessments of what I was actually accomplishing at this crucial stage of my public career.

None of these famous personages was as important to me as a kindly, thoughtful gentleman who died that year. Papa, who had been unemployed for several years, early in the 1940s was appointed custodian of the Department of Agriculture building in Tallahassee, Florida. The job gave him some responsibility and the opportunity to make many new friends among the workers in the building. He was delighted. But after a few years, he seemed to lose interest and to be constantly short of energy. Mama noticed with increasing concern that he frequently fell asleep in his chair. She took him to a hospital, where doctors determined that the problem was kidney failure. There was no dialysis machine in those days, and no other effective treatment. Papa grew weaker and soon passed away. The fact that medical science today could have spared him and enabled him to live many more years has been a constant spur to me in advocating government support for medical research so that others need not die prematurely.

7

Pepper v. Smathers

*Defend me from my friends; I can defend myself
from my enemies.*

—MARÉCHAL VILLARS

In the summer of 1945 the letters began to come, one after
another, each more insistent than the last. A Florida constituent was asking for a favor, a *big* favor. "Trust I can return the
favor some day," he wrote cheerily. "If you hear anything favorable, how about calling me collect. . . ." Even his mother
wrote, mentioning his father, thus putting me on notice that at
least three votes were at risk. The mother wrote, "We know
you are a very busy man and a very big man. . . . truly wish
we had many more in the Senate like you, we need good men
like you so badly to reconstruct this poor old world. We will
continue to hope and pray that all goes well—and for your
success, too, Senator." The son feared he was becoming a pest:
"I want to thank you and your office force for 'putting up' with
me *so* constantly." But there was no noticeable diminuendo to
this chorus of entreaty. Indeed, in one communiqué the son

189

seemed to be chiding me for ineffectiveness: "Another law-yer—32 years old—got out of the service last week. Senator Morse of Oregon was *his* benefactor—so it is being done." Obviously, I would have to spend less time reconstructing "this poor old world" and concentrate more on extricating my Florida friend from the U.S. Marine Corps, the objective of his relentless assault on my self, my staff, and the United States Post Office.

Clearly, this was no ordinary constituent. During my campaign for reelection to the Senate in 1938, a tall, handsome, earnest young man approached me after I had addressed students of the University of Florida. He was president of the student body and, he said, an admirer. He wanted to be my campaign manager on campus. Well, why not? I thought. I knew something about his family—his uncle had served with me in the Senate. The young man obviously knew how to win elections—he had got himself elected, hadn't he? (I was unaware of how emphatically he would impress that point on me some day.) So I appointed young George Smathers to manage my campaign on the University of Florida campus. Later he asserted—and reasserted—his claim to a favor in return for his support of me in my Senate campaign of 1938.

Shortly after his graduation from law school, Smathers asked me to recommend him (tantamount to appointment) for assistant U.S. attorney for the Southern District of Florida. District Attorney Herbert Phillips resisted the appointment. He did not trust Smathers, he said, and did not want him. I also received a telephone call from Dade County Sheriff D. C. Coleman, who asked if it was true that I was going to name Smathers. When I said yes, Coleman declared, "You'll always regret it." "Why do you feel that way?" I asked. "He's able, bright, liberal. I want to encourage that kind of young man to become involved in politics." Coleman replied, "I know him. I know his family. You will regret it if you give him that appointment." I ignored the warning.

But the war came along and Smathers joined the Marine Corps. In 1945, the war had not been won, but Smathers decided it could be done without his services, which "could be better utilized in the Justice Dept." On June 11, he was assigned to the Marine Air Corps station at Cherry Point, North Carolina, and he wrote that "it looks like I will be here permenantly [*sic*]. . . . Can't possibly tell you how anxious I am to get out and start 'doing.' " A day or two later he wrote that he was "snapping in on my new job, but frankly dislike it very much." On June 13, he wrote again, describing his role as "equivalent to being 2nd deputy Sherrif [*sic*] of Collier County— only I can't wear a star nor high top boots." He wanted to be rescued "from this mental Sahara." If his anxiety seems extraordinarily acute, and it does, there is a ready explanation. He wanted to end his military service so he could begin a political career. He was even willing to run in absentia if he had to, and if it was possible legally, for a seat in the U.S. House of Representatives. At one point he thought it necessary, or at least prudent, to assure me that if I would help him get elected, he would never run against me.

Well, that possibility did not loom large among my concerns in 1945. I was concentrating on my forthcoming trip to Europe and on an agenda of domestic legislation that would address urgent needs of the American people. At the same time, I did not have the luxury (no member of Congress ever does) of ignoring my constituents, including George Smathers. I told Smathers that his best chance for an early return to civilian life would be for a high government official to inform Marine Corps officers that he was needed for a particular key post. Perhaps I could persuade Attorney General Tom Clark to open up a job for Smathers and to ask the marines for his release. That is exactly what happened. At my request, Clark appointed

Smathers a United States attorney assigned to the Southern District of Florida, a perfect launching pad for a political career. The Marine Corps honored Clark's request and gave Smathers his cherished discharge.

The former marine officer had barely shed his uniform when he trained his sights on the House seat of Congressman Patrick Cannon, whose district included Miami. Cannon was a shrewd campaigner who knew how to take advantage of his incumbency. One of his tactics particularly vexed Smathers. Cannon was able to obtain from the military lists of Florida men about to be discharged. Then, at government expense, Cannon would send telegrams to the families of men from his district, telling them the date of discharge and implying a role for Congressman Cannon in the impending release. Smathers wrote to my aide, Jim Clements, asking: "Isn't there some method by which you could get the war department to level a blast at him or at least claim that Pepper has had some hand in securing these discharges?" When Cannon was about to succeed in having a new Veterans Administration office established in Miami, Smathers, agreeing that this was a "good idea," again wrote, urging that I step in and make it appear that the project was engineered by me. He was not trying to build me up; he was trying to bring Cannon down. In addition to diverting credit and publicity from his opponent to me, Smathers further tried to seal our relationship with flattering messages, such as: "Just finished listening to your speech on reciprocal trade—it was magnificent. Wish to hell more of your constituents could see and hear you in action. If you send that speech around, I'd like a copy. Those fellows with me say it was far superior to any others they ever heard."

In 1946, after an energetic campaign, George Smathers won the Democratic primary, tantamount to election. We had been photographed together. Early in the campaign, he called me every two or three days for advice. He was regarded as my

Members of the Florida delegation. Standing, left to right: George Smathers, Bob Sikes, Herbert Burke. Seated: Paul Rogers and me.

Mildred and I (first and second from left) watch as President Kennedy signs a bill, of which I was one of the sponsors, proclaiming Sir Winston Churchill an honorary U.S. citizen.

Mildred (seated) and I, entertaining Mrs. Eleanor
Roosevelt (seated center) in our Coral Gables,
Florida, home.

With Senator Hubert Humphrey. Mildred is on the left.

With President
John F. Kennedy.

With Lyndon Johnson
on Capitol Hill.
Standing to my left is
Senator George
Smathers.

With President Johnson.

Mildred and Lady Bird Johnson. I am at far left. Congressman Charles Bennett is second from right.

With Mildred at campaign headquarters in Miami, 1964.

With Prime Minister Golda Meir in Miami in the
early 1960s.

Mildred (seated) and I look on as President Jimmy
Carter signs my Mandatory Retirement Act in 1978.

With President Carter on Air Force One during his
reelection campaign.

To Senator Claude Pepper
Orville Wright

The photo that Orville Wright sent me . . . and, almost
half a century later, with Astronauts Young and Crippen.

With British Prime
Minister Margaret
Thatcher in 1981.

Visiting with Pope John
Paul II at the Vatican.

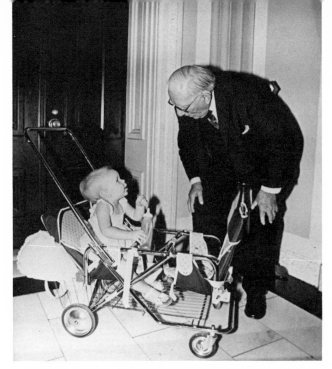

Taking advice from a younger constituent in 1983.

With the National Easter Seal Poster Child in 1984.
(Photo by Charles Geer)

Anthony Quinn joins me at a
Congressional Arts Caucus in
September 1984.

A visit with Israel's Prime Minister
Menachem Begin.

Laying a wreath at a Holocaust
Memorial in Jerusalem with
Congresswoman Lindy Boggs,
Congressman Tony Beilenson, and
Mrs. Beilenson.

Jack Sparling's cartoon appeared after the
House passed the minimum wage/
maximum hour bill in 1938.

At my desk in the Rules Committee Office
at the Capitol, 1985.

With Florida's Governor (now Senator) Bob Graham in
Tallahassee.

Receiving Dr. Jonas M. Savimbi of Angola.

Sitting with six tons of petitions protesting cuts in Social
Security cost of living allowances, July 1985. (Darryl
Heikes/*U.S. News and World Report*)

With Helen Hayes at the
Achievement in Aging Award
Dinner, December 10, 1986.

My official Rules Committee portrait.

The Congressional baseball game. Suited up are my fellow
House members, David Bonior, Marty Russo, and
Mike Synar.

Dodd Hall at Florida State University in Tallahassee, the site of the Mildred and Claude Pepper Library.

This photograph of me in my House office by John McDonnell of the *Washington Post* won First Place in the 1986 White House News Photographers' Association Annual Awards.

I appeared on the cover of *Time* in 1938 and again in 1983. (Reprinted by permission from *Time*)

candidate. I was pleased to have this young, obviously intelligent, and plainly ambitious lawyer as a colleague and fellow member of the Florida congressional delegation. When he arrived in Washington, I gave him all the help and advice I could, not just about the bewildering and shifting power centers of the capital, but also about setting up his office, organizing his staff so that it would be responsive to constituents. George Smathers and I would be a congenial and effective team, I thought, and so we were for most of the four years (he was easily reelected in 1948) he served in the House.

Forces dedicated to my destruction had been mobilizing after my reelection in 1944, when Ed Ball raised $62,000 in a single afternoon, seed money for a war chest that would ensure my defeat in 1950. The spark that ignited Ball, if one was needed, was my vote to uphold President Roosevelt's veto of a tax bill he described as "more for the relief of the greedy than the needy." Not only did I vote to sustain the veto, I defied Senator Barkley and the rest of the party leadership by making a speech praising the president's action. As far as Ball and the Florida business community were concerned, that was pouring salt in a wound that had been festering since 1938, when I vigorously supported minimum wage–maximum hour bills. In addition, Florida doctors opposed me because I advocated what they saw fit to call "socialized medicine." I had not opposed any civil rights legislation since the antilynching bill of 1937, and thus I also had earned the enmity of white racists. I was fully aware of these obstacles to my reelection and confident that I could prevail against them. But as 1949 slipped into history, I was being blindsided by the two factors that would loom largest against me. One was McCarthyism. The other was my protégé, Smathers, who was perfectly willing to resort to McCarthyism.

There were signs of trouble, but I tended to discount them. They began to surface six years before the 1950 election. One

I noted in my diary on March 6, 1944: "Louise McGregor came up with a monstrous scandal story that Mildred was having an affair with Sen. Tydings . . . just the beginning of many [lies] during the campaign." In March 1948, I wrote: "Waller came and we discussed my problem, trying to be an honest liberal and represent Florida, and raised the possibility of my resignation and removal to another state to continue my political career. He was very sympathetic to my difficulties. Troubled by the civil rights issues and foreign policy especially." The first time the word *defeat* found its way into my thoughts and into my diary was on March 6, 1948, when another close friend came by. "Ches [Dishong] feels people strongly for Marshall Plan, against civil rights program and will defeat me if I cross them on these things."

The fact that there would be no Roosevelt coattails to help me in 1950 was a concern, partly mitigated by the announcement—at last—by President Truman of a domestic program that I could support enthusiastically. In January 1949, I wrote of the president's new budget: "It expands social functions— health, education, social security, etc. It is the best attack upon our needs ever made in many respects. It proposes to do more for more people than has ever been recommended by a President. The President has really got New Deal religion and he is now walking in the footsteps of Roosevelt." I would not, as I had feared, have to run against the domestic as well as the foreign policy of my party's leader in 1950. That gave me heart. And all along I was comforted—lulled may be the better word— by the South's habit of reelecting incumbent senators who did not get caught with their fingers in the till or a chorus girl in their beds.

Since the presidency was beyond its reach, the South exercised power by controlling congressional committees. Because Congress was (and is) ruled by a seniority system, Southern politics focused on electing and then reelecting members of

Congress so they would become committee chairmen, power-ful antidotes to Northern presidents. Also, there was still a one-party system in Florida and the rest of the South. Democratic challengers were forced to think twice about taking on Demo-cratic incumbents, especially those with considerable seniority. Money was hard to come by for a challenger, because the busi-ness community generally supported the seniority-laden in-cumbent. That would not be the case in 1950 for incumbent Senator Claude Pepper of Florida.

The road to McCarthyism was being paved by a faction of the Republican party skilled in exploiting public fear of com-munism. Democrats gave them ample opportunity. Alger Hiss, a State Department official who had been at Yalta with Roo-sevelt, was accused of having been a Communist by Whittaker Chambers, an admitted former Communist. Truman's secre-tary of state, Dean Acheson, a friend of Hiss, told the Senate Foreign Relations Committee that "I will not turn my back on Alger Hiss," causing an uproar in Congress and in the country. Acheson also was measured in his criticisms of the Soviet Union, and the Republicans kept his feet to the fire for that.

As to George Smathers, we had been spending a lot of time together. With Senator Spessard Holland and Congressman Paul Rogers, we called on President Truman, seeking funding for a Florida flood-control project. Truman told us of his budget problems. He vowed that he would hold the military budget at $15 million—that that was enough and he would not let the armed forces spend any more. He didn't "give a damn" how much they protested. (In 1987, the Pentagon was spending $15 million every three minutes.) Smathers and I often were in-vited to speak before the same conventions, and we frequently flew to Florida together. On one such occasion in May 1949, the thought that Smathers might run against me first entered my mind. I wrote: "Smathers is very handsome and striking, has good mind and manner and is clever. Makes very favorable impression. He is ambitious and seeking to run either against me or for Governor." I added a gratuitous thought: "Don't think he can beat me."

I continued to pay no attention to supporters warning me that I would need to "change" my policies or face defeat. In fact, I worked up a bill to increase the minimum wage to seventy-five cents an hour—the first minimum wage bill had called for twenty-five cents an hour. Clearly I had made peace with the president after the "dump" effort of 1948. When Jimmy Byrnes delivered a withering attack on the Democratic platform and the president's program, I told Truman I intended to reply. I had written in my diary: "He said he hoped I would and none could do it better; that he would like to but it would make headlines all over the country. . . . The President confirmed that Byrnes had been asked to speak in the last campaign and refused." In this conversation, Truman does not sound like a president bent on defeating "that son of a bitch, Claude Pepper." Nor does his invitation to me a short time later to participate in the signing of the agreement establishing the North Atlantic Treaty Organization.

Meanwhile, conflicting rumors circulated. One week, it appeared that Smathers would run against me. The next week, it seemed unlikely. In August 1949, I received some direct word from Smathers's brother, Frank. He told me that George would not run against me if I could get him appointed solicitor general of the United States, if I could get the governor to promise that George Smathers would have a "voice" in naming a new senator if any vacancy occurred, and if I would agree to support Smathers for governor in 1952. My answer was swift, unequivocal, and brief: No.

Truman came to Florida a few days after I had refused to consider the Smathers "deal." The president delivered a talk on foreign policy, and at his request, I rode in his motorcade from the Miami airport and sat on the platform during his speech.

Convinced by now that Smathers would run against me, I called on the president one day at the White House. He had promised to help me win reelection, but there wasn't a lot he could do overtly in a race between two Democrats. Nonetheless, I wanted to be certain that President Truman had put the events of 1948 behind him. So I asked him point-blank if my support of Eisenhower for the nomination that year would be held against me. Plainspoken as always, Truman asked, "Have you ever seen any evidence that I was prejudiced against you?" I thought briefly, then replied, "No, I don't recall that I have." Truman said, "Well, if I had been, you would have known about it." How true that comment rings. Never in his public life was Harry Truman the least bit bashful about telling people off or letting his feelings be known. Obviously, Truman did not appreciate my support of Eisenhower nor my opposition to many of his policies. But the president who advised people who could not stand the heat to stay out of the kitchen understood politics, a game where you must win over your enemies or you won't have enough friends to win elections.

The Florida campaign of 1950 for the Democratic nomination for a seat in the U.S. Senate is regarded by many historians as the most vicious to that point in our history, and perhaps the dirtiest of all time. I never knew what hit me. I was as bewildered as a sandlot baseball player showing up for the game and finding that the opposition is the New York Yankees. I was outspent by about 10 to 1, outhustled—and in the vilification contest I was like a hummingbird fallen into a nest of screech owls. I heard myself described as part of a sinister "Red network." I was an advocate of "treason." My supporters were Communists, Socialists, "fellow travelers," and Northern labor bosses. Before the campaign got under way, my feeling was one of chagrin that Smathers, no longer in need of my benefactions, would attempt to oust me from the office that enabled

197

me to help him and, if I do say so, many others. But I was not prepared for the slanders, innuendos, and vituperation that he and his supporters, led by Ed Ball, spread from one corner of the state to the other. I had always campaigned as if I were an applicant for a job, convincing my prospective employers of my own virtues and not even mentioning my competitors. In Florida in 1950, such a method of electioneering was suddenly as out-of-date as the kerosene lamp. Some excerpts from Smathers's opening campaign speech make the point:

> The leader of the radicals and extremists is now on trial in Florida. Arrayed against him will be loyal Americans who believe in free enterprise, who want to preserve their right to think, to work and to worship as they please. Standing against us will be certain Northern labor bosses, all the Communists, all the Socialists, all the radicals and the fellow travelers. . . . Surely we will not turn from the noble principles of Jefferson and Jackson to the careermen of Communism. . . . Florida will not allow herself to become entangled in the spiraling web of the Red network. The people of our state will no longer tolerate advocates of treason. . . . The outcome can truly determine whether our homes will be destroyed; whether our children will be torn from their mothers, trained as conspirators and turned against their parents, their home and their church. . . . I stand for election on the principle of the Free State against the Jail State.

Now wait a minute, I thought. Claude Pepper of Tallahassee, Florida, and Camp Hill, Alabama, stands for tearing children out of their mothers' arms? He advocates treason? He wants to interfere with the rights of people to think, work, and worship as they please? What manner of nonsense is this? And who is the fellow spewing it—the same person I visited the White House with a few months ago, who flew with me to an Elks convention even more recently, the fellow I had helped get out of the Marine Corps and into Congress? Run against me, George Smathers—that's your right—but trying to transform me into a draconian figure who threatens the republic is your wrong.

The strategy was not devised by Smathers. Six years earlier, Ed Ball and a group of Florida businessmen had determined to defeat me and they had plenty of time to figure out how to do it. While raising millions of dollars, they collected every photograph of me with Negroes and put them away for the campaign. They monitored my every statement on civil rights and on the need for the United States to be more tolerant of the Soviet Union. There was no secret about my votes in the Senate to choke off Southern-led filibusters bottling up civil rights legislation. In their news releases and political fliers, I was identified as a "nigger-lover" and as a Red. On several occasions when I stepped down from platforms from which I had been speaking, Negroes would be posted to shake my hand. I wasn't about to spurn them even though I knew I was being photographed by people who wished me no good. No, Smathers, who was still in the Marine Corps when this well-financed, no-holds-barred campaign was launched, was not the strategist. He was the tool selected by Ball and his friends, as some of them later admitted. But Smathers had one option—he could have rejected the worst of the smear tactics. He never exercised that option. Winning had come to mean everything to him. "How" he won was incidental.

Although I paid little attention at the time, a similar campaign for a Senate seat was being waged in California. Richard Nixon had been elected to the House of Representatives by pinning the "Red" label on his opponent, Jerry Voorhis. Now he was in the midst of a vicious campaign against Helen Gahagan Douglas, who was dubbed "the pink lady" by the Nixon forces. Senator Joseph McCarthy had not yet surfaced in a major way, but the big-money interests that would enable him to thrive were hard at work and ecstatic over a recent discovery: that anyone who ever expressed a liberal thought or cast a liberal vote could be labeled a "pinko" and in many cases be defeated at the polls.

Anti-Communist fervor had a grip on America. The fear was disproportionate to the threat. The words *left* and *liberal* began to take on ominous connotations. The so-called upper classes that Franklin Roosevelt so effectively "betrayed" saw their chance to brake the New Deal social revolution, and even to reverse it. The mix of racism and anti-communism was subtly brewed. Citizens became leery of each other without reason and watched what they said and wrote lest they be suspected of "leftist" leanings. Liberal politicians scrambled toward the center or even to the right. The climate was perfect for a demagogue to pin labels on decent, honorable people, and soon Joe McCarthy came along to fulfill that role. McCarthyism, however, preceded Joe McCarthy.

My congenital optimism, which has been a blessing more often than it has been a curse, blinded me to the effectiveness of the "Red scare" on ordinary Americans. After my initial shock, I was even able to joke a bit about Smathers and what he was doing. On Sunday, March 5, I wrote in my diary: "Smathers started in West Fla. Saturday. It rained on him." The following month I was still confident, though it is difficult now to understand why. This passage from April 2, 1950, explains it: "Opposition will probably step up their attack but believe it will react upon them." From the moment I read Smathers's first campaign speech, I had believed that his tactics would boomerang, that voters would be turned off by his total lack of restraint. Eventually, I like to think, they would have been. After allowing themselves to be mesmerized by Joe McCarthy for a few years, the American people finally saw through him.

But in a brief political campaign, such simple and easily under-stood labels as "Red" and "nigger-lover" caught on quickly, in part because they were fortified by distorted accounts of my visit to Moscow in 1945 and by half-page newspaper photo-graphs of me shaking hands with blacks.

That linking me with Negroes was a campaign tactic is not a product of my imagination or paranoia. One night I spoke in Leesburg, Florida, and happened to notice a black man stand-ing near the steps leading to the platform. I could hardly help noticing, since the rest of the crowd was several yards distant. At one point, a white man approached the black and spoke to him, and the two walked away. My supporters had been struck by how nervous the man appeared to be, and one of them had asked him to explain his presence. He told this story: He was the janitor at a nearby movie theater. That afternoon two men in a sports car had driven up to the theater and asked him if he would like to earn twenty-five dollars. Of course he said yes, and they told him all he need do was go to the park where Senator Pepper would be speaking, position himself near the platform, and, as soon as the speech was over, rush up and shake hands with the senator. He should retain his grip until a flashbulb burst, then return to the theater to collect his money. Similar incidents occurred frequently, with newspapers op-posed to me generously devoting half a page or more to these photographs. This was the kind of blatant racism indulged in those days by many Florida newspapers, most gleefully by the *Orlando Sentinel*. It was appalling. And effective.

And where did George Smathers stand on the issue of race?*

---

*My own attitude on race evolved, as did that of the South and indeed the nation itself. Some years earlier, after the Supreme Court struck down a Texas law that prevented Negroes from voting, I issued a statement to my alarmed constituents, assuring them that "white supremacy will be main-tained." My views, no less than anyone else's, were formed by region, an-cestry, era, and associations. I could have bitten my tongue when I discovered

Foursquare on the side of bigotry. After his opening campaign speech, Smathers informed the Florida Peace Officers Association that he would defend, free of charge, any policeman indicted for violation of civil rights laws.

In his subsequent speeches, Smathers adopted the practice of referring to me as "Red Pepper." He frequently referred to my trip to the Soviet Union and my interview with Stalin. My opposition to Truman's proposals to aid Greece and Turkey was described as due to my being "soft on communism." Once in a speech on the Senate floor I had described Stalin as a leader we could trust, and that ill-advised remark was blown up and presented as support for the "Red Pepper" red herring. As further evidence of my leftism, Smathers would cite the names of a number of organizations I had addressed after my trip to Russia, groups later labeled subversive by the attorney general or the House Un-American Activities Committee. Not mentioned was that *when* I spoke to them, none of the groups was considered subversive by anyone, including George Smathers.

When some friends from organized labor helped a voter registration drive focused on Negroes, Smathers charged that "Northern labor bosses" were paying ten to twenty dollars to blacks to register and vote for me—ridiculous on its face, since we didn't have that kind of money even if we had been inclined to spend it that way. An organization called the Order

I had made such a statement. It was a throwback, a slip, a yielding in a frightened moment to political pressure. I did not believe in white supremacy. My record dating from my term in the Florida House of Representatives shows that I slipped only twice in a long public career. The "white supremacy" statement was one time; my opposition to an antilynching bill in my early Senate days was the other. Even in arguing against the bill, I pointed out the need for the North to help the South to educate its people, including blacks, to provide decent jobs, adequate health care, and housing for people of all races. We all slip now and again. My mistakes were temporary. I quickly regained my balance and have kept it faithfully over the years.

of Smathers Sergeants was formed by "red-blooded young Americans to keep order on election day and make up a permanent anti-Communist force"—a new way of saying "to keep newly qualified Negroes from voting." On my behalf, Northern labor bosses had sent "the carpetbaggers of 1950" into Florida, Smathers charged, referring to the little help being given by labor to the Negro registration drive. For one of the few times in the campaign, I responded in kind, noting that Smathers was born in New Jersey and referring to him once as a "damnyankee intruder." His response was to decorate his speaking platforms in orange and blue, the colors of his alma mater, the University of Florida, while telling audiences that I had learned the law under the "crimson of Harvard." *

Even my support for compulsory health insurance—now the law of the land—was cited as evidence of my communistic beliefs. This attack was particularly pleasing to the American Medical Association, which poured money into Florida to help Smathers win, or rather to make certain that Pepper lost. **

One speech from the Smathers campaign of 1950, aimed at audiences of "rednecks" in northern Florida, has become a classic of American political lore. The speech was intended to stir the passions of uneducated people by using words they would not understand in a way that implied great evil. It went like this:

> Are you aware that Claude Pepper is known all over Washington as a shameless *extrovert?*
> Not only that, but this man is reliably reported to

---

*Decades later, Smathers told a journalist that "crimson just happened to be Harvard's color" and that his remark was not intended to tie me to communism.

**When "socialized medicine" under the name Medicare was approved by the U.S. Senate in 1965, Florida Senator George Smathers was recorded as voting aye.

practice *nepotism* with his sister-in-law, and he has a sister who was once a *thespian* in wicked New York.

Worst of all, it is an established fact that Mr. Pepper, before his marriage, habitually practiced *celibacy*.

Ever since that text first appeared in 1950 in *Time*, Smathers has denied that he or anyone in his campaign ever made such a speech. For years, his Senate office staff would respond to inquiries by saying this speech was a campaign legend with no foundation in fact. Well, it strikes me as a little odd that *Time* would make that up and publish it not ten or twenty years after but rather *during* the campaign. Besides, the brief passage contains some unintended humor; on reflection, George Smathers should be able to come up with many worse incidents to disavow.

Two additional facets of the campaign had enormous impact on the outcome of the race. One was the appearance of a forty-nine-page booklet just before the election titled *The Red Record of Senator Claude Pepper*. The other was an article in the *Saturday Evening Post* by the respected writer and editor Ralph McGill, the subtitle for which read: "The toughest job in Florida politics is knocking over spell-binding pinko Senator Pepper." It was a one-two punch that few, if any, political candidates could absorb. There was too little time for an effective response to either. After months of hearing about "Red Pepper" chatting with Stalin, about "Red Pepper" being endorsed by the Communist *Daily Worker*, about the crimson of Harvard and the alleged kinship with Henry Wallace and Paul Robeson, now here surely was final affirmation. The *Saturday Evening Post*, with its homey, all-American cover art by Norman Rockwell, was something of a bible. Surely it would not refer to Claude Pepper as a "pinko" if that were not true. And for any voters still holding fast to the view that Claude Pepper was a loyal and unfairly maligned American, the book must have been the crowning touch. Who would dare distribute *The Red Record of Senator Claude Pepper* if he did not have the goods on him?

Just one week before the election, the book was distributed to all corners of the state. The shipment to the Miami area alone, according to a doctoral thesis written many years later,* weighed nine tons. Lloyd C. Leemis of Jacksonville, who claimed to be a former FBI agent, was the author or compiler of this vicious collection of propaganda rarely equaled or even approached in the most sordid political campaigns. Obviously, it cost a lot of money to produce and distribute, and the Smathers campaign had a lot of dollars—estimates ran as high as $2 million. Two former FBI agents were on the Smathers payroll, hired to follow me everywhere and report back on where I spoke, what I said, the crowd size, and so on. And at the Seminole Hotel in Jacksonville, the Smathers campaign had twenty-four automatic typewriters running twenty-four hours a day, sending original letters to names on every mailing list the handlers could get their hands on. My total campaign fund was $200,000, enough to pay for a similar typewriter operation and nothing else.

The Red Record consisted of photographs and superimposed headlines from the *Daily Worker* and other Communist publications. I was depicted as anxious to give Russia the secret of the atom bomb, billions of taxpayer dollars, and America's natural resources. The centerpiece, however, was a double-page montage, a photograph of me with Henry Wallace and Paul Robeson at the rally in Madison Square Garden in 1946. Superimposed was a quotation from me, denying that I had been on the same platform with Henry Wallace since he quit the Democratic party or with Paul Robeson since he indicated his favorable disposition toward communism. This statement was

---

* "Political Feud in the Palmettos: A Chronology and Analysis of the 1950 Florida Senatorial Campaign" by Richard D. Hutto.

absolutely true, but since the photograph was not dated, it appeared to be a clear, inarguable refutation of my words. The damage was compounded by a number of Florida newspapers that reprinted the photograph. It was devastating. Readers' eyes would move from my words denying association with Wallace and Robeson to the photograph of me, big as life, sitting there with both of them. To the charges, fortified by the book, that Claude Pepper was a Red and a "nigger-lover" was added indisputable evidence that he was a damned liar as well. I might have difficulty voting for this man myself.

Naturally, Smathers has always denied having anything to do with the book. But then at one time or another, he has disclaimed responsibility for so much that one almost ends up wondering where George Smathers was during 1950. He insists that the book was the project of Leemis, who compiled it, but Leemis did not have that kind of money to spend. There cannot be any doubt that the financing came from that hate-filled band of greedy men organized by Ed Ball, men who would go to any extreme to destroy a public official who supported Social Security, minimum wages, health care, and so on. Such programs made life bearable for millions. But they cost a little money, and that made life unbearable for the insatiably greedy.

Early on Sunday morning before the Tuesday election, a young woman approached me as I campaigned in Saint Petersburg, handed me *The Red Record* book, asked me what I thought of it. That was the first time I had seen it or heard of it. I will never forget the feeling of revulsion that gripped me as my eyes fell on the cover, which was a dreadful, snaggle toothed picture of me. I had never laid claim to being handsome, but this photograph was just indescribably ugly, monstrous, inhuman. That people who fancied themselves decent Americans would resort to such tactics to win an election defies belief to this day.

On May 2, 1950, the voters of the state of Florida went to

the polls. Registration was the highest it had ever been. The campaign had been waged over a period of four months. There had been virtually no discussion of issues, no debate over the accomplishments of one candidate in fourteen years in the Senate or the record of the other candidate during three years in the House. As is true of all elections, a fraction of the voters followed the campaign closely and objectively, but many, many more knew only what made the headlines and the radio broadcasts (television was not a factor in 1950). The final vote count was Smathers, 382,949; and Pepper, 319,178. I had lost by more than 60,000 votes, an overwhelming defeat, but I cannot help wondering today why, in view of the nature of the campaign, I was able to do that well.

In detailing the tactics that cost me my Senate seat, I fulfill my obligation to history—and I hope a bit more. Sympathy for injustices committed nearly four decades ago is not my objective. Long ago I learned that there is life beyond and outside of the United States Senate. Even on the day of my defeat— May 3, 1950—I had a sense that a phase, not a life, had ended. "We lost! or did we win?" I wrote in my diary. If Providence had another role for me, I would find it and fulfill it, and I believe that I have. But the lesson of the 1950s, of which the Florida primary is only a part, should not be lost on America. It is a simple, yet profound lesson: That this nation's strength is derived from the freedom of its citizens to think and speak as they choose, a freedom that must not be abridged by name-calling, questioning of motives, or assassination of character.

When the returns began to come in, I was with some dear friends and supporters in my old law office in downtown Tallahassee. Although the trend was clearly against me, we waited until the last precincts had reported. I was disappointed, not dejected. My religious beliefs sustained me, as did my friends and family. In a throwback to my years growing up in rural Alabama, we sang. At one point, I took the lead in singing

207

"Swing Low, Sweet Chariot," not exactly a cheer provoker, but one verse struck me as particularly appropriate, and I sang it loudly and with gusto: "Sometimes I'm up, sometimes I'm down, but oh Lord, I'm heavenly bound; swing low, sweet chariot." Someday, George Smathers and I would have to answer to our Maker for our deeds and misdeeds. I felt comfortable with myself.

At last I went home to be with my loved ones and to learn of yet another assault of this most abusive of campaigns. While I had been downtown, three carloads of goons had driven repeatedly around my family's home, shouting obscenities, jeering, booing, and calling me the vilest names in their apparently limitless lexicon of vulgarity. Mama, poor soul, already brokenhearted because I had lost, was bewildered and pained by this brutal exhibition of animosity toward her son and her family. This episode and the campaign in general outraged David Brinkley, the television commentator, who told me years later that the Florida campaign of 1950 would always stand out in his mind as the dirtiest in the history of American politics.

Smathers and Ed Ball aside, I did not conduct a state-of-the-art campaign. First of all, I made very little use of Mildred, who was an effective campaigner and the first of my entire entourage to sense that we were heading for defeat. Also, I allowed my friend and executive assistant, Jim Clements, to run the campaign, assisted by another friend and aide, Robert Fokes. Clements was in the last stages of cancer, of which I was not aware. But I did know that he drank too much, closed the office at night, and did not get along at all with Mildred, one reason she did not have a larger role. In addition to weak management, my funding was inadequate, a pittance compared to the amounts deployed to elect Smathers. But the greatest failure was my inability to recognize that McCarthyite tactics, however repugnant, were effective.

They were utilized elsewhere. I have already mentioned the

Nixon-Douglas race in California. More important to me at the time was the case of Senator Frank Graham of North Carolina. Graham was a distinguished educator and a man of ability and integrity who came within 5,000 votes of winning a majority in the North Carolina primary of 1950. That race had been a clean one, and Graham was so far ahead of the field that the second-place finisher considered dropping out, which would have given Graham the seat without a runoff. But Graham's foes began digesting the news from Florida. There was a new way to defeat an incumbent senator, especially one who had said a good word for civil rights and for the desirability of peaceful collaboration between the United States and the Soviet Union. Graham was vulnerable on both counts. He had not been as far out front on either issue as I had been, but he was a man of convictions and his convictions were known. Ten days into the runoff campaign, this decent public official had been thoroughly smeared as a lackey for communism and a "nigger-lover." His best friends, Graham told me, were afraid to speak to him on the street. After being all but guaranteed another six years in the Senate, Frank Graham went down to a crushing defeat.

McCarthyism claimed several senatorial victims in 1950. Besides Graham, former president of the University of North Carolina, and myself, McCarthyism engulfed the majority leader and majority whip of the Senate, Scott Lucas of Illinois and Francis Myers of Pennsylvania; Millard Tydings of Maryland, a decorated war hero and chairman of the Senate Armed Services Committee; Elbert Thomas of Utah, chairman of the Education and Labor Committee; and Elmer Thomas of Oklahoma, chairman of the agriculture subcommittee of the Senate Appropriations Committee.

With respect to George Smathers: He was a well-born, handsome, athletic young man when I first came to know him. He was clever and able. He was also self-centered, egotistical, ruthless in pursuit of his personal goals, and insensitive to the feelings of others. Gratitude was an emotion unknown to him. The favors I did for him did not foreclose his opposing me politically, but my defeat was not his aim—my destruction was. With Ed Ball's help, he very nearly succeeded. At the end of the campaign, I was so discredited that I did not even try to raise money to pay off my campaign debts.* It would have been futile. I had no income beyond my soon-to-end Senate salary of $12,500 a year, except for a small amount in uncollected fees from my law practice. I can never feel warmly toward George Smathers; Mildred died completely unforgiving.

Over the years, I have tried to adjust so that relations between George Smathers (now a Washington lawyer) and me are at least civil. He contributes to my campaigns, calls on me for favors now and again, and was instrumental in getting me admitted to certain clubs and organizations from which his friends had "blackballed" me. I try, not always successfully, to set aside the personal rancor and to look on the Smathers campaign as just a shabby period in American history. McCarthyism was an aberrant phenomenon of those times. Perhaps such periods of excess are part of the price we must pay for democracy. I think of George Smathers as part of that phenomenon, as one of a group of ruthless men determined to achieve selfish ends by destroying anyone standing in their way. There will always be such people, but as America matures their chances of prevailing, I trust, will never again be as good as they were in 1950.

What I can never forget are the hurt and humiliation inflicted on my mother, who was then seventy-three, and my wife. Mildred suffered many embarrassments. People both in Florida and in Washington whom we had always regarded as our friends no longer invited us to dinners or cocktail parties. All over Florida, my photograph was removed from the office

*Eventually, I paid off every cent.

walls of people who had been my supporters for years. It wasn't simply that I had lost. It was that my reputation had been so distorted that it had been effectively destroyed. From Florida's "boy wonder" in politics I had gone in fourteen years to being a "has-been" out of step with his state and nation at best, a traitor at worst. Some true friends—many, in fact—remained loyal, which is what true friends do. But Mildred and I learned firsthand the meaning of the phrase "fair-weather friends." When we did receive invitations during those final months of my Senate career, often we would be the object of sneers and snide remarks. I'd like to say they didn't bother me, but they did. Most of all, they deeply hurt Mildred who, after all, was an innocent bystander.

Mildred should not have had to pay the price of my near-destruction, and yet she paid a heavy price indeed. She was a gallant companion at my side during all the Senate years, during my twelve-year "exile" from public life, and during seventeen years of my service in the House of Representatives.* But she did not live to see the full extent of the mellowing toward me of the people of Florida and of other parts of the nation. She did not share in my ascension to the chairmanship of the House Rules Committee, a more important post than that of chairman of the Senate Foreign Relations Committee, which I would have become had I won in 1950. She did not share in the warmth of handshakes and friendly greetings that make my travels around the state and the nation so pleasant. When my honor and integrity were questioned by so many, Mildred steadfastly and nobly bore up. She deserved to share in the vindication of recent years.

I referred to the Smathers-Ball campaign organization as "ruthless." Too strong a word? I think not, though "vengeful"

---

*Of the seven victims of McCarthyism in 1950, I am the only one ever again elected to public office.

may be just as appropriate. Not long after the primary, I spotted Ed Ball at a New York cocktail party sponsored by the Florida Industrial Development Council. I congratulated him on "his" victory. When he mumbled something to the effect that it was good to have won "the last round," I replied that maybe it was not the last round. Ball shrieked so that everyone in the room could hear, "Claude, if you ever run for public office in Florida again, we'll lick you so bad you'll think this time was a victory."

At the banquet that followed, leading public officials and prominent Florida businessmen were seated at the head table. There was only one absentee—the recently defeated but still senior senator from Florida, Claude Pepper. Ed Ball, who was in charge of the event, informed me that there was "no room" for me at the head table.

Over the years, I have often thought back on the events of 1950. Ed Ball's bitterness toward me, I now realize, began much earlier than I had thought. Early on, Ed Ball tried to take over the Florida East Coast Railroad. I thought it should be merged with the Coast Line Railroad and represented that line pro bono publico before the Interstate Commerce Commission. Ball and his banks were represented by James M. Byrnes, a former Supreme Court justice. Ball sat in the hearing room beside Mildred, for we had often been together in social settings. In the course of my argument, I said: "Mr. Chairman and members of the Commission. If I wanted a man skilled in the art of finance, outstanding in his financial ability, to be the head of a financial institution, I know of no one I would select ahead of Mr. Edward Ball. But if I wanted a man to head up a great public utility, a man sensitive to the public interest, a man concerned about the public well-being, the last man I would select would be Mr. Edward Ball." I pointed to him in the hearing room.

Ed Ball's long effort to remove me from public life had many origins, and I believe this was one of them. After 1950 I had little contact with him. I was practicing law and he was expanding his economic empire in Florida. After several years I saw Ed Ball at the state capitol in Tallahassee, and afterward we encountered each other on a narrow path on the capitol grounds. I said, "Ed, you and I have been fighting each other for a long time. Let's fight someone else and stop fighting each other." I put out my hand and he extended his, saying, "Why, I agree with you; it's a deal." He never did oppose me again. When, in his nineties, he died, the *Miami Herald* asked me to write an article about him. I did, emphasizing the years when we were friends, praising his contributions to Florida's growth. I wrote that I would remember the good days and try to forget the period of enmity. The first one to call and thank me for the "kindness and tone" of my remarks was Fred Kent, Ball's attorney.

Let me return to my election-day comment in my diary: "We lost! or did we win?" I look back now on that terrible year and compare what has happened to me with what probably would have happened had I won. I would have become chairman of the Senate Foreign Relations Committee. But Florida was becoming more conservative and I might well have been defeated in 1956 anyway. Or in 1962. Or perhaps I would have survived and been in the Senate to this day. Foreign affairs would have preoccupied me.

Instead, in losing I returned to law practice for twelve years, improved my financial position, and became Florida representative for Cravath, Swaine, and Moore, one of the leading New York firms. We won a $40 million lawsuit for Bethlehem Steel Corporation. I paid my debts, including my campaign debts. In twenty-three years in the House of Representatives, I have been chairman of the House Select Committee on Crime and for six years chairman of the House Select Committee on Aging, which enabled me to understand and champion the nation's elderly. I got laws passed lifting mandatory retirement practices. I received ten honorary degrees to go with four awarded when I was in the Senate. For four years I have been chairman of the powerful House Rules Committee, which governs what legislation goes to the House floor and decides on the rules for its consideration. I enjoy the friendship and respect of my colleagues. If Mildred were just with me, I would be as happy as I have ever been in my life.

Maybe I won after all.

8

The Hiatus: 1951–1962

It is difficult to make a man miserable while he feels he is worthy of himself and claims kindred to the great God who made him.

—ABRAHAM LINCOLN

On the morning of January 3, 1951, my faithful staff and I gathered in my office in room 253 of the elegant Old Senate Office Building, now the Russell Senate Office Building. Robert Fokes, my administrative assistant, had resigned the previous summer shortly after the election to get himself established in Florida. Everyone else was present. There was great sadness among my excellent and loyal staff. I tried to keep the spirit light and upbeat. A number of friends came to tell me goodbye. Near noon, my colleague from Florida, Senator Spessard Holland, called to say he would like to stop by on his way to the noon opening of the new Congress. It was a strange encounter. He said nothing to indicate regret, offered no condolences. In a casual, pleasant way, we just carried on an inconsequential conversation for a few moments. I never considered him a warmhearted person, perhaps the reason he was not more liberal in his political philosophy. But our chat was friendly, probably because neither of us said what he was really thinking. Soon he left for the Senate floor.

For the first time in fourteen years, I was not to attend the opening of the Senate. I felt strange and somewhat empty. It helped that many senators made kind remarks about me on the floor that day, and a beautiful speech eulogizing me was made by Senator Matthew W. Neeley of West Virginia. He was an eloquent speaker and his tribute, which he read into the *Congressional Record,* moved me very deeply.

Senator Olin Johnston of South Carolina, who was going to take over my Senate suite, had kindly told me to take my time in vacating the offices, so I took a few days off to move my belongings somewhere else. My staff thoughtfully had bought from the government the black leather chair in which I sat in my private office and had also acquired from the government my seat on the Senate floor. The office chair is now in the Senate Room of the Mildred and Claude Pepper Library at Florida State University in Tallahassee, and my old Senate chair is in my House office in the Rayburn Building in Washington, in constant use by visitors.

Mildred and I still owned and lived in our comfortable apartment at 1661 Crescent Place in Washington. I divided my time in January between Washington and Tallahassee, where our and my family's home was. I had resolved to enter the private practice of law and to do so from offices in both Washington and Tallahassee. The new Cafritz Building was just being completed in Washington; I reserved space for a comfortable suite there and was able to influence its design since the building was not yet complete.

But in Tallahassee, there were problems finding and furnishing suitable office space. For a time I worked out of the den in my home. I was now a private citizen, a lawyer who was broke, a lawyer without an office, without a desk, without a partner, and with a mountain of debt, personal and political. I had announced that my firm would be called Pepper and Clements, my partner being Jim Clements, who had been my faithful friend and executive assistant in the Senate for so many years. But he was gravely ill with cancer in Miami and was not able to join me personally for the opening. Robert Fokes had been succeeded as my administrative assistant by Mildred (Millie) Waller—no relation to my former partner, C. L. Waller—who had served devotedly on my staff for many years, and she was of great help in setting up the Tallahassee office in January and the Washington office in February. We finally found office space in Tallahassee in late January. It was small, but it had to have some furniture, so I bought some without having any idea how to pay for it. On February 1, the law firm of Pepper and Clements at last opened for business in Tallahassee. Its first employee was Esther Wilfong, who had been an able and a loyal secretary in my former law firm of Waller and Pepper and had remained with Waller in the firm and later when he became a district and circuit court judge. Waller had died in 1945.

I borrowed money to furnish the small office. I had no clients. I felt frustrated, sinking to such a bare-bones existence after my years in the Senate. In my diary, I wrote: "Let the record be clear that after fourteen years as a senator with considerable power I ended that public service borrowing money to pay personal debts and to buy furniture and set up offices at Tallahassee and Washington."

On March 1, 1951, my Washington offices opened. Mildred and Millie Waller helped me select $1,200 worth of furniture on credit and get the offices set up. What we needed now were clients. But wealthy people and business firms already had lawyers, and rank-and-file citizens did not seek out senators to handle their legal problems, fearing I suppose, that their fees

217

would be too high. Little did they know. A surprising number of people who came by did not want the services of a lawyer. They wanted favors, just as they did when I was in the Senate. Had they not heard of my involuntary retirement from that body? Of course they had, but old habits die hard.

With Mildred helping me immeasurably in so many practical ways and being the stout supporter of my morale as she always was, we shuttled between Washington and Tallahassee. Fortunately, a client came in with a $1,000 retainer, my first post-Senate fee. That was heartening. Then Louis Wolfson, who owned the Washington Metro Transit System, gave me a $7,500 retainer to represent the system. But the biggest boost to my financial situation came from Dr. Julius Hyman, a distinguished scientist and the developer and discoverer of the three best known insecticides of that era, aldrin, dieldrin, and chlordane. Dr. Hyman was involved in litigation with a relative who was principal owner of the firm where the scientist had discovered the insecticides. The two disagreed over how large a share of the proceeds from the discoveries should go to Dr. Hyman. He paid me a $25,000 cash fee to represent him.

Since Jim Clements was too ill to play any role in the firm, I began to look around for partners. I found a good one, a young lawyer working in the appeals division of the Internal Revenue Service. As a tax lawyer, Thomas LeFevre was perfect for the Washington office, and he accepted my rash guarantee of a salary of $8,500 a year. His salary and Millie Waller's, rental costs, travel and living expenses, and trying to pay for the furniture demanded a considerable amount of money from me, and income did not rise rapidly enough. For months, Millie Waller spent much of her time trying to fend off furniture dealers demanding payment. I was so discredited from the campaign of 1950 that many Florida businessmen would not come near me. They were turned off by my voting record on minimum wages and by my longtime support for organized labor. To my surprise, labor didn't give me any business, either, because the unions already had their own counsel. I had to fight my way up slowly, and I was determined to do it. I never let the situation get me down; Mildred would not have allowed it even if I had been so inclined. With painful memories of 1950 still fresh, I even told myself, "Maybe I shall not want to run again with all that it entails." But even in a diary entry, I hedged, adding: "Yet I probably will." I didn't *have* to be in public office for the status it bestowed. But I *wanted* to be in a position to legislate for the satisfaction it gave me. Unequaled satisfaction.

I stayed close to politics and political talk, frequently lunching with youthful and still loyal supporters at Florida State University, including the student body president, Rubin Askew.* Many of these young people and other friends urged me to run for senator or governor in 1952. An equal number advised against it. My closest and most loyal political friend and adviser, Jim Clements, was unable to provide his always wise counsel because of his illness.

Although in January I had described myself as being at a "low ebb in Tallahassee and in the state," by mid-February things had brightened a bit: "Feel for the first time I'm going to make money at law practice."

On March 2, I was in Washington getting matters settled in that new office when Jim Clements died in Miami. I rushed there to comfort his family and to speak at his funeral. Jim and I were as close as two men can be. Three and a half decades after his death, I still have a sense of loss.

In early 1952, I opened a law office in downtown Miami in a space being vacated by a friend. I brought in two able young lawyers to join LeFevre and me as partners—John B. Orr, Jr.,

---

*Later a two-term Florida governor and a candidate in 1984 for the Democratic presidential nomination.

a member of a prominent Miami family, and Earl Faircloth, former student body president at the University of Florida. The firm became Pepper, LeFevre, Orr, and Faircloth.

Both in Florida and in Washington, we began to acquire more clients. I must have said something to Mildred that sounded unduly optimistic because she told me she had ordered $300 worth of peat spread on the lawn in Tallahassee. I had to warn her that this declaration of victory over austerity was a bit premature.

Meanwhile, the fortunes of the Truman administration had taken a nosedive. Numerous scandals involving Truman appointees dominated the headlines, and I felt strongly that after twenty years of Democratic rule, the nation was ready for a change. Truman, as unpopular as he had been before his stunning upset victory in 1948, was eligible to run again, having been specifically exempted from terms of the Twenty-second Amendment, barring anyone from being elected president more than twice.* I thought Truman would run—and lose. Despite my devastating 1950 defeat, labor leaders and others were urging me to run in 1952 against Senator Spessard Holland, a fine gentleman but a reactionary with a dismal record. I agreed that it would be a service to Florida and the nation to remove Holland from the Senate, but I hoped someone else would do it. I needed more time to build up my law practice and to get on my feet financially. Things were just beginning to go well, but I knew the process would take years.

In no sense was this hiatus period an exile. Mildred and I

---

*My House colleague, Representative Charles Rangel of New York, regaled a group of Democrats flying to Florida for a fund-raiser in 1986 by noting that had I been Roosevelt's running mate in 1944, I would have become president in 1945 "and Claude Pepper might still be president." He was technically correct in that the exemption would have applied to me as it did to Truman. But it is unlikely that the nation would keep the same president for forty-one years, or that any human being could survive four decades in that demanding job. Rangel, of course, was joking.

made many trips back and forth to Washington, maintaining friendships and contacts. As already noted, we kept the Washington apartment and the family home in Tallahassee; after I opened the third law office in Miami, we had an apartment there, moving later to a lovely Spanish-style home in Coral Gables with a swimming pool.

We did not spend those dozen years bemoaning our fate and lusting to return to public life. There was a considerable downside to that period of our lives, but Mildred and I were much too busy to indulge in self-pity. The downside included growing older, of course, not just ourselves but our loved ones, particularly Mildred's parents and my mother, who suffered a heart attack and several other illnesses that left her frail but uncomplaining. Especially hard on Mama was a charge of jury tampering lodged against my brother Joe, who pleaded guilty and served sixty days in jail. We were afraid that would kill Mama, but she faced up bravely. Joe, too, was very manful about his act, which was more a mistake than a crime. He resisted efforts for a reprieve or pardon, saying he wanted to atone. He served his time and soon rejoined the rest of the family in our special pew at church, which we attended faithfully whenever I was in Tallahassee. My brother Frank and his family and my sister Sara and her children always joined us.

My spirits reached a low ebb one night in May 1954 when I wrote in my diary: "Last night I had some bad thoughts about my situation, financial and political. I have never admitted the word or thought failure in the lexicon of my thinking. And I do not, but the startling thought strikes me occasionally that it might be possible. Yet it will take quite a lot to get me down and with God's help I shall not be downed." My mood probably was affected by the fact we had to close a small law office we had opened in Daytona Beach for lack of business.

Then a fuss arose over my appointment to the board of the American Cancer Institute, which as a senator I had been instrumental in founding. Three doctors resigned because, they said, I supported "socialized medicine," which was untrue because national health insurance is not socialized medicine. When more resignations followed, I withdrew as a director. I also was forced to reduce the size of the Washington office, where overhead was running more than $100,000 a year. I considered a number of options to the practice of law. A group planning a world's fair in Miami asked me to become president. Labor friends wanted me to become head of a government workers union. I was offered the presidency of the Miami Beach Hotel Association at $50,000 per year ("Not bad!" I told my diary), and later a client said he would pay me $250,000 a year to run an insurance company. But I cherished the independence of practicing law and the freedom it gave me to return to politics some day if I so desired.

Our lives were not all that different from the Senate years. We attended events such as presidential inaugurations and luncheons and dinners with old friends. I made dozens of speeches to various groups, chiefly in Florida but occasionally in Washington and elsewhere in the country. I had many invitations from various organizations, labor unions, Democratic groups, and civic clubs such as Lions, Rotary, and Kiwanis.* I was close to and able to help my family financially and in other ways. On the advice of my doctors, I gave up alcohol during this period—at least for a time; I never did use it very much. More and more, Mildred and I regretted that we did not have any children. During the early years of our marriage, we didn't want children because we were both so involved in our careers.

---

*Although I had been a member of Kiwanis since 1925, serving as lieutenant governor for the Western Division of Florida and once addressing an international convention, I was turned down in 1953 when I tried to join the Downtown Kiwanis Club of Miami. Some person or persons continued to blackball me until 1986 when, under the sponsorship of George Smathers, I was admitted.

Since Mildred was in her mid-thirties and I was in my late thirties when we married, the childbearing period passed very quickly. We enjoyed our nieces and nephews, some of whom stayed with us for brief periods, but we regretted that we did not have a son attending law school and a lovely daughter reaching maturity.

Inevitably, over the course of these dozen years, I would encounter my old nemesis Ed Ball. The first time was in 1955 when I took a client to see Ray Green, then Florida's state controller. Ball was in Green's office, and: "He and I chatted about age and health. . . . I said, 'Ed, we are growing old and should stop fighting.' He said, 'You threw a brick at me without cause and I threw one at you.' I said, 'You threw a brick at me in '44 without cause.' Ball and I walked out together, Alphonse and Gastoning at the door as to who should lead." We talked more and I found him to be the same small and vindictive person toward anyone who ever opposed him that he always had been. I told him he had worked hard and should retire and have fun. "He said he had always had fun. The only fun he knows is making money, eating, and drinking. (He said fun is exercising power.) I told him a story. He laughed and we called each other by first names as we separated." The second meeting occurred in 1962 when I suggested we fight someone else and stop fighting each other. He agreed and we shook hands cordially. That is the incident I prefer to remember in thinking back on Ed Ball.

In 1957, Mildred and I traveled abroad, sailing on the *Queen Elizabeth* to London where we attended events associated with the American Bar Association Convention. We also went to a garden party at Buckingham Palace and traveled on to Paris, Rome (where we had an audience with the Pope), Madrid, and Lisbon. Several months after our return I ran into former President Truman and former Secretary of State Dean Acheson at the Mayflower Hotel in Washington. Truman invited me to his room, where we discussed President Eisenhower's drop in popularity and his detachment, after several bouts with illness, from the presidency. I volunteered the thought that Truman, if interested, might be able to win the presidency again. His response was simply to say that he was six or seven years older than Eisenhower, which I took to mean he felt he was too old for the job. (Truman was seventy-four in 1958, two years younger than Ronald Reagan in 1987.)

Mildred and I enjoyed a full social life during the hiatus years, in Washington, Miami, and to a lesser degree, Tallahassee. There were always visitors coming through, and we had many close friends in all three cities.* I headed a Muscular Dystrophy fund-raising drive in Florida and also led the United Fund drive in Miami Beach. I participated in panel discussions on many topics, including the problems of old age. Mildred kept her membership in the Women's National Democratic Club, and we belonged to the Army and Navy Club in Washington as well.

One of the many visitors we entertained in Miami was Eleanor Roosevelt, who came to the city for a public address at a forum sponsored by the Washington Federal Savings and Loan Association, of which I was an officer. In 1960 we invited a number of guests to join Mrs. Roosevelt and us at our home in Coral Gables. She was upset at the time because the State Department had turned down her request to visit China. After the department refused to issue a visa to her, the Chinese, following suit, she thought, refused to admit her. She spoke freely about her late husband, insisting that President Roosevelt "had no premonition of death at all. She agreed with what Churchill had told me, that his mental faculties were in full, unimpaired

* In December 1958, I noted that we went to a party given "by the Ernest Grahams honoring their son, Robert, and his bride-to-be." As Bob Graham, that son served two terms as governor of Florida and in 1986 was elected to my old seat in the United States Senate.

force at Yalta.'' Later we attended a UN dinner with her. And Frank Sinatra, who sang after dinner, came over and sat at our table. "She was not particularly talkative with him, I thought. She was very friendly to Mildred and me—the most friendly she has been since I left the Senate."

The period from 1951 through 1962 was, as I look back, in many ways strikingly similar to the 1980s. We were worried about Communist takeovers in Latin America, particularly in Guatemala and Nicaragua; Communists were gaining the upper hand in Indochina ("Maybe we shall draw the line somewhere, some time," I wrote). In South Africa, whites were killing blacks. In the Middle East, one crisis followed another, the major one being Nasser's seizure of the Suez Canal, bringing France and Great Britain to the brink of war. Many people, famous or infamous, died during that period—Stalin, succeeded at first by Malenkov; Joe McCarthy; Adolf Eichmann (hanged); Marilyn Monroe; Eleanor Roosevelt. The Fifth Amendment was under attack during this terrorized period of McCarthyism. In a television debate, I defended the amendment "and insisted that all persons charged with crime or suspected should be given their constitutional rights . . . in this time of hysteria about communism, many forget that if we lose our constitutional rights we have lost the battle for liberty under law." My old friend Hugo Black, an ardent defender of the Fifth Amendment, came to Miami and at lunch said he felt "deeply that the present trend is away from the American way and the Constitution and bodes ill for the future."

In those years the space age began in both the Soviet Union and the United States. I wrote: "The headline is the President's approval of a project for the U.S. to build a satellite to revolve around the earth. It is to be about the size of a basketball but will be visible at twilight. It will run for a period of days and return to the atmosphere to be destroyed. It will course 250 miles above the earth. This is the first man-made satellite we think, though the Russians claim to have one under way. A momentous event!" To someone who had met one of the Wright brothers, the venture into space had very special meaning.

Two major developments during these years foreshadowed long-range crises to come. One was the Egyptian seizure of the Suez Canal, which underscored Western Europe's dependence on Middle Eastern oil; the other was Castro's rise to power in Cuba, giving communism its first major foothold in the Western Hemisphere. President Eisenhower handled Suez about as well as it could be handled. From my diary: "President Eisenhower said to be following a bold new course of wooing the Arabs against the Russians, even against Britain and France . . . but this may be wisdom as that is key area and the Arabs are the key there. [But] what's to be done about Suez and dependence upon Middle East oil? West Europe is at the mercy of Nasser—really Russia. Yet an alternative is hard to find." As to Cuba, I have always felt that we should have enforced the Monroe Doctrine and kept communism, which spreads like weeds, from being planted on this continent and hemisphere. In the 1980s, many of my fellow liberals attribute my support for anti-Communist forces in Angola and Nicaragua to my growing Cuban constituency, or to over correcting the "soft on communism" label wrongly acquired in the campaign of 1950. That is wrong. I have been consistently anti-Communist all my life, even though I saw, earlier than most, that we would have to find a way to live with the Soviet Union.

The 1950s and early 1960s were, of course, years of the Cold War. With their customary brutality, the Soviets put down uprisings in Poland and Hungary. Nikita Khrushchev eventually emerged as Stalin's successor, attended UN sessions in New York, and acted as if he had taken leave of his senses, shouting and yelling speeches and even banging on a desk with his shoe. His forces shot down a U-2 spy plane and captured its pilot,

Gary Powers; when the president denied that we had any spy planes over Russia, Khrushchev produced Powers. Later he stalked out of a summit meeting with Eisenhower. Cheered by Castro's success in Cuba, the Soviets supplied him with funds, food, planes, and weapons; in August 1960 Raul Castro, Fidel's brother and foreign minister, delivered a three-hour speech on the close friendship between Cuba and the Soviet Union. As the military buildup in Cuba continued, the Soviet foreign minister, Andrei Gromyko, warned in a speech at the UN that an attack on Cuba by the United States "means war." From my diary: "I made speech emphasizing we should put naval and air blockade around Cuba, not let the buildup interfere with Cape Canaveral, and continue our resolve to get rid of Castro and Communism as aggressor in Cuba." In the end, of course, came the Bay of Pigs disaster and the Cuban missile crisis, the latter brilliantly handled by President Kennedy, who must share with President Eisenhower the blame for the failure of the former.

The major domestic issue of the times was segregation. It affected everything—adversely: people's lives, politics, education, law enforcement. In my first year out of public life, there was one bubble of hope, which quickly burst. The Florida Student Government Association adopted a resolution opposing segregation in institutions of higher learning. The University of Florida promptly withdrew from the association. And the state house of representatives, which in 1929 had condemned Mrs. Herbert Hoover for inviting a black congressman's wife to the White House, loudly and with much cheering passed a bill withdrawing state funds from all state institutions if the Supreme Court prohibited segregation. "Such is democracy in the country claiming to save the world for democracy," I wrote in disgust. In a talk with an ignorant, albeit typical, Southern sheriff named Bill Towles, I was appalled to hear him say that he had promised to resign his office if a single

Negro voted during his term. He even asked me if I had ever shaken hands with a Negro. He knew damned well that I had.

May 17, 1954, was a day that the South, and much of the North, had long feared. I wrote: "Well, it has come. The Supreme Court has determined segregation in the schools must go and over-ruled the old "separate but equal" facilities doctrine. The time for it taking effect is still open and the manner of enforcement also. It will allow time for plans and adjustment. But Talmadge and Holland sound off and there will be much sound and fury. I fear the effect may be to keep liberals out of office in the South a long time as every demagogue will jump on this issue." A day later:

> Reactions are more violent re. Supreme Court antisegregation decision. Some threaten not to follow it; others denounce the court. Time for working out compliance will ease the strain but the demagogues will be busy. Some commendable public statements have been made by officials . . . mournful statement by Lister Hill re. the court and the segregation question. I wonder what Sparkman has said. They have never dared to take the liberal position regarding race. Sparkman's repudiation of the Democratic platform in his last race precludes him from national nomination.

The end to the "separate but equal" doctrine handed down in *Brown* v. *Board of Education* would change the face of the nation. It was one of the most important court decisions ever. From the start, the difficulties to come were easily discerned. On September 20, 1954, I attended a lunch of the Florida Bar Association and heard Eugene Coole, attorney general of Georgia, speak on the court decision. He was anything but "cool." I wrote: "An awful exhibition of reactionary and bigoted

Southern thinking . . . the sentiment in Georgia is no doubt nearly solid for continued segregation. How will the problem be solved? Yet this is less drastic than slavery being abolished. Still that was by war and by a President. I understand the prejudice but I deplore it."

In 1956, a young black woman sought admission to the University of Alabama, my alma mater. She was turned away in the first of several such incidents, all of them accompanied by varying degrees of violence. That same year, a young black man was admitted to the University of Florida law school, which prompted the governor to announce that he would argue personally an appeal of the Supreme Court ruling. A "manifesto" opposing the ruling was signed by nineteen senators and ninety-five congressmen. In Tallahassee, one of my hometowns, blacks were boycotting the bus system. In September, I wrote: "Many riots in Tennessee and Texas on integration. But militia holding mobs in check and judges (U.S.) issuing injunctions." A day later: "Rioting in Kentucky on integration and militia had to step in to protect the Negro pupils. One must admire those Negro children who will brave such physical threats as well as the unfriendliness they must face from many of the pupils. Yet it is heartening that some pupils refused to leave school upon parents' call and cried out from the windows 'the law is the law.' The children would solve the problem if left alone. They will in the long run."

Millard Caldwell, a former Florida governor, called the Supreme Court "Communist" because of the Brown decision. The home of the editor of the *Miami Herald*, which took a moderate position, was bombed. Eisenhower had to send troops to Arkansas in order to integrate the schools there, and later Kennedy had to dispatch federal marshals to get James Meredith admitted to the University of Mississippi. A modest voting rights bill introduced in the Senate in 1957 drew united Southern opposition: "Russell sounds off in the beginning of the filibuster re. the President's civil rights bill. It is so distasteful to see the whole Southern delegation (now that I'm not there) fight against the bill to ensure general voting rights for Negroes as if it permitted the raping of every woman in the South. When will we grow up?"

It's a good question today, and not only in the South.

By the mid-1950s, my law practice had grown to the point where it was solidly successful. In 1952, I had obtained a charter for what became the Washington Federal Savings and Loan Association. My understanding with the organizers was that my firm would receive one-half of the association's legal business, and as the firm grew and prospered, my fees increased substantially. I was also engaged late in the decade by Abe Zable, a hotel broker from Atlantic City, New Jersey. Zable had heard about two young Jewish men who were running a small kosher hotel in the mountains of New Jersey. He called on them, suggesting they operate the same kind of business at one of the major hotels in Atlantic City. They didn't know how to go about it. Zable promised to handle the details and got them into a major hotel. There was a contract, but the young men refused to honor it. Zable came to me in Miami and asked me to sue Larry and Robert Tisch. I won nearly $1 million in damages and was paid a $400,000 fee. The Tisch brothers went on to own several hotels and the Loews Theater chain, and in 1986 Larry Tisch became chief executive officer of CBS while Robert was named postmaster general of the United States. We became friends, despite the circumstances of our introduction.

But the case that really made us, so to speak, took place in 1955 and 1956. One of my law associates, Don Wilkes, who had worked for the large and prestigious New York firm of Cravath, Swaine, and Moore, telephoned from New York, saying officers of the firm wanted to talk to me about becoming their Florida representative in a huge lawsuit involving their client,

Bethlehem Steel Corporation. A manufacturer of hatch covers for cargo ships was suing Bethlehem and other firms for $40 million, alleging breach of contract. Because the manufacturer failed to produce the hatch covers on time, Bethlehem canceled the contract. The case had been in Federal District Court in Tallahassee for a year, and Cravath, the general counsel, decided to change the Florida representative. Earlier, I had some preliminary talks with attorneys for the plaintiff, Seaboard Company, about handling their case. I feared there might be a conflict, but was assured there was none by Federal Judge Dozier Devane, who was to try the case. Ralph McAfee of Cravath found that Seaboard had not listed me as one of its attorneys, so I was free to hear the best offer of each side and choose. As I recorded in my diary, when McAfee told me "I could fix the fee and it would be okay," I accepted that offer, of course. We agreed that I would be paid $60 an hour, my associates who helped me would be paid $40 an hour, and there would be a $100,000 bonus if we won. I was very emotional about this sudden turnabout in my fortunes and wrote: "I am humbled and grateful that after all the heartaches I have suffered to get established again, I now am apparently about to get on my feet and out of debt and have my office on a sound basis. I thank thee Lord and will try to prove worthy."

The association with the Cravath firm was a happy one. McAfee, the managing partner, and I became close friends. Two associates in the New York office, Allen F. Maulsby and John R. Hupper, were assigned to work with me. When in New York, I used any office that happened to be vacant for the day. We worked day and night, usually dining together, then returning for more work. McAfee and I visited a number of shipyards where the hatch covers were made. I saw how a big law firm operates—to be hired, secretaries had to be able to take dictation at a rate of 250 words per minute. The library had a researcher who could be called day or night to come up with a memorandum on a point of law in very short order. For expenses, one just put down the total, with no need to itemize.

The case came to trial on January 9, 1956. Early on, John Hupper and I became convinced that a key witness had testified falsely. But how to prove it? The testimony involved large amounts of money spent in building hatch covers. We put the figures up on a blackboard and went over them studiously, time and again. One Sunday in the Cravath offices in New York, Hupper was at the blackboard and suddenly he exclaimed, "We've got it! We've got it." He said that we had proved "within three cents" that the witness had falsified the figures. We went through the figures again—the addition, multiplication, subtraction, and the result was always within three cents of our theory. I had to know the figures backward and forward, since I would be cross-examining the witness. We called our theory the "postage stamp theory" because of the three cents involved, the price—then—of a stamp.

In court, I began questioning the witness. The opposing counsel objected, and Judge Dozier Devane said, "I'll have to stop you, Mr. Pepper. I sustain the objection."

I said, "Your Honor, please, I am just beginning my cross-examination of this witness and if you will allow me to continue you will see what I am seeking to show."

Replied the judge, "I have already ruled."

I tried again: "Your Honor, I don't need to argue the merits of cross-examination for revealing the truth in a trial, but, Your Honor, this man is telling a falsehood and if you will allow me to do so, I will prove it to Your Honor and this jury on the blackboard right here in your presence." Judge Devane turned red in the face and said, "This is the first time I have had such defiance by a lawyer. I don't know what I am going to do; the case is recessed for lunch."

We were dumbfounded. We could establish that testimony

was false, but the judge would not allow us to. I offered to resign from the case because the judge apparently was prejudiced against me. If he disciplined me, that would prejudice the case. McAfee said, "Let's go on to lunch and we'll think about it." We were joined by a former president of the Florida bar. I told the two of them that when court resumed, I would be willing to apologize to the judge in case I had inadvertently and unintentionally offended him; that I need not again assure His Honor of my great respect and my long friendship; that although I was obliged to represent my client to the best of my ability, I would never knowingly do anything to offend His Honor. The former bar president told the judge what I planned to say, and he responded that if I did, the case could continue, but I would not be allowed to resume my line of questioning. In my opinion, this was one of the key turning points in the case. The jurors, most of whom knew me personally, knew that I would not say I could prove false testimony unless I was prepared to do so. My comment that so offended the judge probably won the case.

In my summation, I told the jurors that although I was a liberal in politics as many of them knew, I thought Bethlehem as a big-business firm had treated little Seaboard with great fairness. Then I made my final point: "The plaintiff says the defendant formed an evil conspiracy to perpetrate a wrong upon this plaintiff. If this defendant conceived such a conspiracy, when did it begin?" I went through the record showing that Bethlehem time after time had virtually begged Seaboard to perform the contract, until finally the company had to cancel it. "Where was the evidence of conspiracy?" I cried. The jury did not deliberate long. Its verdict: "Not guilty." After three months, suddenly it was over. My firm earned a fee of $300,000, and Cravath appointed me its chief Florida counsel. As such, I represented the Westinghouse Company, Time Inc., and other Cravath clients until I went to the House of Representatives in

233

1963. Friendships formed with Cravath personnel have lasted to this day, although my closest friend, Ralph McAfee, tragically died in 1986. I was privileged to read the lesson at his funeral service and to renew my association with Allen Maulsby and John Hupper. Maulsby is now the senior partner of Cravath, Swaine, and Moore and my "postage stamp" partner, John Hupper, is not far behind.

Caught up as I obviously was in the practice of law, there still was something gnawing at my innards. In the midst of the exciting Bethlehem case, I made this confession: "I find myself so occupied with this Bethlehem case that I think less and less of politics. Yet I know loving law as I do that my best service can be rendered in politics. That's where I belong. I wish the next campaign were further away." This was written in March 1956. In 1956, George Smathers was up for reelection.

Almost from the day I left the Senate, even during those chaotic days when I labored to get a chair and a desk and an office, supporters pressured me to run for either senator or governor. Some, dismayed by Spessard Holland's attitude on race and his conservatism, argued that it was my "duty" to run, even if I lost. Deep down, I knew I probably could not win; in any event, I had to do something immediate about my financial situation. Still, I did not dismiss the possibility out of hand. I believed I could survive any attempt to renew the Red issue, but on race I would have to change or be extremely vulnerable. "What makes me hesitate," I wrote on September 23, 1951, "is the position I would be forced into on the race issue. I don't want to have to take an un-American position."

An option I had once considered—moving to New York and running there in a climate more hospitable to my views—was suggested again by a friend, A. J. Paul. When I was next in New York, I took this idea seriously enough that I accepted a long-standing open invitation to have lunch with Cardinal Spellman. He was conservative, I knew, but I wondered if he thought I could get some of the huge Catholic vote in New York. He was blunt. "He said he thought I would better stay in my own state; that there were tough problems in New York; that he imagined there could be jealousy in New York by those who might be passed over by a newcomer. I don't know whether this was honest advice or whether it represented an indication the Irish Catholics of New York would not be for me." It had always been a wacky idea; an Alabama accent was not likely to go over big in the Bronx or Brooklyn, or even in Manhattan.

On a trip to Washington, I arranged an appointment with President Truman. Happily, my trip coincided with a speech to the Senate by Winston Churchill, now showing his age but still a commanding figure and gallant personality. I marveled at his oratorical skills, which remained largely intact. From my diary: "He wore morning coat, striped trousers, polka-dot bow tie, white shirt and soft rolled collar and French cuffs; big watch chain on vest. No wrist watch for him."

At 4:00 P.M., I was received by the president. He was cheerful and looked well.

> Wanted me to run against Holland.* Said Chairman McKinney** had interviewed 31 Democratic senators, and Holland was the only one that was severe in his opposition to and criticism of the President. The President said he would help me every way he could and so would the Democratic National Committee. He said, however, he wanted me to run for what I felt I wanted. Said he had wanted to be gov-

---

*This further undermines Smathers's claim that Truman prevailed on him to beat "that son of a bitch, Claude Pepper."

**Frank McKinney, chairman of the Democratic National Committee.

ernor of Missouri . . . when I asked him confidentially if he were going to run, he said all he had achieved he owed to the Democratic Party and he would not let the party down, but he would give his right arm to be able to get someone else. Said he wanted to go back to the Senate. Said he never regretted anything more than my defeat in '50. To Democratic National Committee and talks with India Edwards and Chairman McKinney. They said if the President approved, they would help me all possible.

But the following day the president injected a note of caution. Through India Edwards, the DNC's vice-chairwoman, he sent word that he did not want to see me defeated again. He repeated his promise to help, but I gathered that McKinney and Edwards had probably told him that I could not defeat Holland. Amid all the conflicting advice and pressures, one factor kept emerging: my terrible financial position. I owed several thousand dollars; not all office salaries had been paid. Albert Lasker, who along with his wife Mary was interested in my political career because I had been effective in health legislation, urged me not to run, arguing that another defeat might end my political career.

I wrote in my diary on January 26, 1952:

In my den with Joe and Frank, Tom, Jack and Earl* present, I told them I did not want to be governor and since there was so much defeatism about Holland among my friends and we knew his crowd had so much money I would just stay out of any race this year and get myself in a better economic situation before I struck again. They all agreed, though Joe

*My brothers and my law partners.

236

and Frank with some tears. I got Esther out with
typewriter, got quiet in living room with her and with
several proposed statements before me, dictated a
statement. Allen Morris, Stan Cawthorn, Loyal
Courtney, Tom, Jack and Earl, Joe and Frank, and
Mildred all present for the revision. It went to press
room at 4 P.M. Frank read it on WTNT at 4, Mama
and several of us listening. Tears from some. It was
over for the present. We shall see what Providence
has decreed.

I felt much relieved.

On Saint Valentine's Day, Mildred and I attended a reception for President and Mrs. Truman at the Women's Congressional Club. He told me he thought I had made the right
decision under the circumstances. Four days later, I made another decision that would profoundly affect my future. I opened
a third law office, in Miami. Had I not done so, it is entirely
possible that I would never have had the opportunity to serve
in the House of Representatives, where I have served the Miami
area for twenty-four years—and counting. Once again I had
taken a step that I really could not afford, but Miami was such
a booming area that I felt if I ever was going to make some
money from the practice of law, I would have to be in a position to share in the large and growing Miami market.

My temporary exit from politics did not foreclose my interest
in it. Richard Russell of Georgia announced that he was a candidate for president, although he had no prospect of winning
any votes outside the South. President Truman still had not
made his intentions clear, but I thought he would run and
probably defeat the likely Republican nominee, Senator Robert Taft of Ohio. But if General Eisenhower should upset Taft,
all bets were off. Russell, a decent person, was the Dixiecrats'
cat's-paw in a renewed effort to rid the party of Truman. On

237

making his announcement, Russell was asked the inevitable question: Should Truman beat him out for the nomination, would he support the president in the election? Russell refused to say. Harry Byrd and Jimmy Byrnes were manipulating Russell. That their efforts could help elect a Republican president did not concern them.

Russell telephoned, asking my support in the Florida primary, and friends urged me to give it to him since he had no chance to be nominated and I could shore up my standing with Southern politicians by backing a Southerner. Truman would not be on the ballot in Florida. Meanwhile, Senator Estes Kefauver of Tennessee defeated Truman in the New Hampshire primary. In Maine, write-in votes for Eisenhower came close to beating Stassen, the only name on the ballot. On March 20, I noted: "Taft withdraws from New Jersey primary. Eisenhower intimates he will come back to campaign, taking the offensive. Taft seems licked and Eisenhower the next President." Ten days later, Truman announced he would not accept renomination. "His decision was wise for him and the country," I wrote.

While I was trying to decide whom to support, some interesting political byplay occurred in Florida. Drew Pearson wrote in his syndicated column that Smathers had encouraged me to run against Holland. When other reporters descended on me, I confirmed the report. When Smathers denied what he knew was true, I told reporters, "Since he [Smathers] had stabbed me in the back, I wasn't surprised that he was ready to stab Senator Holland in the back." It was a front-page story in all the major newspapers.

Shortly afterward, Senator Paul Douglas of Illinois and his wife, Emily, dined with Mildred and me. Douglas was convinced that Adlai Stevenson wanted the nomination, especially if the Republicans nominated Taft. Douglas preferred Kefauver, but doubted that he could win. He said he wanted to see a Southern president. When I suggested that the party could do worse than turn to Douglas, who was certainly capable of being president, he refused to hear of it. He was supporting Kefauver and did not want there to be any conflict. He also thought that if Averell Harriman, Barkley, Kefauver, and Stevenson all stumbled, Truman would accept a draft. But I think that India Edwards,* who was closer to Truman, had a better reading on his situation—he would not accept a draft because of Mrs. Truman, if for no other reason, Edwards said a day later.

After a fair imitation of Hamlet, Stevenson agreed to accept the nomination, and with Truman's backing, he won it easily. His running mate was Senator John Sparkman of Alabama,** who used to toil alongside me from four to seven in the morning at the University of Alabama power plant. I thought the ticket too conservative and the platform too vague, purposely drafted that way to appease the South. But what about the large urban centers of the North? It was an unhappy time for the Democrats. Stevenson tried to distance himself from the unpopular Truman, and the president resented it. At one point, Stevenson even referred to "the mess in Washington," employing the phrase that was the Republicans' campaign theme. Truman was furious. Then Sparkman opined publicly that the administration had mishandled the steel strike, during which Truman illegally seized control of the mills.

But Stevenson's biggest problem was the nomination of Eisenhower by the Republicans. Stevenson could have beaten Taft; probably no one could have beaten Eisenhower. For a brief period, Eisenhower's running mate, Senator Richard Nixon of California, gave Democrats some hope. Nixon was found to

---

*Interestingly, Truman offered to appoint India Edwards as chairwoman of the Democratic National Committee. She declined on the ground that men would not work for a woman in the top job.

**Sparkman was handpicked by Truman, not Stevenson.

have an $18,000 slush fund provided by wealthy backers; the scandal almost cost him his place on the ticket. That would have ended his political career, and the country would have been the better for it. On September 23, Nixon delivered his famous "Checkers" speech. I wrote: "[It] was the cleverest demagogic ham I've seen. It was almost frightening to think how dangerous he is and what a reception he got with it. It was full of holes but they were cleverly concealed." Nearly everyone was fooled, even Eisenhower, who kept him on the ticket. Eisenhower was a very tolerant man. He even spent a day campaigning in Wisconsin with, of all people, Joe Mc-Carthy. On November 4, it was a landslide for Eisenhower and Nixon, and the Republicans also won control of the House and Senate. I worried: "If Eisenhower just lives and we don't get Nixon, as I fear we may; Eisenhower should have loved his country too much to risk that, whatever the political advantage. . . . Nixon is a bad egg and Eisenhower will rue the day he ever accepted him to use the communist smear against Stevenson. I foresee he will disgrace the administration as Vice-President and the country should, God forbid, he become President." Well, my time frame was a bit off here, but my character analysis, unhappily, was right on target.

Early in 1954, friends urged me to run for Congress. The notion had struck me years earlier when I was still in the Senate and becoming frustrated over Florida's increasing conservatism. I had always done well in liberal Dade County and now I had a law office and apartment in Miami, the county's metropolis. Once I had dismissed the thought, believing a former senator would not be happy in the House. Well, I had to ask myself: Do you want to be in government for the prestige, or so you can accomplish good things? The answer was the latter. But in 1954 I was still saddled with debt, so I set the thought aside for another day. It bothered me to be out of Congress. I felt like an athlete benched when he was at the peak of his game. I had to watch the players on the field, knowing I could do better than many of them if only I could get back in the game. Joe McCarthy was riding high, destroying careers and lives, yet for a time no one in the Senate had the guts to take him on. To do so was to invite him to direct his invective on oneself. Even President Eisenhower was cowed. I longed to be in the Senate to do battle with McCarthy and all that he represented, and I know I would have done so, no matter the political cost. "What is to be done with this new Caesar?" I wrote in my diary, "since all run from him."* I could not run for anything, however, in 1954.

Adlai Stevenson came to Miami that year to address a Jefferson-Jackson dinner. The following morning, Mildred suggested that I call him. I did and he invited us to come to his room for what turned out to be some fascinating conversation:

> He asked what I was going to do and I told him I thought I would run in '56 for Senate. Could spend my last years, I thought, most usefully in public service. He listened intently. I reminded him I was the first victim of the McCarthy technique. We complimented his speech. I told him I was organizing the Democratic Party from bottom up with young men and thought we would control delegation in '56 and be for him for the Presidential nomination. He said for the four walls only I could not support him for he would not be a candidate; that he had wanted to be governor again; that he had seen what was forthcoming; that in a way the Democrats deserved to lose to clean up some things and to let the people see the

---

*When the Senate finally condemned McCarthy, he predictably labeled the chairman of the committee that investigated him, Senator Arthur V. Watkins of Utah, an "unwitting handmaiden of the Communist Party." Watkins, a conservative Mormon, lost his bid for reelection.

falsity of the G.O.P. claims; that he thought the Democrats would come back if things didn't get too bad (I suppose he meant if the McCarthy crowd didn't take over). I told him he would have to accept the nomination again for there was no one else capable of leading; that some effort was being made to get Symington and [John F.] Kennedy on a ticket but this no good; that he was in it now and would have to bear the ordeal which would not be like now. He listened with heavy heart, it seemed. He said he had to spend hours on his speeches—it was a labor.

Stevenson's speeches were always first-rate, and I'm sure he did not exaggerate the difficulty of writing them. In fact, one of his weaknesses as a candidate was that he neglected other aspects of politicking to work on his speeches.

In Washington, two senators, braver than their colleagues, spoke out against McCarthy. Both Republicans, they were Ralph Flanders of Vermont and Margaret Chase Smith of Maine. Flanders said that McCarthy's sideshow was diverting attention from the real fight against communism, and wrecking the Republican party as well. Surprisingly, President Eisenhower said he approved of Flanders's comments. At last two senators of conscience had taken the risk of being trampled by McCarthy; their doing so had smoked out the president and would lead to McCarthy's disgrace and downfall, though McCarthyism would live on through the years.

By 1955, much of the Florida electorate was anticipating a rematch between Pepper and Smathers. In Washington one day I had lunch with Bobby Baker, secretary to the Senate majority, who later became enmeshed in a scandal that sent him to prison. But he was a powerful person in 1955 because he was so close to Senate Majority Leader Lyndon Johnson. From my diary:

Baker says Smathers very close to Lyndon Johnson and votes with Democrats when they really need him; that Smathers is Johnson's intermediary to conservative Democrats and [Hubert] Humphrey to the liberal Democrats; that the three really are the leaders of the strategy board. A commentary on the times. That Johnson dislikes Holland who has hardly any Democratic friends in Senate due to his arrogance and voting with Republicans; that he is sure Johnson would raise money for Smathers against me, but for me against Holland. . . . This raises the question I have considered as to whether I should oppose Smathers or Holland. Holland is the real machine menace because he is becoming the Byrd of Florida while Smathers will never be a power to influence things much.

As always, there was conflicting advice. Joseph Davies, the former ambassador to Russia, told me at lunch that he and I, so "pilloried" for our views on Russia, were now being vindicated by events. The nation was shocked when President Eisenhower suffered a coronary thrombosis, which inevitably led to speculation he would not run in 1956, which would help all Democrats. In September there was a hopeful sign from the Republican state of Maine that I noted in my diary: "Maine elected Democrat as governor: Muskie." And a man who had been one of Smathers's top ten campaign officials in Okaloosa County in 1950 told me that "none would support him now and only two would speak to the son of a bitch." I talked with Billy Graham during one of his visits to Florida and he was encouraging, saying he had noticed that "Claude Pepper always fights for the little man."

In December, I decided to talk with Lyndon Johnson. "Had long talk with Lyndon Johnson by phone . . . he said Smathers had just visited him. . . . Smathers said he had been campaigning, wouldn't be able to help much in Senate until after election. Smathers more interested in his [Johnson's] personal success than Holland. Smathers voted with Johnson more than Holland did. Johnson would not 'underwrite' a Smathers commitment" not to oppose me if I ran in 1958 against Holland and not against Smathers in 1956. But the majority leader said he believed Smathers would say no more than that he'd vote for Holland in 1958. Johnson said he had been "devoted" to me for a long time and would not feel any "displeasure" toward me should I run against his friend Smathers. If I did, he said he would take no part in the primary.

In January 1956, Stevenson called. When I told him the situation, he advised that I wait for Holland. In February Smathers announced his candidacy, and in March he let me know that he would not help Holland in 1958 but would assist me if I ran. I wrote: "Would like to forget the past and be friendly with me and work with me; that he would assist me when he could in Washington. Smathers is not dependable and not intellectually honest but self-interest and vanity will induce him to keep this bargain." Labor, I believed, would enforce this commitment. "Labor is his weakest front and my strongest. If he double-crosses it, labor will be more embittered against him in the future, and it seems that this is the best arrangement for me under the circumstances. After all, Holland is the real power in the state now. Break that and we can regain the state for democracy and the people. Smathers can be taken care of later if he does not show himself worthy of confidence." So Smathers, without a major opponent, won overwhelmingly, so much so that I was moved to comment: "Maybe I was fortunate not to be able to get into race this year." I turned my attention to the presidential election.

Stevenson, as I had foreseen, was nominated again. Kefauver had withdrawn in his favor. In August, I wrote: "Kefauver probably second place on ticket, though it might be Kennedy." Stevenson threw open the nomination, and Kefauver barely defeated Kennedy, who got his first major national exposure. As an alternate delegate, I spoke for Kefauver. But the ticket was foredoomed. Eisenhower, like Roosevelt before him and Ronald Reagan after, was a candidate who could win regardless of problems of health and age that would sink a less magnetic personality.

In 1957, I received some advice that I should have followed: "Nelson Poynter said Holland unbeatable and he didn't want me to run; to wait and run from new Dade district in '60." Elsewhere, there were more encouraging signs. "Mr. Proxmire won Senate seat from Wisconsin for first time for a Democrat in 25 years. He a liberal, 41 years old, who had lost twice to same opponent running for governor. It looks like a Democratic liberal trend in 1958 and '60. Seems a good augury for us." But it only seemed so. In June 1958, I announced my candidacy for the Senate. In the fall, I lost to Spessard Holland, who received 408,084 votes to my 321,377, not a bad showing but a defeat nonetheless. I made no attempt to raise money. Holland had a huge campaign chest. I went $90,000 into debt, every penny of it paid from my law office earnings over the next few years. "The campaign cost me terribly. It will take me some time to pay out. But I have no regrets. I did my best and I fought a decent fight." Some of my friends had borrowed money in their own names, and after I lost, immediate repayment was demanded. Some of them couldn't pay, so I paid for them. At the end of the year, I wrote: "The moral debt was mine and I have honored it." One great advantage grew out of this campaign—I carried Dade County (where Miami is located) by 25,000 votes. This was a factor in my decision to run for the House from a new district created in time for the election of 1962. Goodwill from my losing effort helped me win in the first primary.

Early in 1960 it seemed inevitable that Nixon would be the Republican nominee for president. The Democratic front-runner was Senator John F. Kennedy, but I could not see him gaining the nomination. In February, Kennedy made clear he would not accept the vice-presidential nomination, and there were reports the top spot was "within his grasp." "Not so," I wrote. "It will be Stevenson or Symington. I hope the former." Kennedy called me for advice about the Florida primary. "He said he thought he could not beat Smathers if he ran as a favorite son, especially on account of the race issue. He was a friend of Smathers; thought Smathers was really for Johnson on account of the pressures there . . . thought running against a favorite son in South different from West." On a visit to Florida, former President Truman told me he thought "Jack was a nice fellow but he had never liked his daddy." In March, Gardner Cowles, publisher of *Look* magazine, told me he thought Kennedy would win the nomination. "He will not," I wrote. But Kennedy seemed to be getting all the attention:

> Joe Timulty of Boston and Miami Beach, close friend of Joe Kennedy and his family, talked a lot about Joe who said he should take all bets he can get on Jack Kennedy. Joe first tried to see Truman here and Truman told the intermediary to say he couldn't contact him. Later Truman indicated he would like to see Joe and he refused, saying "what's the use—he's against us." Said Joe fell out with Roosevelt because the President brought up about Joe having a mistress in London; Joe was angry and protested this invasion of his personal affairs and seemed to infer (I understood) something about Roosevelt's personal affairs. [Timulty] said Mrs. Roosevelt told him she could always tell when Joe Kennedy was in Washington by the way the President acted.

Well, Joe Kennedy's son was a lot more charming than Joe was. He won the Wisconsin primary, defeating Hubert Humphrey, who blamed his loss on Catholic Republicans crossing over to vote for Kennedy and vowed to recoup in Protestant West Virginia. Meanwhile, I had decided to support Stevenson again and told him that I expected him to be drafted. "He asked if I seriously thought that was possible. I told him it was probable and would occur about the fifth ballot, I thought. I told him I went on the [Florida] delegation to help his nomination. He warmly thanked me for keeping on as his friend after so many years. I told him we must beat Nixon and he said at all events—'that terrible fellow'."

In May, I recorded: "Kennedy scores smashing victory in West Virginia, gaining 60 percent of the vote. While he spent a great deal of money and was obviously the only real candidate of the two, yet his success is considered a refutation of the religious issue as a bar to the nomination. Yet I think he will not be nominated." He was having difficulty making a believer of me. In June, when Kennedy said he was "positive" he would be the nominee, I wrote: "No." Eleanor Roosevelt visited us at our home in Miami. She wanted a ticket of Stevenson and Kennedy, in that order. It would win, she insisted. "If Kennedy the nominee, she thought he could win but it would not be as certain as if Stevenson headed the ticket." My old friend, Averell Harriman, gave me a tip. He urged me to switch my support to Kennedy because he would win and I would have entrée.

As an alternate delegate, I went to the Los Angeles convention with Mildred. Smathers headed the delegation and was committed to Lyndon Johnson. Convinced now that Stevenson could not make it, and more and more impressed by Kennedy, I tried to persuade some of the delegates to back him. Our suite was near Kennedy's, and I saw him often. I told him that he had supporters in the Florida delegation, but Smathers was insisting they stay with Johnson until the last vote was counted. It was odd—Kennedy and Smathers were close personal friends, and Joe Kennedy had given $150,000 to Smathers's campaign in 1950. Kennedy told me: "I can't do a thing with him." As it turned out, Kennedy didn't need him. Despite an emotional show of support for Stevenson,* Kennedy won on the first ballot. Johnson went nowhere. But Kennedy wisely chose him as his running mate, despite opposition from labor and liberals and even Bobby Kennedy.

In the first Kennedy-Nixon debate in September, I knew the party had chosen well. "Kennedy got the better of it in striking and intelligent appearance, quick grasp of issues, and able and fluent speech." Southern Democratic governors, who had been distancing themselves from this Catholic candidate, were convinced. They endorsed him. He defeated Nixon in an election that should not have been so close and would not have been, in my opinion, but for the religious issue now happily dispelled.

Following the census of 1960, a new congressional district was carved out in Dade County and I was urged to run for the seat by the state AFL-CIO, by several newspapers, and by countless friends. I was particularly impressed by an editorial in the *Saint Petersburg Times*, one of two liberal newspapers to support me in 1950, written by the owner, Nelson Poynter, saying: "Claude Pepper should run for that new seat in the House of Representatives created in Dade County." I no longer was troubled about going to the House after being in the Senate. What I wanted to do was legislate; I could do that equally well in either body. Senator Paul Douglas came to campaign for me, saying he was glad I was running for the House and

*I was to learn later that by not allowing his name to go before the convention until almost the last minute, Stevenson lost an opportunity to be appointed secretary of state. He was Kennedy's choice for that post, but when he continued the fight for the nomination, the Kennedys felt he did not deserve a reward.

hoped that someday I would knock off Smathers and Holland—"They are no good." Hubert Humphrey made one of his all-out rousing speeches for me. Newspaper coverage was kinder than usual, one article noting that going from the Senate to the House was a trail blazed by such as John Quincy Adams (who stopped off at the White House in between) and Henry Clay.

The old Red smear surfaced briefly in the campaign when fliers circulated with the photograph of Robeson, Wallace, and me. I met the issue head-on this time, as I should have the first time. In a televised debate with the other candidates, I opened by saying that "anyone who suggested I was connected with or sympathetic to communism was ignorant and a fool, or a scoundrel." I later issued a statement saying that the new smear attack was "the old ventriloquist game. You appear to hear one Charlie McCarthy or another but the master's voice is always the same—the Birchite reactionaries" and a few unscrupulous politician-doctors. Two of my campaigners were warned that the Ku Klux Klan would "burn them out" if they did not get away from Claude Pepper.

I was through playing games. In April, a delegation of Negroes called on me, asking what role I wanted them to play. "I told them I wasn't running out on liberalism . . . and I was grateful for their open support."

At my request, President Kennedy wrote a gracious letter, praising my record in the Senate and expressing the hope that I would be returned to public life. An amusing incident occurred: I had scheduled two fund-raisers rather close together, one to be addressed by Senator Kefauver, the other by Vice-President Johnson. Johnson's office telephoned, seeking assurance that the turnout for Johnson would be greater than for Kefauver. Both gave good speeches to appreciative crowds, and Lyndon Johnson, when I saw him off the following morning, gave me a tip that has proved out countless times over the years. I asked him to suggest another speaker if I needed to hold another fund-raiser. Without a moment's hesitation, the vice-president said, "I'd suggest Congressman Jim Wright from Texas. He's an eloquent, forceful speaker who always makes a great speech." As it turned out, I didn't need Representative Wright. But I have had many opportunities through the years to affirm Johnson's high regard for him. His oratory, legislative skills, and warm personality enabled him to rise through the ranks of the House leadership. At the beginning of the one-hundredth Congress, Jim Wright reached the pinnacle when he was elected Speaker of the House.

On May 8, 1962, primary election day, I was able to write: "The day! We won!" No longer was a Democratic primary victory tantamount to election, but the Republican turnout had been light and we anticipated no major problem in winning the general election. And there was none. Ed Ball and the business interests so opposed to me in the past knew that Dade County's new Third Congressional District was liberal (it consisted of part of Miami and northern Dade County) and that they probably could not beat me anyway. In later years I heard that Ball told associates that he would not oppose me as long as I ran for the House, but would oppose me if I ran again for the Senate.

Whatever the case, Mildred and Claude Pepper, after a dozen years, were returning to where they could do the most good.

The "hiatus" years were marred by many grievous personal losses. I have already mentioned the death of Jim Clements. Also, two educators who had strongly influenced the course of my life passed away—C. C. Mosely, my high school principal, who did more to stimulate me to rise than anyone; and Dr. George H. Denny, president of the University of Alabama, whom I always referred to as "my other father." *

* Dr. Denny, on an autographed photograph he gave to me on February 22, 1939, paid me the finest tribute I have ever had: "To my dear and

But the most pain accompanied the loss of my mother. She was a woman of intelligence, talent, and strength. She played the piano and organ beautifully and taught herself to play guitar and violin. She also danced, and thus was the liveliest and most important presence at those song-filled Christmas eves of my youth.

Mama had been hospitalized twice after suffering heart attacks during the 1950s and early 1960s, but she recovered and became characteristically active. One week before she would have celebrated her eighty-fourth birthday, Mama invited my brother Frank and his family to dinner at the house in Tallahassee that Mildred and I had shared with her and Papa for so many years. About eight o'clock, she said, "Well, children, I think I had better go in. I'm not feeling so well this evening." About midnight, she asked the woman who took care of her to call the doctor to come immediately. Dr. George Garmany came in an ambulance and took Mama to Tallahassee Memorial Hospital. En route, Dr. Garmany told us later, she pleaded, "Oh, Dr. Garmany, please don't let me die. You have saved me so many times. Please save me again." My younger brother Frank called me in Miami and I took the first plane I could catch, arriving at four or five in the morning. The doctor told Joe, Frank, our sister Sarah, and me that Mama had suffered a stroke and a heart attack. We all stood, moist-eyed, around her bed. From time to time, she would fling her arm, as if trying to communicate. But she could not. She died at 1:00 P.M., June 8, 1961.

She had lived a full but hard life, experiencing years of poverty and struggle. But in the role of the dedicated and loving mother and wife, she never faltered. She fought hard for the

distinguished friend, Senator Claude Pepper, whose brilliant rise from the obscure hills of Alabama to national fame is based on high character, unremitted industry, broad social sympathy and superb natural gifts, is dedicated this tribute of affection, loyalty and this expression of pride and faith and good will. I have no better friend. I ask for none."

family, and was a source of great strength to us all. She was proud of my being a senator, and crushed by my defeat. I regret more than I can express that she did not live to see me returned to the Congress. She would have enjoyed, even more than I, the honors given me and the vindication won after so many bitter struggles.

Of the many gifts God has bestowed on me, the most precious, the most irreplaceable, were the two great women in my life—Mama and Mildred.

A man so blessed has no right to complain about anything else.

9

At Home in the House

Duty is the sublimest word in our language. Do
your duty in all things. You cannot do more.
You should never wish to do less.

—ROBERT E. LEE

I took my seat in the House of Representatives twenty-seven
years after being sworn in for the first time as a United States
Senator. John Kennedy, whom I had met at a horse show in
Ireland when he was in his teens, was president of the United
States. Lyndon Johnson, who had been secretary to a Texas
congressman, was now vice-president. Roosevelt, Truman, Eisenhower, Byrnes, Lodge, Wallace, Borah, Taft, Vandenberg,
Barkley, McCarthy, the great and not-so-great names from my
previous incarnation in Congress were no longer a part of the
Washington scene. Rayburn was not Speaker of the House but
a building. For me, it was not a time to reflect on the past.
The Senate, as I had often said, was a ministry where great
good was possible; the House is no less so. I had left a lucrative

253

law practice because I "wanted to do something that meant something." It was time to get started.

The first time I was addressed as "Congressman" (by Senator-elect Edward Kennedy, by the way), I was startled. For the fourteen years I was in the Senate and for the dozen years after when I practiced law, almost everyone called me "Senator." Almost everyone still does, even after twenty-four years in the House. The title "Congressman" is an honorable one, but when applied to me for the first time it sounded so strange. My new office quarters (home was still the apartment Mildred and I moved into in 1939) were rather weird as well. Instead of the spacious suite of my Senate years, I was relegated, with other "newcomers," to the ancient Longworth Building, where there was a small office for me, a large office for my staff, and nothing else.* Did I mind? Yes, a little, until I gave the matter some thought. I realized that it was entirely appropriate for "The People's House," as the House of Representatives has been known down through the years, to be less ostentatious than the more majestic Senate. Almost immediately I became aware of several advantages a congressman has over a senator:

—It is much easier to campaign in a geographically limited congressional district than crisscrossing an entire state.

—A congressman gets to know more of his constituents personally because they are fewer and all live nearby.

—The House is a friendlier place than the Senate, its 435 members being allegedly less important, and thus less self-important, than the 100 senators.

—It is even easier to achieve one's legislative goals from a House seat than from a supposedly loftier perch in the Senate.

*As I acquired seniority in the house, I also acquired more commodious office space in the new and larger Rayburn Building. And as chairman of the House Rules Committee, I now have a spacious and comfortable office in the Capitol itself.

Senators can talk a bill to death by filibustering; House rules forbid the filibuster and sharply limit debate.

—A representative belongs to fewer committees than a senator. Thus he can know more about legislation and wield more influence on conference committees trying to reconcile differences in bills passed by both houses.

—Addressing the House on important occasions is like making a speech before an audience. Addressing the Senate is like talking to a grade-school class when most of the students are out for recess and those who aren't are unruly.

I loved the Senate. I dearly love the House.

During the Senate years, my chief concerns were the minimum wage, foreign policy (Lend-Lease; relations with our allies, including the Soviet Union), and a health policy for the nation. In the House there are and will continue to be fair treatment for the elderly, crime prevention, and—still—a health policy for the nation.

It is most gratifying to me to see how much of the work of my old Senate Subcommittee on Wartime Health and Education is still in place. Shocked when I learned during World War II that nearly three million young men had been rejected for military service because of physical or mental impairment, I persuaded the Senate to establish the subcommittee and to allow me to chair it. The subcommittee was:

—the first to recommend a national health insurance system that would enable all Americans to obtain the health care they need.

—the first to recommend home care as an essential component of any future health-care system.

—the first to recommend "capitation," the use of a set fee in financing a future health-care system.

—instrumental in establishing that the federal government

had to play a major role in financing research aimed at preventing and curing disease.

Of the National Institutes of Health, only one—the National Cancer Institute—existed when the subcommittee was created in 1943. Legislation establishing that research organization has a poignant history. Senator Homer Bone, crippled by cancer, introduced a resolution calling for such an institute, with $500,000 a year to be appropriated for its support. Then he personally came around to each of his Senate colleagues, asking us to sign his resolution, which he knew was too late to help him. All of us signed, and the bill became law. For many years, only the $500,000 appropriation was available for cancer research. It was totally inadequate.

One of the first to sense this was Mary Lasker, a genuine "angel" who has done so much to obtain federal aid for disease research. She urged me to seek $100,000,000 for cancer research, to remain available until spent. She asked Representative Matthew Neeley of West Virginia to lead the fight in the House. For months, I held hearings, with Mrs. Lasker producing the nation's leading cancer authorities to serve as witnesses. Finally, Senator Robert A. Taft, the conservative Ohio Republican (who, incidentally, died of cancer), introduced a bill calling for a $75 million cancer research fund to remain available until spent. We joined forces and boosted the annual appropriation for the National Cancer Institute from $500,000 to more than $8 million. The amount has grown until currently it is $1.1 billion. All through the years I have pressed for increased funding because the only hope for a cancer cure—and we must find one—is research, which costs money. Hardly an American family has not been touched by cancer. The money is well-spent.

After my beloved Mildred died of cancer in 1979, I realized how little had been achieved in the battle against this disease. I held committee hearings that increased public awareness and also made clear the need for an international conference on cancer and aging. Thus, in 1981 the United States invited many nations to the first world conference on cancer research, at an estimated cost of $500,000. But for budgetary reasons, the United States put up only $250,000 and was about to cancel the conference. I appealed to American Bankers Life company in Chicago to provide the needed $250,000, and the company did so. The conference, held in Washington, was chaired by Dr. Louis Thomas of New York's Sloan-Kettering Institute and eight Nobelists participated. It was widely acclaimed as a major success.

By 1950, six more institutes of health had been established: the National Institute of Mental Health; the National Heart, Lung and Blood Institute; the National Institute of Allergy and Infectious Diseases; the National Institute of Dental Research; the National Institute of Neurological and Communicative Disorders; and the National Institute of Arthritis, Diabetes, and Digestive and Kidney Diseases.*

Between 1961 and 1974, five more institutes were established: the National Institute of Child Health and Human Development; the National Institute of General Medical Sciences; the National Institute of Environmental Health Sciences; the National Eye Institute; and the National Institute on Aging. In 1986, Congress voted to establish the thirteenth health research agency, the National Institute on Arthritis. In a sense, this was a reestablishment. The original arthritis institute had acquired so many additional, unrelated research programs that its purpose was diluted. With the help of House colleagues, I was able to push through an amendment establishing an institute devoted to arthritis research alone.

In 1983, a devastating new—or just recently recognized—

---

*In 1967, I was given the Albert and Mary Lasker Foundation award for being principal sponsor of all the institutes except that for dental research. I treasure that award.

disease demanded our attention. It was Alzheimer's disease, a form of early senility that incapacitates the victim and also inflicts great suffering on his or her family. Senator Albert Gore, Jr., and I introduced bills to establish twenty research centers in various regions of the country to seek a cure and to provide treatment. Budget restraints reduced the number of regional centers to ten. I shall continue to press for the other ten, which health experts agree are urgently needed.

How many millions of lives have been saved and how many millions of people have been enabled to lead healthier and happier lives because of these health institutes is impossible to say. But it is a safe bet that every American family has benefited, directly or indirectly. The notion that the health of its citizens is a legitimate concern of the federal government—an idea opposed as "socialized medicine" for so many years by the American Medical Association—led in 1965 to enactment of the Medicare and Medicaid programs to assist the elderly and the indigent. They were a godsend to both groups; the elderly had been spending an average of 20 percent of their income on health care, far more than most of them could afford. Unfortunately, with the constant escalation of health-care costs and with many illnesses (including Alzheimer's) not covered by Medicare, the elderly again are spending 20 percent of their income for treatment and medicine.

As chief sponsor of five of the first National Institutes of Health and a co-sponsor of the sixth, I take considerable pride in what has been accomplished, but there is so much more to be done. Currently, I am pressing for congressional passage of a bill that would provide complete coverage for the elderly without costing any more than the severely limited Medicare program costs now. Inspiration for the legislation comes from a program that Chrysler Motor Company has put in place for its employees, based on public- and private-sector collaboration, cost controls, and disease prevention. The bill also would extend comprehensive coverage to the poor, provided states are willing to pay into the fund 90 percent of their anticipated outlay for Medicaid. In 1965, we thought we had provided substantial medical care for the elderly, but that is no longer the case. Too many diseases are not covered. As to Medicaid, the level of inclusion is so low that only the truly destitute are protected. Thus the American middle class is vulnerable to catastrophic illness. We must do something about that through the proven principle of insurance, whereby care shall be provided primarily by private suppliers with governmental supervision, with all patients paying what they can and should.

For example, say a man working for General Motors earns $50,000 a year. He and his wife have $100,000 in liquid assets, own their home, have two automobiles, furniture, and so on. One day the husband receives the sad news that came to me in 1977—that his wife has cancer. Under stress, he suffers a severe heart attack. In such circumstances, how long do you suppose the $100,000 in liquid assets will last in paying doctor, hospital, and drug bills? Medical care, especially for catastrophic illnesses, is so expensive that it can bankrupt middle-class families.

In 1946, I first introduced in the Senate a bill calling for adequate health care for all Americans. This remains foremost among my legislative goals. I plan to realize it. We must reach the point where every man, woman, and child in the United States, after paying whatever is possible and reasonable, will be able to obtain whatever health care is needed. Today, the great rewards of research sponsored by both government and private enterprise should not be available only to those with sufficient wealth to pay the bills. The United States lags behind every other developed nation in the world in providing health care for its people. We must change that. And we shall.

When I moved to the House, the elderly became a major concern for none of the base political motives occasionally attributed to me. Some have said my interest derived from the fact that I was approaching elderly status myself, being sixty-two at the time I took my seat. Others have said that with retirees flocking to Florida, winning a reputation for legislation benefiting the elderly was simply good survival politics. The truth is that as a young boy I was taught to respect and be considerate of older people, including, of course, all four of my grandparents. I was in my late twenties when I introduced in the Florida legislature the bill exempting old people from a fishing license fee. But I believe the major reason I have become so involved with the elderly and their needs stems from my preoccupation with health matters. As a group, older people naturally have more health problems than do the young. In fact, older generations require three times as much health care as the young.

Another motivating force is my career-long advocacy and defense of Social Security. In 1937, I introduced in the Senate the controversial Townsend Plan, which called for payment of $200 a month to every citizen sixty-five or older. Social Security became an obviously better way to provide income to older people, so I switched from pushing the Townsend Plan to supporting and defending Social Security.* In March 1944, when I was a mere lad of forty-three, I introduced a resolution designating the second Sunday in October as "Old Folks Day," and of course I was active and influential in the passage of Medicare and Medicaid in 1965. I have worked in both the Senate and the House to obtain federal help in providing housing for the elderly and I was the original author of a bill that established a program to provide meals to the elderly.

*In 1982, after President Reagan had been rebuffed in his attempt to pare billions from Social Security benefits, I campaigned on that issue for twenty-three Democratic candidates for the House and Senate. The president accused me of demagoguery. I was simply telling the truth about what he had tried to do.

With all this background, it was only natural that I would urge the formation of a House Select Committee on Aging. With others, I began pressing for such a committee during the early 1970s, but the Speaker of the House, Carl Albert, was opposed. So was the chairman of the powerful House Rules Committee, which decided what legislation would be sent to the floor for a vote and what would not. Finally, on October 2, 1974, Representative Bill Young of Saint Petersburg, Florida, offered an amendment to a bill that was being considered. His amendment called for formation of a Select Committee on Aging, and it passed. (Unlike standing committees, select committees cannot legislate. But they can and do hold hearings, and issue reports and studies that lead to legislation.)

It seemed obvious to me and many of my colleagues that Claude Pepper should be chairman of the Committee on Aging. I conveyed this notion to Speaker Albert, who had the authority to appoint chairmen of new committees. But the speaker apologetically informed me that he had already promised the chairmanship to Representative William Randall of Missouri. Albert did name me the ranking Democrat, which meant I could become chairman if Randall retired, which in fact he did a little more than a year after the committee became operational.

I assumed the chairmanship and made one additional assumption—that the nation's elderly, all thirty-seven million of them, were now my constituents and that it was my duty to safeguard their interests in every possible way. They soon came to rely on me, and on the Select Committee. Rarely does a day pass that old people do not stop me in the corridors of the Capitol, in airports, or in restaurants and thank me for caring about them when many others—often including their own children—do not. A surprising number of young people also come up to me and thank me for what I have done for their parents or grandparents. Their undisguised affection warms my heart and gives me far greater satisfaction than I could ever attain from winning a major lawsuit, no matter how large the fee. And their heartfelt gratitude makes it easy for me to withstand criticism that I am fiscally irresponsible, a pleader for "special interests," and so on. There are worse ways for a government to spend money and our government, no less than many others, has found them. Brightening human lives is not wastrel government; it is government at its very best.

The House Select Committee on Aging quickly became a force. At first, many House members were reluctant to serve on it; now there is a clamor to be appointed whenever a vacancy occurs. When the committee became operational in June 1975, the number of congressmen serving on it was thirty-five; today, sixty-five members of the House serve on the committee and thirty are members of the Subcommittee on Health and Long-term Care, of which I am chairman.* It is the largest committee of Congress, and the subcommittee is also the largest in Congress. One in every seven members of the House serves on the Select Committee on Aging, an indication of the force the committee's recommendations have always carried.

When I became chairman in 1977, I enlarged the committee staff and sent out strong signals that this would be an activist committee. We held hearings and conducted research into the problems of older Americans, which proved to be more numerous and less intractable than I had imagined. Several volumes would be required to detail the accomplishments of this comparatively young committee, but the highlights include expansion of home care for the elderly, which is not only more pleasant

*In 1983, forced to choose between continuing as chairman of the full Committee on Aging or becoming chairman of the House Rules Committee, I chose the latter because of that committee's power to control legislation. As Rules chairman, I felt I could continue to help the elderly as well as other constituencies, and I have. I was allowed to continue as chairman of the Subcommittee on Health and Long-term care.

for the individuals but much less expensive for the government, and a package of reform bills to reduce abuses against patients in nursing homes.

Mandatory retirement at age sixty-five or seventy or any age is now against the law, with some exceptions. This is a tremendous civil rights triumph in which the committee and I take great pride. We fought the U.S. Chamber of Commerce, the National Association of Manufacturers, and many powerful corporate boards and executives. Hardly anyone knows how long and lonely this effort was. Once the law was in place, opponents who fought it vigorously conceded that their fears were unfounded. Some very sheepishly admitted that they were wrong and we were right.

In 1977, the Select Committee heard testimony that punctured the myth that people become incompetent as they age. Some do; most don't. Witnesses were Averell Harriman, then 85; Colonel Harlin Sanders, 86; Ruth Gordon, the actress who had just won an Academy Award for her role in *Rosemary's Baby* (and who would not reveal her age); Will Geer, actor, 75; my old friend Thomas (Tommy the Cork) Corcoran, 76, from the Roosevelt years; Dr. Arthur Flemming, 71, U.S. commissioner on aging, who had just been exempted from mandatory retirement by an executive order from President Carter; and Francis Knight, 71, director of the U.S. Passport Office. These people were not just competent, they were energetic, experienced, highly skilled, and too valuable to their professions and their country to be consigned to rocking chairs. Millions of other Americans older than 65 but still able to contribute had been forced to retire. With a few exceptions to be phased out gradually, that cannot happen to workers today. Now "mandatory" retirement comes only when they are no longer able to do the job. In 1978 my bill abolished mandatory retirement at any age for federal government workers and raised from 65 to 70 the age at which nonfederal employees could be forced out.

President Carter signed my bill in a moving Rose Garden ceremony with dear Mildred sitting in a wheelchair beside the president and me. The final step outlawing mandatory retirement altogether (again with a few exceptions) became law in 1986. President Reagan proposed a Rose Garden signing ceremony, but I was in Florida campaigning for reelection so I urged him to go ahead and sign the bill, which he did.

This was the righting of a great wrong. Now it is as illegal to discriminate against a person because of age as it is to discriminate in employment because of sex or race. Now millions of people doing creditable work can continue as long as they wish and as long as they continue to perform. This is restoration of a civil right that should never have been denied.

Another accomplishment of the Select Committee was adoption by an administration of an agenda for reform in housing, income security, and other pressing concerns of the elderly. This occurred in 1977 after the entire committee met at the White House with President Carter.

We proposed to the president "An Agenda for the Elderly for the Last Quarter of the 20th Century." The agenda required that

—A national health security system should be created.

—Federally funded home health care should be provided.

—Pending national health insurance, Medicare and Medicaid should cover annual checkups, professional and nutritional counseling, and diagnostic services.

—Eyeglasses, hearing aids, dentures, and other necessary medical appliances should also be covered by Medicare and Medicaid.

—Nursing homes should be audited for abuses of the elderly by staff.

—Nutrition programs must be expanded.

—Congress should grant airlines permission to offer standby and other discount airfares to the elderly.

—Housing needs of elderly Americans must be met.

—Security against crime victimization and con games must be improved for the defenseless elderly, who are disproportionately the victims of criminal activity.

—Funding of jobs earmarked for the elderly should be increased under the Older Americans Act.

—Discrimination in employment because of age must end.

—A single national retirement income policy should be established.

Well, we have not achieved everything on the agenda, but efforts continue. We did gain an increase in the number of days covered for home-care reimbursement. We passed bills reforming the operation of nursing homes. We won increased funding for geriatric training for the nutrition program for seniors. We got the bill through establishing the ten Alzheimer's research and care centers. And we passed a bill allowing states to provide alternatives to institutionalized care when it is less costly to care for the elderly at home. In 1986, we got the arthritis institute established, and we won a major victory by creating a "seal of approval" to help seniors identify good supplemental insurance programs.

In transportation, we won the rights for airlines and Amtrak to offer special discount fares for the elderly, and we also passed a bill requiring the Department of Transportation to design vans equipped to meet the needs of the elderly and handicapped.

As to crime, we succeeded in getting many states to stiffen laws against elder abuse and to step up enforcement. We made it more difficult for charlatans to defraud seniors through such consumer frauds as quackery, phony business investments, and land frauds promoted through the mails, and we forced senior housing projects to provide better security. As already mentioned, we brought an end to mandatory retirement, and we passed legislation increasing the amount of outside income an individual can earn and still receive full retirement benefits under Social Security. Not a bad record. A good one, in fact. But there's more to be done.

Perhaps the most widely publicized hearings ever held by the committee were those conducted in 1978 to let the public know how widespread was the fraud and abuse in the sale of Medicare supplemental insurance (Medigap). Laws were passed requiring companies to meet certain standards and to make elderly customers fully aware of what they were buying. The hearings were televised by the American Broadcasting Company network, and some of the people depicted as having ripped off vulnerable oldsters did not appreciate the exposure. They filed suit against the committee staff that had prepared the case against them, against ABC News, and others, including the committee's dedicated and superefficient staff director, Kathy Gardner. After eight years in the courts, the case was dismissed and the fine people involved were all fully exonerated.

There has been much additional good that can be traced to the House Select Committee on Aging—an attack on medical quackery that exposed a $10 billion scandal, establishment of the hospice benefit under Medicare. But the greatest achievement of all, I believe, is that the national attitude toward old people has made a 180-degree turn. More and more, younger generations have come to realize that in their elders they have a precious and useful asset, not a burden. Old people are the same persons they were when they were young. Some may not hear so well, may have to wear glasses, maybe are a step slower when they walk. But they are not useless, and they must not be treated as outcasts, as more and more Americans have come to realize. Not all of this gratifying change in attitude stemmed from the Select Committee or from Claude Pepper. But they both helped.

Increased concern for the elderly has its political aspect, of course. Older people vote in greater percentages than any other age group. Both major political parties try to identify with the elderly, although Republicans have a more difficult task because of their historic opposition to Social Security and because at intervals prominent Republicans like Barry Goldwater and Ronald Reagan advocate making it "voluntary" or seek to trim its benefits.

Many Americans erroneously credit me with being one of the founders of Social Security. This is understandable: I am one of the few men in public life who was active in 1935, when President Roosevelt initiated Social Security. But I did not get to the Senate until 1936. Also, I have always supported the concept and have fought attempts to reduce benefits. The United States can afford Social Security, as even President Reagan seemed to realize at last, judging from his campaign speeches and pledges in the presidential campaign of 1984.

In 1981, the long-term solvency of the Social Security program seemed in doubt. President Reagan tried to meet the problem the way he attacks all domestic issues—by seeking sweeping cutbacks in benefits. The president identified $62 billion in "savings" that could be made—at what cost in human suffering and deprivation he did not say. Congress went along with $22 billion in reductions, but refused to go further. A large number of Republicans, some out of conviction and others out of concern over the next election, declined to support the president. In 1982, my party sent me to campaign on the issue of Social Security cutbacks in congressional districts all over the country. Democrats gained twenty-three seats in the House that year. Most of the new representatives were those I had campaigned for, holding up their arms while they pledged to resist cutbacks in Social Security benefits. Republicans cried "foul" but they could have met the same promise if they believed in Social Security as firmly as I did, and do.

The fact remained, however, that Social Security was headed for disaster if something was not done. Feeling that he and his party had been unfairly "burned" on the issue (he was partly right—they had been burned, but not unfairly), President Reagan tried to play a cat-and-mouse game, trying to trim or delay the cost-of-living increase awarded to recipients to compensate for inflation. But he wanted bipartisan sponsorship so Republicans would not further tarnish their image as the party that would gut Social Security if it could. The Democrats, with Speaker O'Neill taking the lead, were not buying. At last, the president proposed that a bipartisan commission be appointed to study the problem. Congress agreed, and a commission of six Republicans and five Democrats was named. I was one of the Democrats, appointed by Speaker O'Neill.

At first, it appeared that the commission had driven itself right into gridlock. White House aides made clear that the president was determined to avoid political fallout, that Republicans would not support any solution that did not have the imprimatur of Speaker O'Neill. For his part, the speaker made known that he would not accept any proposal that did not have the approval of Claude Pepper, the party's most trusted spokesman on Social Security. I publicly declared I would oppose any reductions in benefits. It seemed the commission would simply throw up its hands and go out of business. But we couldn't. Millions of recipients, present and future, were depending on us to find a way to save the system.

For months, we explored all aspects of the system. We had two major objectives—to keep it as a social insurance program, which it had been from the beginning, and to ensure its solvency for at least the next seventy-five years. Given the enormity of the problem, I regard it as miraculous that we succeeded as well as we did, although I was not happy with all of the changes. I vigorously opposed taxing benefits of individuals with incomes over $25,000 and couples with more than $32,000 annual incomes. But overall, we strengthened the program with $160 billion in new funds and taxes—even anticipating the years when the millions of "baby boomers" will become eligible for benefits. Congress accepted most of the commission's proposals. On the House floor, Representative Jake Pickle of Texas proposed an amendment to increase from sixty-five to sixty-seven the age at which benefits would accrue. I opposed the proposal, but it was adopted, leaving me at least technically in a breach of my pledge that no benefits would be reduced. The amendment does not take effect until the next century. Before then, I will do everything possible to bring about its repeal.

I will also resist recurring efforts to turn Social Security into a welfare program. It is not welfare. It is an insurance program to which the beneficiaries and their employers have contributed. Today, a Social Security recipient can retrieve his monthly check from his mailbox with pride and with the world looking on because he paid for half of that benefit during his working life. I am also determined to rectify the problem of very low benefits for women, attributable to the lower salaries they were paid, often for the same work men did for considerably more money.

With all the attacks President Reagan has leveled at Social Security over the years, and with all the attempts he has made to trim benefits, I think it is interesting that in his campaign for reelection in 1984 he made a public pledge that he would not touch Social Security, not even the cost-of-living adjustment for inflation. In fact, he declared that if the rate of inflation fell below 3 percent, which is the automatic "trigger" for an increase in benefits, he would ask Congress to approve an increase anyway. On this issue, Reagan is a president who has come full circle.

I trace the beginning of the president's "conversion" to the White House Conference on Aging in 1981. Justly fearing that reports to be released at the conclusion of the conference would

269

be critical of the administration, the White House "stacked" the committees, particularly the Social Security committee. When its handpicked members issued a report favoring cutbacks in Social Security, attendees flocked to me, asking that I do something. I led 500 of them, all clamoring for rescission of the report, to the committee rooms. A new resolution was adopted and an embarrassed administration withdrew its puppets. The elderly took charge of all committees, as they should have in the first place. New accounts, which described me as a "hero" that day, berated the White House for its blatant, politically motivated, interference.

Committees I have chaired and served on have been the highlights of my service in the House of Representatives. When I first took my seat, I was assigned to the Banking and Currency Committee, which certainly was not my choice. But I was so overjoyed just to be legislating again that I did not complain. The chairman, Wright Patman of Texas, was a good friend, but I have no memories of anything significant that the committee accomplished during the short time I was a member. When I was at home in Miami during the Christmas recess in 1964, Speaker John McCormack telephoned. In his peculiar, high-pitched Boston accent, he said, "Claude, this is the Speaker. I want to tell you something if you won't tell anyone but your missus." I replied, "All right, Mr. Speaker. I'm agreeable to that." He went on, "I am going to appoint you to the Rules Committee." He knew I would be delighted, and I was. The House Rules Committee is one of the most powerful in the entire Congress, since it controls the flow of legislation and determines how much time will be allowed for debate, whether the measure can be amended, and so on. I thanked the Speaker warmly for the honor and opportunity for service he had offered to me. A number of very powerful members, including Tip O'Neill, the future Speaker, were on the committee and I looked forward to working with them.

For years, the Rules Committee's chief purpose seemed to

be to bottle up civil rights legislation. Its chairman, Judge Howard W. Smith of Virginia, did not believe in civil rights, especially for blacks. He was stubborn and cantankerous, and ruled the committee with an iron hand. His method was simple: If he knew committee members were going to bring up bills he didn't like, he refused to call a meeting. I experienced this technique early on. It was inevitable that I would try to introduce legislation of the sort Chairman Smith would oppose; we were ideological opposites. I drafted a bill to provide medical aid to underprivileged people in the Third World, which had the support of the administration, the House leadership, and a majority of the Rules Committee membership. I carefully selected a date on which supporters of the bill could be present, and the afternoon before that date I telephoned Judge Smith and told him I intended to call up my bill at a scheduled committee meeting the following morning.

He said, "Well, if that's the way you propose to play the game, there won't be any committee meeting tomorrow morning."

Astounded, I replied, "Judge, I'm not trying to play games. I have a bill supported by the president, by the leadership of the House, and by a majority of our committee, and I want to bring up my bill tomorrow morning."

Said Smith, "Well, if that's the way you propose to play the game, there won't be a committee meeting tomorrow morning."

This can't be, I told myself. One man can thwart the intentions of the president, House leaders, and the majority of a House committee? I told Smith I would call him back. Then I telephoned Speaker McCormack and told him what had happened. The Speaker said, "Claude, why call me? I can't do anything about it." I said, "Well, Mr. Speaker, I suppose I just wanted to unburden myself on somebody. I think that's a hell of a way to run a railroad."

It was. Smith could use his considerable and unwarranted

271

power to push through legislation that he did want. Some of his fellow Southern reactionaries were trying to get through the Judiciary Committee a bill prohibiting United States district courts from considering or deciding any matter involving civil rights. But the chairman of the Judiciary Committee opposed the bill and refused to bring it up for a hearing. Smith, naturally, favored the bill and announced at a Rules Committee meeting that he was calling up the bill for consideration. He did. Then he persuaded a majority to support it and sent the crazy legislation to the House floor, where it passed. Fortunately it never got through the Senate.

Eventually, the House diluted the powers of its committee chairmen to prevent bigoted autocrats like Smith from behaving like kings or dictators. After becoming chairman of the Rules Committee myself, I got a measure of grim satisfaction in asking the staff to remove a portrait of Judge Smith from the committee's hearing room. There were two portraits on facing walls, one of Smith, the other of Representative Richard Bolling of Missouri, who had preceded me as chairman. When the staff asked me where to place the Smith portrait, they say I replied, "Under the front steps of the Capitol might be a suitable and safe place." I don't recall being quite that harsh. But the memory I have of the haughty and imperious Judge Smith is obviously a vivid and unpleasant one.

The Rules Committee has been the subject of controversy since the beginning of the Republic. Its control over legislation always rankled the House leadership, which regarded such authority as one of its own prerogatives. Speaker "Uncle Joe" Cannon and Speaker Thomas "Czar" Reed both gained control of the Rules Committee and pretty much determined the direction of the country for a while. Any bill they didn't want enacted never reached the floor. They controlled the calendar and thus what the House did. And if the House did nothing, the Senate and the president were stymied because it takes approval of all three (except in case of veto overrides) for a measure to become law. It was Speaker Sam Rayburn who finally resolved this power struggle. Rayburn managed to appoint a Rules Committee majority that would work in harmony with the House leadership. When Dick Bolling was chairman, he persuaded the House to make the Rules Committee a part of the leadership, thus enhancing the committee's prestige and making it a part of the "team."

The functions of the Rules Committee are complicated and not of great interest to the public in general. They are of major importance, of course, to members, lobbyists, and anyone who works directly with the Congress. Suffice it to say that the power to decide what bills will go to the floor for consideration by the entire House is greater than that of any other congressional committee. Thus as I gained seniority, I realized that some day I would be in line to become chairman. But House members can chair only one committee, and I wondered how I would ever be able to give up my chairmanship of the Select Committee on Aging. I gave the matter a great deal of thought and solicited advice from friends and colleagues. Dick Bolling retired from Congress at the end of 1982, leaving me the senior Democrat on the Rules Committee. Before the new Congress assembled, I telephoned Speaker O'Neill and told him that I had made my decision. Because of the great opportunity to influence legislation for the benefit of all, I wanted to be chairman of the Rules Committee. I was not turning my back on the elderly—I could in fact help them more as Rules Committee chairman and I would retain my chairmanship of the Subcommittee on Health and Long-term Care. Tip O'Neill had mixed feelings. "Claude," he said, "I just hate to have you give up the chairmanship of that Committee on Aging. But if you want Rules, I'll appoint you chairman of the Rules Committee." I am satisfied now that the decision was the right one.

Before my involvements with Rules and Aging, I had an

oppportunity to contribute in another area of vital concern to me—crime. There had been a number of airplane hijackings, usually involving a Miami-bound Eastern Airlines jet forced to fly to Havana. Sale of illegal drugs had long been a major problem in Florida, and now it was getting worse; organized crime was heavily involved. The torch had been put to many American cities, including Washington, D.C., in violent outbreaks protesting the Vietnam War and the assassination of the Reverend Martin Luther King, Jr. Crime was no longer a local problem, and yet the Congress wasn't doing much to deal with it. One day when Mildred and I were scanning the newspaper headlines and deploring the various criminal acts they reported, Mildred made a suggestion. She said that Congress ought to take a role in the battle against crime and added, "Claude, why don't you offer a resolution to establish a House Select Committee on Crime?" It was a splendid idea. I followed through immediately.

The timing was right. My resolution zipped through the Rules Committee and was adopted by the House on a lopsided vote. It is House custom for a member who successfully proposes creation of a new committee to become chairman, so in 1969 I was appointed to head the House Select Committee on Crime. We had seven members and an appropriation large enough to pay for an excellent staff. For six years we battled against a variety of criminal activities. We held hearings and compiled studies on organized crime, street crime, white-collar crime, drug smuggling, and much more.

Our purpose was to gain a clearer understanding of the criminal world and to determine what new federal legislation might be needed to cripple it. Thus we held our hearings in all parts of the country, hoping to stimulate public support for a revitalized effort to put criminals where they belong—behind bars. Much of the testimony we heard and the exhibits we produced were unpleasant, even shocking. In New York City, we collected information on drug abuse. The witness was the city coroner, who calmly laid out heart-wrenching photographs of young boys and girls, needles in the arms of some, lying dead from overdoses of heroin in alleys, on stairways, on bare floors, in gutters. What a waste!

Unfortunately, we cannot claim anything resembling victory in our war on drugs. We tried to shrink the market, which probably has grown tenfold since 1969. We studied how to prevent distribution of drugs in the nation; today they are more widely available than ever. We sought means of interdicting shipments of drugs from other countries; billions of dollars' worth reach our shores every year. Perhaps this is a war that cannot be won, but we have no option other than to keep trying. In 1986, Congress passed a bill to pour $1.7 billion into an expanded war on drugs and President Reagan signed it, only to cut the amount considerably in his budget recommendation. The bill includes an amendment I introduced providing $100 million for education and treatment. We must awaken our people to the dangers of drug abuse and we must enable those who wish to quit using drugs to find help.

One of the most celebrated episodes in the history of the House Select Committee on Crime involved Frank Sinatra. Our staff produced evidence that the singer was a director of a country club in Massachusetts dominated by organized-crime figures. Well, organized crime was one of our chief concerns, so we scheduled hearings. Sinatra's attorney was notified that we wanted to question Sinatra on a certain date and that it would be in his best interest to have his client there on that date. The attorney called me with assurances that Sinatra would be present and would testify. But he pleaded with me not to issue a subpoena. For some reason, Sinatra strongly objected to subpoenas, probably because it is against his nature to be compelled to do anything. I wanted Sinatra's testimony and it did not matter to me whether he came before our committee voluntarily or under subpoena. On receiving the attorney's promise that the singer would appear, I agreed not to issue a subpoena.

One day before the hearing, I received a telephone call from a journalist representing the British Broadcasting Corporation in Washington. He asked if Sinatra would be testifying at our hearing the following day, as scheduled. I told him yes. "Well, I doubt that he will be there," said the journalist, "because he is in London at this moment."

I was outraged. I immediately called the attorney, told him that he and Sinatra had breached their pledge to me and that I wasn't interested in any explanation they might wish to offer. I told him that I was going to issue a subpoena and place copies of it in every U.S. Customs Office at major Eastern seaboard ports and in every major embassy in Europe. It didn't matter to me if Sinatra tried to travel in Europe or chose to return to the United States. In either case, he would be served with a subpoena. Not even Frank Sinatra, I shouted, could defy a committee of the United States Congress. The attorney begged me for just one more chance. He vowed to produce the singer, and again he asked that I not issue the subpoena. The attorney knew that I was deadly serious about my threat and that his client would be arrested if he again failed to appear. So I gave him one last chance.

On the appointed day, an angry Sinatra appeared in the hearing room and was sworn in as a witness, although not a very helpful one. He admitted owning stock in the country club, but was very offhand about it. He recalled giving "a few hundred dollars" to someone at a club where he was performing, but this was such a "minor matter" to him he could not recall any more details. Our evidence was more convincing than Sinatra's testimony. That evidence held that Sinatra was a director of the club and that the club was dominated by figures from organized crime. I think I delivered a lesson in citizenship to Frank Sinatra—that in the United States, when you are called on to testify, you do so. Celebrity status means nothing. The law is the great equalizer.

At another hearing we interviewed a genuine organized-crime "godfather." He was Raymond Patriarca, the dominant Mafia chieftain for all of New England. As is usually the case with a criminal about to testify, a "contract" was put out on Patriarca by other elements of organized crime who wanted him silenced. We brought him down to Washington on the eve of his testimony under heavy guard provided by U.S. marshals. The mobster testified under very unusual circumstances, with shoulder-to-shoulder marshals facing him and another cadre of marshals at his back. They did their job so well that Patriarca lived on into the 1980s and finally died of natural causes.

The bizarre scene that took place in the halls of Congress when Patriarca testified proved to be the death knell for the Crime Committee. Speaker Albert didn't like select committees anyway, and so he put this one out of business. In six years, we didn't cure crime—we didn't expect to—but we did important and lasting work. Our hearings brought out many faults in law enforcement, not all of which have been corrected. We were the first to recommend that mere use of marijuana be treated as a misdemeanor rather than a felony; we demonstrated that the problem of drug abuse by teenagers (and even younger children) was not confined to the large urban centers but existed in small and medium-sized communities in every section of the country. Our twenty-one recommendations formed the basis for a wide-ranging crackdown on the use of heroin. We put a spotlight on securities fraud, leading to stronger enforcement by the Securities and Exchange Commission and a sharper focus by that agency on protecting victims.

After the murderous prison riot at Attica, New York, in 1971, and other prison disturbances elsewhere, we studied and recommended better riot-control techniques. The committee visited Attica and held a hearing there after conferring with Governor Nelson Rockefeller, who sent us to Attica in his plane. There had been many deaths in the riot. Prisoners held several hostages, some with knives at their throats, and announced that if law enforcement officers came in, they would take the lives of the hostages. Officials deployed some sharpshooters with orders to shoot the prisoners, but when they entered the walled enclosure they fired a hail of bullets that killed many hostages as well as prisoners. I have often thought it would have been far better to have sent a gunship helicopter over the wall. Inmates had knives but no guns. The worst they could have done would have been to throw rocks at the helicopter. Officers manning machine guns could have directed all prisoners to fall flat or be shot. While inmates were on the ground, other officers could have moved in and taken charge. This possibility was among the committee's recommendations for a response in future situations of a similar nature.

Perhaps our greatest achievement is one about which there is little public knowledge. My special concern about plane hijackings prompted me in 1970 to introduce a bill authorizing the Federal Aviation Agency to install weapon detection devices at all of the 531 commercial airports in the country. The need for such devices was generally recognized, but they weren't being installed and hijackings continued. A squabble over who would foot the bill between the FAA, the airlines, and the airports was causing the very dangerous delay. My bill called for appropriation of federal funds to the FAA to install these metal detectors and to get the job done before more passengers were forced to fly to hijacker-preferred destinations. I also pointed out in testimony the danger always present in such circumstances that someone could be killed. In May 1972, all eleven members* of the Crime Committee demanded that the

*The committee had been increased in size from the original six members.

FAA take immediate action. In August, an initial appropriation of $3.5 million was made and the work finally got under way. Further appropriations were needed, of course. In any event, airline passengers today fly with reasonable assurance of safe passage because the detectors have been functioning well for several years now at all commercial airports. It happened much sooner than it would have without the House Select Committee on Crime.

10

Friends and Foes, and Sad Farewells

The job of being a professional politician, in spite of the odium which some persons have falsely attached to it, is a high and difficult one.

—HENRY CABOT LODGE, JR.

The year of my first election to the House, 1962, was also an election year for George Smathers. Although the senator who succeeded me had acquired the reputation of being the close friend and partner in many social "excursions" of Jack Kennedy, beginning when they were in the House together, the Florida electorate returned him for what would be his third and final term. When Spessard Holland's term expired in 1964 and when Smathers decided not to run in 1968, there was some pressure on me to run again for the Senate. I was not tempted. So quickly had I become involved in the work of the House, so many friends had I made there, so numerous were the opportunities to achieve my legislative goals there, that I no longer yearned to return to the Senate. I was rising in seniority in the House and I had what was considered a "safe seat." I could, as I often told supporters, do what I thought was right, meaning I did not have to trim my sails on race or other issues—as probably would have been necessary to win a statewide election. I felt comfortable in the House. There was no need to go elsewhere. A member of the Senate is thought to have more prestige than a member of the House, but prestige had long since ceased to be what I wanted from public life.

One difference between my Senate and House years is that I never achieved the degree of intimacy and mutual dependency with a president that I enjoyed with Franklin D. Roosevelt. I enjoyed friendly relations with all of the presidents, despite some of the rocky episodes with Truman and Eisenhower. After the smoke of political battles cleared, we became friends. Eisenhower's two terms occurred while I was not in the Congress, but we knew each other well from the time of my conference with him in Europe in 1945 and my foredoomed attempt in 1948 to "dump Truman" and replace him with Eisenhower as the Democratic candidate for president. Mildred and Mamie Eisenhower were good friends, and the general won a permanent spot on my good side when he once said, "That Mildred Pepper really is something, isn't she?"

Ike as president was something of a disappointment to me, although he was hugely popular in the country. One thing that really stuck in my craw was the way Eisenhower let the sleazy Joe McCarthy intimidate him. A forceful rejection of McCarthyism by the popular president of McCarthy's own party would have limited the damage of that scourge and shortened its life. It never happened. In fact, at McCarthy's insistence, Eisenhower omitted a paragraph praising General Marshall from a speech the president was going to deliver. Marshall, one of McCarthy's many undeserving targets, was entitled to the unstinting admiration Eisenhower felt toward him and to have it publicly expressed. In many ways, the incident was typical of the Eisenhower presidency—cautious to a fault. Although the years of his presidency were stable ones and his leadership was generally wise, it is significant that he is best remembered for the one major bold action he took—condemning and warning of the dangers of the military-industrial complex. It came in his farewell address at the end of his second term. I sat bolt upright when I heard it, sensing that this was Eisenhower at his tardy finest.

As noted earlier, I had known John F. Kennedy since his youth. I saw him a number of times when Mildred and I were in England in 1936 and Joseph P. Kennedy was ambassador to the Court of St. James. On a number of occasions after that I saw him at the Kennedy home in West Palm Beach, although invitations dropped off sharply after Joe Kennedy decided I was too liberal and started to contribute money to my political opponents. Of course, I followed Jack Kennedy's career closely—his wartime heroism; his well-publicized books (*While England Slept, Profiles in Courage*); his election to Congress for the first time in 1946; his defeat of my former colleague, Henry Cabot Lodge, Jr., for the Senate in 1952; his overwhelming reelection in 1958; and the tremendous impression he made in almost winning the Democratic nomination for vice-president in 1956.

But in 1960, I was slow to perceive this bright, attractive young man as presidential timber. One reason was that I had been through the Al Smith campaign of 1928 in the South, and I knew how strongly opposed the Bible Belt still was to having a "Rome-controlled Catholic" in the White House. Also, I thought that Adlai Stevenson would make a splendid president, and I remained loyal to him until it was clear that he had no chance to win the nomination a third time. When finally I did swing behind Kennedy, Smathers held the Florida delegation tightly in his control and in support of Lyndon Johnson. So I was of little help.

John Kennedy was always warm and thoughtful toward Mildred and me. When he was still a senator, I was lunching at the Willard Hotel one day when he proudly brought his girl-friend to my table and I met the beautiful Jacqueline Bouvier for the first time. During his campaign in 1960, he unfailingly invited me to sit on the platform whenever he appeared in Florida. The fact that his father had turned against me and made a huge contribution to the Smathers campaign in 1950 did not adversely affect our relationship. In fact, I always in-quired after his father whenever we met. We both understood that the father's disdain for me had no bearing on our friend-ship.

President Kennedy up close was even handsomer and more animated than he appeared on film or on television. His mood could change in a split second. I recall a day in the East Room of the White House. When the president entered he had a very troubled look on his face and seemed to be heading for a dif-ferent part of the room; but catching a glimpse of Mildred and me, he veered sharply, greeted us warmly, and the troubled look vanished. He had been president for two years when he returned to Washington, had survived the Bay of Pigs fiasco, and had avoided World War III by his courageous and wise handling of the Cuban missile crisis. I became his great ad-mirer, although I have always felt that both the Eisenhower and Kennedy administrations did too little to prevent Fidel Castro from planting the seeds of communism in the Western Hemisphere.

On Monday of the last week of his life, President Kennedy came from Palm Beach to Tampa to make a speech. Several of us from the Florida congressional delegation joined him there. He received a warm and exuberant welcome from a large crowd, including schoolchildren who were released to watch his mo-torcade. From Tampa, we flew to Miami on the president's plane, and he spoke there before another large crowd at the airport. I introduced him, and again the audience gave him a tumultuous welcome. At this stage of his life and presidency, John Kennedy had some of the magic of Roosevelt. He could stir crowds to a frenzy simply by being in front of them.

That evening, President Kennedy graciously appeared at a Miami Beach reception to which he had allowed several members of the delegation to invite their friends. He spoke at a dinner for Latin American newspaper representatives, then hurried to his plane. The rest of us had to scramble to get to the plane before takeoff. I sat opposite the president, who was in a forward-facing seat next to a telephone. We engaged in casual conversation until I brought up a matter I considered of some importance. I do not now recall what it was, but it gave me a view of how the president operated. First of all, he listened intently. Then he reached into his inside coat pocket, brought forth a piece of paper and a stub pencil, made a note, and said to me, "That's interesting. I'll look into that."

After landing at Andrews Air Force Base in Maryland, we flew by helicopter to the White House grounds. The president and I were the last to leave the helicopter. As he alighted, he turned to me and said, "Thanks again for that ad." He was referring to a full-page advertisement that Mildred and I had placed in the *Miami Herald* that day, welcoming him to the Miami area and to our congressional district. I watched the president as he walked to the White House entrance. A little dog ran out and put its paws on his legs. He patted the dog on the head and then disappeared into the White House. That was the last time I saw John Kennedy.

On November 22, 1963, Mildred and I were having lunch at the Democratic Club near the Capitol in Washington when a member of my staff rushed excitedly and clearly in distress to our table. "The President has been shot in Dallas," she cried. We couldn't believe our ears, but the messenger was too distraught to be telling anything but the truth. Information was sketchy at first on the seriousness of the president's condition, but too soon we learned the awful truth. We sat there—drained—deep in our own thoughts.

The nation was as shocked and as saddened as it had been on the day FDR died. Although he won the election of 1960 by the narrowest of margins, President Kennedy—young, handsome, vigorous, intelligent—had attained great popularity at home and around the world. His trips to Ireland (his ancestral home) and Europe, his "Ich bin ein Berliner" speech at the Berlin Wall, his Alliance for Progress in Latin America, and his Peace Corps, which sent idealistic young Americans to help people in every corner of the globe, made Kennedy in three short years a president of unusual stature worldwide. To the always traumatic experience of losing a world leader there was in the death of President Kennedy the added shock of assassination and the sorrow of seeing a potentially great president cut down in his prime. John Kennedy was a tough act to follow. The man who had to try was Lyndon Johnson, a politician and a personality as different from Kennedy as Austin is from Boston.

Lyndon Baines Johnson first came to Washington as secretary to a Texas congressman. Later he ran for a seat in the House and was elected. I came to know him well when he was in the House and I was in the Senate. As a very young congressman, Johnson was a favorite of President Roosevelt, who once predicted that Johnson would be the first post–Civil War president to come from the South. During those years when Roosevelt was trying desperately to awaken the nation to the threat a Hitler conquest of Europe posed for this country, Johnson and I met often to discuss how we could help the president.

Lyndon and I had a mutual friend, Charles Marsh, a distinguished publisher from Austin, Texas, who owned eleven Southern newspapers, including the *Orlando Sentinel*. The three of us were very close. After serving in the navy during World

War II, Johnson returned to Texas, was elected to the Senate, and quickly rose to the post of Democratic leader. When he first explored the possibility of running for the Senate, he arranged for me to address a joint session of the Texas legislature. During that visit, I did all I could to extol Johnson for what I knew him to be—a brilliant legislator. As Senate leader, he became one of the most powerful and dominant figures ever to fill that role. I did not support his bid in 1960 for the presidential nomination because I did not think a Southerner could be elected. But I greatly admired his legislative skills and the way in which he gained and retained the support of both liberal and conservative Democrats in the Senate.

Johnson was another Roosevelt in philosophy and compassion for people who needed help. His causes were education, welfare, medical care, housing, and other programs for the needy and for the elderly. Had it not been for the Vietnam War, historians would have adjudged him another Roosevelt. Now the great good that he did is largely forgotten, relegated to only a mention in some history books and biographies; his name and his presidency are shadowed by his inability to extricate the nation from its most unpopular war. It is my opinion that had Lyndon Johnson not been born in Texas, he would have been able, at some point, to step back and realize what that tragic conflict was doing to Indochina and to America. But he could not stand the thought of being remembered as the first president to lose a war. And so he pressed on with a conflict that could be won, if at all, only at a prohibitive cost in lives and money. In the mid-1960s, I broke with Lyndon Johnson on the Vietnam War. My only regret is that I did not do so earlier.

During Johnson's years in the House of Representatives, Mildred and I became very fond of Lyndon and Lady Bird Johnson and saw them frequently. Lyndon, so much maligned these days, was not the person depicted in hostile biographies. He was stubborn at times, crude and profane, but he could also be very kind. During the height of the Vietnam War, I was invited to a briefing at the White House. I brought with me a little girl, the daughter of dear friends in Miami. In retrospect, this probably was not the best time to do this. But President Johnson, beleaguered though he was, could not have been more patient or gentle. And the little girl had a thrill she will never forget—meeting the president of the United States.

Another incident is typical. Once we encountered each other at the White House during the Roosevelt years. Lyndon pulled me to one side and said, "Send Charles Marsh a telegram. His birthday is tomorrow." Marsh suffered a stroke when Johnson was vice-president; he was mentally alert, but could not speak. One Sunday, LBJ and I went to Marsh's home. He was bedridden; Johnson took one of his hands and held it, I took the other. For hours, we sat there, telling our friend the gossip and anecdotes on which Washington thrives.

One night in the spring of 1968, Mildred and I were astounded to hear President Johnson say, at the end of a long speech on the war, that he would "not seek, and will not accept, the nomination of my party for another term as your president." I had to ask Mildred if she had heard what I heard. The war and the president had become very unpopular, and on the day of that speech two of Johnson's emissaries had returned from Wisconsin, whose presidential primary would be held two days later. They had to tell the president that he would be lucky to receive 30 percent of the votes against Senator Eugene McCarthy, who had made opposition to the war the basis of his candidacy. In later primaries, Johnson would have to face a more formidable foe, for Senator Robert Kennedy had also declared his candidacy.

There may have been reasons other than the prospect of a humiliating defeat that caused Johnson to withdraw, including the one that he gave—that he could not let politics interfere with his efforts to bring the war to a close. At the end of his term, he returned to his beloved ranch in Texas, disheartened and disillusioned. He died there, knowing his place in history would be less than he so desperately wanted it to be, and less than he deserved. At his funeral, we tried to think only of his rise from humble beginnings in the Texas hill country to the highest office in the land, and of his skill and devotion in trying to build a truly great society.

The last year of Johnson's term was a violent and tragic one for the nation. Peace demonstrations increased in number and hatred. Martin Luther King, Jr., the great civil rights activist whose "I have a dream" speech in August 1963 had thrilled millions of blacks and whites, was slain in Memphis, Tennessee, on April 4, 1968. Angry mobs torched several large American cities, and racial polarization, against which Dr. King had labored so valiantly, gripped the nation. In June, an assassin's bullets claimed the life of Senator Robert Kennedy after he had won the California presidential primary. After early years as a lawyer for the Senate Investigations Committee headed by Joe McCarthy, Robert Kennedy had served effectively and compassionately in the school desegregation crises of the early 1960s. He was the attorney general and the one his brother, the president, relied on most for advice during the Cuban missile crisis of 1962. He became a spokesman for the underprivileged and his untimely death was a great loss to the nation.

The Democratic nomination that year went to Vice-President Hubert Humphrey, a warm and able man who lost in a close election to Richard M. Nixon. Humphrey simply could not divorce himself completely from the Vietnam War policies of the Johnson administration. Nixon had come back from his defeat for the presidency in 1960 and a loss in a race for governor of California in 1962 to win his party's nomination and then the general election over a bitterly divided Democratic party. My opinions of Nixon appear elsewhere in this volume. When the returns for 1968 were complete, I knew the voters had rejected a man who would have brought honor to the presidency and elected a man who would disgrace it. I didn't look ahead and see Watergate. I looked back on Nixon's years in the House, his witch-hunting, his McCarthyite campaigns, his obviously flawed character. In his presidential years, he scored some triumphs, particularly in foreign policy, but in the end he failed his country, his party, his family, and himself. When he resigned in August 1974, I was relieved because I knew his vice-president, Gerald Ford, was a decent human being. I knew Jerry Ford well from our years of service together in the House, where he was the Republican leader.

Betty Ford and Mildred also were close friends. We saw the Fords often during the House years and quite frequently after he became president. Jerry Ford was one Republican president whom I opposed on various issues only with pain and reluctance. This incident underscores the down-to-earth openness of both Fords and our relationship to them: Comedian Bob Hope used to entertain at dinners to raise funds for the National Parkinson Foundation in Miami. Mildred was chairwoman of these dinners, which were always huge successes. One year, Mildred heard that President Ford would be in Miami the night of the Bob Hope dinner. Hope and I separately placed calls to the White House to see if President Ford would arrange to attend the dinner. We were unable to get a firm commitment. On the evening of the dinner, I received a telephone call from a presidential aide telling me that President Ford would arrive at the dinner within fifteen minutes. Hope and I went out to the entrance to await the president. He arrived as scheduled, and Hope took him up on the stage and introduced him.

After the president made a few remarks, he turned his head and asked, "Where's Mildred?" He caught sight of her seated at the head table and said, "Mildred, come on up here. I'm going to tell this crowd why I am here this evening." Mildred joined him and President Ford said, "You know, Mildred and my wife, Betty, are good friends. Mildred called Betty this morning and said, 'Betty, you've just got to get the president to come to my dinner this evening. We're counting on you to do so.' So Betty got after me and said, 'You've just got to go to that dinner.' And so you see that's why I'm here with you this evening." Mildred and the crowd were delighted.

Then Ford asked Mildred if she would like to say something. She turned to the audience and said, "Friends, I want to tell you what a wonderful person our First Lady is. She is lovely and beautiful, someone of whom we can all be proud." Then she added, "And the president is a wonderful man, too. We are all very proud of our president." Then she turned to Gerald Ford and said, "So good a man deserves a better party." She brought down the house. The president and, believe it or not, Bob Hope were speechless.

I always have felt that President Ford was right in pardoning Richard Nixon, given the agony the country would have gone through if Nixon had been indicted and tried, as he no doubt deserved. But the pardon probably cost Ford the election of 1976 that brought Jimmy Carter to the White House.

During my lifetime, there have been four certitudes about presidential politics: A Catholic could not be elected president. Nor could a Southerner. Nor a woman. Nor a black. The last two remain to be disproved; the first two already have been, by John Kennedy and Jimmy Carter. Carter, a former governor of Georgia not well-known in national Democratic circles, stunned the experts by winning the nomination and election in 1976. He had come along at just the right time. After four years of the baleful Watergate scandal, the forced resignations of Richard Nixon and Spiro Agnew, and the pardoning of the former by President Ford, the nation was in no mood for a politics-as-usual president. Jimmy Carter was not from that mold. He was an intensely religious man, obviously intelligent, and most important of all—honest. I came to know him well as he campaigned in the Florida primary, which he won; during the general election campaign, Mildred and I came to know Rosalynn and Jimmy well. We were frequent guests at the White House. It was gratifying for me to know that at last no one was automatically barred from the presidency because of where he was born or lived. The Civil War at last was over.

In the fall of 1978 when friends gave a marvelous tribute to Mildred and me in Miami Beach, Rosalynn Carter represented the administration and delivered a warm and generous eulogy to both of us. As president, Jimmy Carter had many problems. He had difficulty projecting himself as he was. On television, he was uneasy and unnatural, coming across as weak when in reality he is a strong person. His Camp David accords represent a foreign policy achievement unmatched by his successor. But as Lyndon Johnson could not overcome Vietnam, Jimmy Carter was dogged by the Iranian hostage crisis, his handling of which gave the impression of a weak and ineffective leader. In 1980, the electorate rejected his bid for a second term. I campaigned for President Carter and remain convinced that his stature, like Truman's, will be enhanced with the passing of the years. As President Reagan became enmeshed in his own hostages-for-arms crisis late in 1986, he was already making President Carter look better.

When Ronald Reagan was seeking the presidency in 1980, he and I appeared together on September 7 on a broad thoroughfare in Philadelphia before a large assemblage of senior citizens. As a representative of the Democratic party on this occasion, I told the audience that candidate Reagan in the past had often suggested converting Social Security from a social insurance program to a "voluntary" system. I related the record of my party in creating and expanding Social Security and cited President Carter's record in support of programs for the elderly. "Why risk Reagan when you've got a proven friend in the White House?" I asked. When his turn came, Reagan turned on the charm and took the pledge: He would work to preserve Social Security. No doubt he won the votes of most who were there and of senior citizens generally.

But when he became president in 1981, Reagan called on Congress to reduce Social Security benefits by $62 billion. Cuts of $22 billion were made, affecting adversely the most important programs for the elderly—Social Security, Medicare, Medicaid, housing, the meals program. Congress restored most of the cuts, but I was alarmed by the difference between Reagan and his rhetoric.

In other respects, Reagan's record concerned me greatly. Under his administration, our national debt soared toward $3 trillion. Our trade deficit topped $150 billion. Foreign policy ineptitude led to the "Iranscam" scandal that plunged the administration into chaos. He violated his own oft-declared pledge never to deal with hostage-takers and in doing so he flew in the face of common sense as well. Trying to divert attention, he announced a "giant step" in health care, a program to protect against the cost of catastrophic illness. The program failed to protect enough people against enough illnesses, including Alzheimer's. I went on television to denounce the plan and call it what it really is: a dwarf's step. Unfortunately for the nation, the Reagan administration's bungling ended its effectiveness two years short of the end of its term.

It was like so many lovely Octobers in Washington, the sky blue, the leaves a brilliant montage of browns, yellows, and reds. It was 1978. During the congressional recess, Mildred had taken a trip to Sofia and had returned with three coats, from which I chose one as a present. She was so happy. It was our sixteenth year in the House of Representatives, the bitterness of the past had been largely dissipated, we were comfortable financially. Mildred and I were planning to take an afternoon flight to Miami, and Charlotte Dixon, Mildred's devoted companion and aide, was helping her to get ready. Life was good.

292

As we rode to the airport, Mildred said to Charlotte, "My, we had such a pleasant drive in the country this morning, didn't we?" Charlotte looked perplexed. "No," she said. "We didn't go on a drive this morning." Said Mildred, "Oh? I thought we did." Soon we alighted at the airport and Mildred asked Charlotte where her bags were. Charlotte said, "Mildred, I'm not going on this trip. I never planned to." I gave little thought to these lapses until later.

When we got on board, Mildred sank into her seat and half sang, half said, "I'm going home." I looked at her closely and asked if she felt all right. "Sure," she replied.

But of course she wasn't all right. We reached our home in Miami, and I made a speech that evening, since Mildred seemed to be completely herself. But when I returned, she was on the floor. "I can't get back up," she cried. I helped her get back into bed.

The next morning Mildred felt nauseated. She was due for a physical checkup the following day, so we let the nausea pass, believing we would find out during the checkup what had caused it and why Mildred had fallen. We headed for our car, parked in a third-floor garage, but before we reached the door Mildred went limp and sank to the ground. I telephoned for an ambulance.

At the hospital, we learned the worst—Mildred had suffered a slight stroke. She remained hospitalized for several weeks, and when she was released her mind was clear but her speech was slurred. She had full use of her limbs. Mildred was a fighter and she would have overcome the effects of a stroke. But a week after her admission to the hospital, doctors informed me that she also was suffering from internal cancer. This was a severe blow. We remained hopeful, and Mildred refused to give up all of her activities.

On the advice of our doctor, I hired two practical nurses so she would have care and attention around the clock. In autumn of 1978, Mildred summoned up her considerable courage and participated in the tribute at which Rosalynn Carter and Governor Reubin Askew of Florida spoke. She clutched the arm of her doctor, Dr. Richard Elias, and walked across the huge dining room at the Fountainbleau Hotel on a boardwalk constructed from the entrance to the head table. For a year, she had taken chemotherapy treatments, and of course I strove frantically to bring her all possible help, including the wisdom of the experts at the National Cancer Institute. In January 1979, Mildred accompanied me to Tallahassee for the inauguration of Governor Bob Graham, and despite the bitter cold refused to leave until the ceremonies were over, at which time she in her wheelchair was helped off the platform. She also attended a luncheon given in our honor by the president and senior faculty of Florida State University, at which plans were made to establish the Mildred and Claude Pepper Library at the university. Afterward, we drove to the campus and selected the building in which the library would be housed. She was enthusiastic and helpful. But soon after she began to experience the terrible pains that accompany the last stages of cancer.

One morning in early 1979 we were at breakfast in our apartment in Washington. She looked up at me with those beautiful blue eyes and said, "Well, Claude, I guess we've just about come to the end of the road." That nearly destroyed me. I broke down completely, rushed around the table, and took her in my arms. "Don't say that, Mildred," I pleaded. "You know I can't live without you."

Mildred saw what the mention of our inevitable, approaching separation meant to me. She never again referred to it, even obliquely. She withstood pain and discomfort bravely and even cheerfully. But the doctors lost control of her tumor, and she grew weaker. I spent a great deal of time at her side, day and night. We talked by telephone many times daily and in the last conversation before she lapsed into a coma, she was vibrant and uncomplaining. She died on March 31, 1979.

When she was very, very ill we exchanged two brief notes. To me she wrote:

> Dear Claude,
> I have compleated a lovey painting & I love you verry, verry much. I mis you when you are in Washington.
> We have been for forty younge years married.
> Can you believe it!
> I love you very devotedly.
>
> > Mildred Pepper

My note to her:

> Dearest Mildred,
> You have not awakened and I will have to run. I hate to leave you so much. I pray for the early time when we can go together as we have done for so long. Darling, you are the sweetest and dearest one in all the world. I love you with all my heart. I just wish I had been a better husband. I leave you until Thursday evening in the hands of Charlotte, so dear to us both. She's the best.
>
> > All my love,
> > Your only husband,
> > Claude.

There were two funeral services for Mildred, both well-attended and as lovely as funerals can be. One was at the Coral Gables Methodist Church in Miami, and the other the following day at the First Baptist Church in Tallahassee where she and I and my family worshiped for so many years. She was buried in our family lot at Woodlawn Cemetery in Tallahassee. I wrote the epitaph for the headstone under which she sleeps:

SHE WAS A PERFECT WIFE, LOVELY OF PERSON AND BEAUTIFUL OF SPIRIT. HER BEAUTIFUL LIFE HAS LEFT A GLOW WHICH WILL ILLUME AND INSPIRE OTHERS FOR GENERATIONS TO COME.

Her name lives on. In Miami, there is a Mildred and Claude Pepper low-cost housing project for the elderly. In the renovation of downtown Miami's lovely Bayfront Park designed by Isamu Noguchi, there will be a fountain that will shoot water sixty-six feet into the sky, and it will be known as the Mildred and Claude Pepper Fountain. The Mildred and Claude Pepper Library at Florida State University contains thousands of our letters, papers, clippings, and a special exhibit of Mildred's gowns and personal effects. Also at Florida State there is an endowed Mildred and Claude Pepper Chair in Gerontology.

In 1981, a beautiful memorial service for Mildred was held at the Washington National Cathedral. Every seat was occupied. The three eulogists were our old friend, Bob Hope; Mrs. George Bush; and Congressman Jim Wright, then the majority leader, now the Speaker of the House of Representatives. Senator Henry Jackson and Representative Lindy Boggs also participated in the service, as did Rabbi Irving Lehrman of Temple Emanuel of Miami Beach.

I have tried to carry on as Mildred would have wanted me to do, terribly lonesome for her person, but sustained even today by her brave beautiful spirit.

She will be with me always.

Epilogue

A major objective [of liberalism] is the protection of the economic weak and doing it within the framework of a private property economy. The liberal, emphasizing the civil and property rights of the individual, insists that the individual must remain so supreme as to make the state his servant.

—WAYNE MORSE

Since politics is a breeding ground for distortion, malevolence, and demagoguery, there is little wonder that the word *liberal*—generously sprinkled throughout these pages—has become a term of opprobrium, even in some circles that regard themselves as "progressive" or moderate. The word has a thousand definitions, it seems; a regrettably common one conjures images of witless government spending, a benevolent attitude toward welfare "cheats," a softness and naïveté toward communism, an indifference to national defense, and a tolerance for avant-garde life-styles. The language butchers have man-

297

gled the meaning of *liberal* beyond recognition. They must not be allowed to prevail.

By now, the reader has observed that I apply the label to myself unhesitatingly. It is crucial, therefore, that my own definition be expounded. If I were preaching a sermon on the subject, I believe I would take my text from Ovid: "Note too that a faithful study of the liberal arts humanizes character and permits it not to be cruel."

In the days of the New Deal and many times since, I have seen what it means to the man jobless and hungry to find employment and to be able to provide food.

I have seen what it means for those without shelter to be able to obtain—with help—a home.

I have seen what it means for impoverished young people to be able—again with help—to obtain a decent education, a goal beyond their unaided reach.

I have seen the handicapped extended a hand that enabled them to lead useful and productive lives.

I have seen the hopelessness in the eyes of the elderly, fearing the onset of illness and infirmity, knowing that without help they have no chance of obtaining the care they will need.

I have seen my native region—the South—locked by discriminatory freight rates into a status described by President Roosevelt as "one-third of a nation ill-fed, ill-housed and ill-clothed."

I have seen working people paid ten or fifteen cents an hour. I have seen them work—I have, in fact, worked with them—seven days a week for months at a time.

I have seen industry, farmers, businesses large and small unable to remain afloat, unaided.

And yes, I have seen people die because research into killer diseases has been too sparse to lead to cures.

My brand of liberalism has a bedrock belief in life—in a better life not just for the elite, but for all. It rejects the notion that those who are underprivileged have earned their fate, that hard work inexorably leads to success. It holds that the health, economic security, and—to the degree possible—happiness of its people is a proper concern of government. It acknowledges the value—indeed the necessity—of individual worth and effort. But it diverges sharply from conservatism by recognizing what should be clear to all: that in a complex, twentieth-century free society, no one and nothing except government is big enough, powerful enough, and universal enough to make life bearable for the masses of citizens. Voices cry out from high places: "Let the private sector do it." Fine, if it can and will. But the truth is it cannot and will not.

Liberalism, as I define it, obviously believes in democracy. It therefore has no room for racism, sexism, or ageism. It has been criticized some for its insistence that no one should suffer discrimination for conditions beyond his or her power to control. Election analysts tell us that the white male vote in the South is lost to liberal candidates before the polls open, and their evidence is persuasive. But what may be true today need not be true tomorrow. Enlightenment comes. Attitudes change. Only a few short years ago, Lyndon Johnson found that he could not drive from Washington to Texas with a black aide because motels along the way would not provide accommodations for Negroes. That is no longer the case. The WHITES ONLY signs at drinking fountains and rest rooms throughout the South have disappeared. Should we despair that there will be no further progress in race relations? Of course not. The pattern of our history is that bigotry is in retreat—slow retreat, to be sure. But everywhere there is evidence that it will continue to ebb.

If its zeal for equality damages its image in some quarters, liberalism will have to live with that. But in other respects, it can and in my opinion must repair the face it presents to the nation and the world. Liberals have allowed themselves to be perceived as foes of something fundamental to most Americans—the national security. Instinctively and in many cases subconsciously, citizens of a democracy sense that the blessings they enjoy must be protected and, if necessary, defended. There can be little doubt that in several recent presidential elections, we liberals allowed ourselves to be painted as antimilitary, as insufficiently aware of our fellow citizens' need to feel at least reasonably safe from attack.

It is important that I not be misunderstood on this point. I grieve over every tax dollar that goes into the building of a bomber, a missile, a weapon of destruction. How much better if that dollar could be diverted to medical research, to education, to helping someone who is lost to find his way. Some of my fellow liberals attack me for my support of the M-X missile program and the anti-Communist forces in Angola and Nicaragua. I am, they say, inconsistent. The opposite is true. Just as I worked alongside President Roosevelt to eliminate discriminatory freight rates in the South and to institute a minimum wage, so did I campaign up and down and all across the country for a strengthened military. Whether the enemy is fascism or communism or something else, I have never wavered in my conviction that the United States must be strong enough to resist it. I have also consistently supported this nation's backing of forces for freedom beyond our borders, whether that was England and France and the Soviet Union in World War II, or the anti-Communist Freedom Fighters in Central America and parts of Africa in more recent years.

Central to my concept of liberalism is that government need not be intrusive. Nor need it be inefficient or prohibitively expensive. The Home Owners Loan Corporation of the Roosevelt era helped thousands of Americans avoid foreclosure and still made several millions of dollars in profit for the government. The loan guarantee that saved Chrysler from bankruptcy brought millions to the U.S. Treasury. I recall the charges of "intrusion" and needless expansion of government power that accompanied my introduction of resolution for the United States to participate in the World Health Organization. That was not the intent nor the result of the resolution. The goal, largely achieved, was to enable the governments of the leading nations of the world to work together to improve the lives and promote the health of their people.

I do not wish my defense of liberalism to degenerate into a political polemic, but I cannot avoid registering a strong and clear dissent from the Reagan administration stance that government is the enemy and not the friend of the people. It is a shortsighted view for which the president and his advisers will be answerable to history. Millions of talented young Americans denied help in obtaining an education become a liability to the nation whereas they could have been an asset, enriching the overall earning capacity of the population. If Ronald Reagan had adhered to the Rooseveltian philosophy he professes once to have embraced, he could have stimulated the economy by building urgently needed public housing, providing thousands of jobs, and bringing the comfort of decent shelter to millions. He would not have attacked the Social Security system, depriving indigents of a pathetic $255 burial allowance that would have kept many from Potter's Field burials. But, I can hear many say, you bleeding-heart liberals always forget that someone must pick up the tab. Well, it is a fact that President Reagan's policies have led to deficits exceeding those racked up by *all* previous presidents, including such notorious "big spenders" as Roosevelt, Truman, and Johnson. Curiously and, I fear, irresponsibly, President Reagan adheres to the implausible notion that government income can be slashed and outgo increased without there being a day of reckoning just down the road.

Undeniably, the Reagan era and the presidential elections of 1980 and 1984, represent setbacks for and widespread rejection

301

of traditional liberalism. But I have lived long enough and watched the pendulum* over a sufficient span of years to know that liberalism is too basic to human nature to ever go permanently out of style. As long as there are people who care about and wish to help others less fortunate than themselves—in short, as long as there are people—the political spectrum will be able to accommodate liberalism.

In a personal vein: My understanding of what constitutes liberalism is perhaps best symbolized and encapsulated by one of the most cherished awards I have ever received—the Franklin Delano Roosevelt Four Freedoms Award. It honors my long and not always successful efforts to live up to the spirit of President Roosevelt's Four Freedoms, perhaps the most important of which is freedom from fear. As a concerned citizen, as a member of "The People's House," and as chairman of a great and powerful congressional committee, I intend to continue to devote my full energies to helping to free people from fear of dictatorial oppression, from fear of illness and poverty, from fear of discrimination, from fear of ignorance, and from fear of opportunity foreclosed. To me, that is what liberalism means. Unabashedly, then, I am and shall remain a liberal.

Claude Pepper
October 1987
Washington, D.C.

---

*The defeats in 1986 of many conservative Republican senators may have been a signal that the pendulum is moving again.

Index